The Neural Teaching Guide

The Neural Teaching Guide showcases the innovative practices of K-12 teachers who are effectively applying findings from educational neuroscience into their classrooms. Educators today have remarkable opportunities to understand how the complex and often malleable functions of the brain affect learning, behavior, and social-emotional dynamics, but what practical strategies come out of this information? Authored by in-service teachers around the country, this book showcases a variety of brain-based approaches – cutting-edge yet intuitive, evidence-based yet accessibly translated – to helping children realize their potential at school. Both novice and veteran K-12 teachers alike will be reinvigorated to enhance students' engagement and curiosity, nurture positive behaviors and self-regulation, support interest-based activities and inclusive interactions, identify biases and struggles, and more.

Kieran O'Mahony is Founding Principal of the Institute for Connecting Neuroscience with Teaching and Learning, Chief Learning Officer of HUE Learn, and Emeritus Research Scientist at Neural Education.

Also Available from Routledge
Eye On Education
(www.routledge.com/k-12)

The Brain-Based Classroom: Accessing Every Child's Potential through Educational Neuroscience
Kieran O'Mahony

Educators as First Responders: A Teacher's Guide to Adolescent Development and Mental Health, Grades 6-12
Deborah Offner

Supporting Student Mental Health: Essentials for Teachers
Michael Hass and Amy Ardell

Harnessing Formative Data for K-12 Teachers: Real-time Classroom Strategies
Stepan Mekhitarian

Nurturing Students' Character: Everyday Teaching Activities for Social-Emotional Learning
Jeffrey S. Kress and Maurice J. Elias

Differentiated Instruction Made Practical: Engaging the Extremes through Classroom Routines
Rhonda Bondie and Akane Zusho

The Neural Teaching Guide

Authentic Strategies from Brain-Based Classrooms

Edited by Kieran O'Mahony

NEW YORK AND LONDON

Designed cover image: © Getty Images

First published 2024
by Routledge
605 Third Avenue, New York, NY 10158

and by Routledge
4 Park Square, Milton Park, Abingdon, Oxon, OX14 4RN

Routledge is an imprint of the Taylor & Francis Group, an informa business

© 2024 selection and editorial matter, Kieran O'Mahony; individual chapters, the contributors

The right of Kieran O'Mahony to be identified as the author of the editorial material, and of the authors for their individual chapters, has been asserted in accordance with sections 77 and 78 of the Copyright, Designs and Patents Act 1988.

All rights reserved. No part of this book may be reprinted or reproduced or utilised in any form or by any electronic, mechanical, or other means, now known or hereafter invented, including photocopying and recording, or in any information storage or retrieval system, without permission in writing from the publishers.

Trademark notice: Product or corporate names may be trademarks or registered trademarks, and are used only for identification and explanation without intent to infringe.

ISBN: 978-1-032-58262-7 (hbk)
ISBN: 978-1-032-58344-0 (pbk)
ISBN: 978-1-003-44968-3 (ebk)

DOI: 10.4324/9781003449683

Typeset in Palatino
by KnowledgeWorks Global Ltd.

Contents

Foreword vii
Acknowledgements x

Introduction 1
Kieran O'Mahony

1 **I Can Hear My Baby Across a Noisy Crowded Room!** 16
By Laurie Donati

2 **Fun in a Box: Purposeful Play** 32
By Wendi Trummert

3 **Y O U LOOK GOOD** 57
By Mary Catherine Pilon

4 **Our Stroke of Enlightenment: Neuroplasticity and Resiliency in Action** 64
By Laurie Donati

5 **Leave with Dignity!** 75
By Dani Hylton

6 **We Are Hardwired Learners No Matter What** 85
By Stephanie Turcotte

7 **Creativity, Brain, Response Art, and the Making of Community** 100
By Valli Rebsamen

8 **Play Card** 120
By Audrey Gallagher

9	**Belonging** 133
	By Paige Wescott

10	**Soft-Start** 150
	By Taylor Cassidy

11	**10/10 Would Recommend: Using Choice to Transition from Co-Regulation to Self-Regulation** 165
	By Gunner Argo

12	**The Dope Dealer** 174
	By Jeannine Medvedich

13	**If I Only Had a Brain: Mirroring Neurons, Authentic Relationships (Regulate, Relate, Reason)** 195
	By Michelle Curry

Index 209

Foreword

When I was first introduced to educational research through my work at the Institute for Connecting Neuroscience with Teaching and Learning, I had no idea how sincerely fulfilling this work would truly be. As a researcher, I am afforded the opportunity to interface with Brain-Based pedagogical models from an aerial perspective. Being at a 30,000-foot level provides me with an overview perspective that hints at the depth and breadth of an immersive educational moment and shows its potential in the lives of educators, parents, and children. Personally, I find it impressive, and it has my full attention. I was in for a shock when I was asked to come down from my sky-high tower and take off my research glasses, to enter the classroom with a teacher who was so busy giving tours, lectures, and keynotes that she was in danger of missing the deadline for finalizing her chapter for this book. I gratefully offered to be her assistant, gladly rolled up my sleeves, and got busy with the editing and crafting.

I was surprised when I realized that this process eventuated a kinesthetic amplification of cognitive pedagogy. In extending my help, I was immediately immersed in one of the pillars of the pedagogic model that we are describing – that being acting as an "intelligent novice". In taking this role, I interviewed the "domain expert", or seasoned educator, who has years of experience and has learned from hands-on course changes and pivots. The concept of "domain expert" coupled with "intelligent novice" is an intrinsic element of the pedagogic model we are describing. Moreover, it turns out that one of the central ideations of the pedagogy is a construct called "making visible". This construct makes it possible for children, teachers, and counselors alike to cofunction with a common vocabulary, a level playing field, and solutions that fit emergent problems. By taking the role of the "intelligent novice", I was able to help the "domain expert" make visible her mental models around her implementation of Brain-Based pedagogy.

As the "intelligent-novice", I came to find out that there is no substitute for the deep understanding that comes from making mistakes and asking the right questions at the appropriate time. I quickly realized that if I didn't ask curious questions, her expertise wouldn't allow her to make visible the meaningful rudimentary elements of her method and approach that made all the difference for her students. In other words, she was hampered by her own aptitude, a common and symptomatic "blind spot" that is copiously documented in the expertise literature. Together, we delved into her historical data. Without inhibition, I repeated back to her what I heard, followed up with probing questions, and asked for clarification. At times, I misconstrued or made mistakes in my understanding, but through deeper discussions we built a rapport that was needed to highlight the mental constructs that she embodies in a pedagogy that made her so successful. We emerged from our numerous exchanges with the account that you will read in her chapter on dopamine.

Given the unique opportunity to experience this pedagogic model from a more immersive position, I witnessed first-hand the genius of this work. Throughout the interaction, I asked many questions, laughed at her humor, and teared up when she shared heart-wrenching and emotionally moving anecdotes about successes she, her staff, and her students have enjoyed since leaning into Neural Education. No longer was I court-side experiencing the story unfold through distant data! This educator gave me a seat right in the middle of her world making me understand the magic of cognitive pedagogy in a new, enlightened way. As I listened to her account, I watched with awe, her students blossoming in my mind's eye. In each case study, she connected broad, cognitive principles with simple, creative, and grounded actions that she composed with her students and staff.

Listening to her storied journey made me deeply understand that a teacher's unique ability to creatively connect findings from the cognitive learning sciences with individualized classroom instruction is where the magic lies. She began at the source with examples and suggested solutions portrayed in the publications of the Institute founder, Dr. O'Mahony, but she adapted many of the strategies to her on the ground classroom needs. For instance, she took the idea of introducing brain-breaks that cross the midline to heart and went one giant step further by creating a physical Brain-Break Wheel that children could Spin to select a random activity that aligned with their need for autonomy, mastery, and purpose through a theory of intrinsic motivation. She fully understood that when the children co-created their learning space, they would express and "feel" the impact of neurotransmitters that supported learning and fostered a strong sense of safety and belonging. All this so they could access their higher order rational brain and process new and existing information with powerful executive functioning. Through becoming the "intelligent-novice", I realized that the neuroscience of learning examples were fundamental and that they served as a springboard for educators to embrace the emergent pedagogy as their own. I, thus, witnessed the genius of an individual educator who took ownership of a Brain-Based pedagogy to uniquely and creatively tailor her teaching to fit the immediate needs of each child with whom she interacted.

When an educator puts on their neural lens, they, themselves, own their teaching. This automatically makes learning more accessible to students. This is because a cognitive pedagogy liberates teachers into their true teaching potential and, in turn, provides teachers with the tools to liberate each child into their true learning potential. This was a powerful revelation for me; prior to undertaking this role of "intelligent-novice", I had not made that connection. An educator who is engaging learners with the highest potential is, in fact, architecting important neural structures in children's brains. These neural structures, architected in the classroom and consolidated during sleep, predict higher order processing capacity for the entirety of a child's life. It assures that students attain strong potential both during and after their formative school years. This is a lifelong gift that keeps on giving!

I encourage you, dear reader, to read these stories with an open heart and an open mind. If you, like me, are a heavy, left-brain thinker who gets caught up in the technicalities of science, I suggest you stand up, plant both feet on the ground, and continuously shift your weight back and forth from left to right leg. This will upregulate your right hemisphere and prepare your brain for the learning experience. Oh, and breathe! In doing this, you open yourself up to letting these stories work their magic. Yes, the science appears to be magical. What I mean is … you can put yourself in a mental state that allows each educator to enter into your consciousness without a need to know how to explicitly implement cognitive learning sciences into your classroom. Trust me, this will pretty much happen naturally just through sheer exposure to these encounters with the learning brain. Cognitive pedagogy is an implicit contagion! Once we're exposed, there is no going back!

All this to say, enjoy the journey. They are treasure troves of brilliance, insight, and inspiration. I wish you well on your Brain-Based pedagogic adventure!

Alison Di Giamarino, MA, BcID, Research in Education

Acknowledgements

A work that involves educators from many disciplines, broad experience, and wide geographical domains tends to cut across the lives and livelihoods of people who are directly and indirectly connected to school systems, learning systems, and communities of support. We are happy to have an opportunity to reach out and acknowledge contributions often immense and selfless, that people have wittingly or unwittingly made in the necessary incubation of a work of this magnitude and scope. A work like this where individual stories and evidentiary accounts of change that takes place immediately or over time because of intentionality of practice is designed to show that there is an alternative. Choice is central to motivation that stems from a place of intrinsic understanding. For over a century (Watson published his infamous manifesto in 1913), teachers have tried to cause improvements and make change within a system that was essentially trying to change itself. It's akin to a child scoring her own tests. Difficult to do and difficult to grow as a result!

In a work that has come together over three or more years of practice, there are a lot of voices that can be heard in the background. Teachers are not alone in their classrooms. Neither are they alone in the outcomes and transformative results that they describe on these pages. Today's results can be traced back to incremental research findings, some that pointed out that there was no advantage in using method A over method B and some that caused us to think about the very soul of our work routines. We stand on the shoulders of those who have paved this journey with academic papers and talks that sometimes were successful at piercing the veil of indifference and conformity. To these nameless many, we offer sincere gratitude and a vote of thanks.

Among these voices that are no longer with us, two individuals stand out as primarily influential in my own journey: JK and JB. Professor of education at the National University of Ireland, John Kevin (Barry) stumbled into my rudimentary lab by mistake at a time when I was breaking rules and forging connections with children who had already been cast aside by societal norms as failures, dregs, and bottom-rung blue-collar working-class children. He came for one 45-minute period and stayed for a month. He was intrigued to witness action-research firsthand, a societal shift right under his eyes with children who, when ignited, had incredible potential. These scholars had already been labeled; they had been stratified; and they were destined to fail.

Yet, within a few short months he and I reversed their life trajectory and turned extant accepted belief systems on their head. For JK's prolonged visit and long discussions about research methods and potential, I am eternally grateful – he was old and wise enough to name it for what it was: revolutionary change in a time of entrenched thinking. Years later in Seattle, at the University of Washington College of Education and the National Science Foundation Science of Learning's first Learning Center – the Life Center – I was fortunate enough to work with the other John in my life, John Bransford. Having recently arrived on the coast from Vanderbilt, Bransford invited me to join in his efforts to advance his work on anchored instruction and its dissemination into k12 systems. A large learning sciences project at The Boeing Company was the site of a research intervention that set in motion a brain-based pedagogic model. The four-year intervention involved adult learners (Aerospace Engineers) who were shifting their manufacturing model from metals to composites in preparation for the groundbreaking 787 (plastic) aircraft. A second project that we undertook was also sponsored by the National Science Foundation and involved a learning sciences longitudinal study that coincided with the removal of two dams on the River Elwha that were responsible for displacing several Native American nations at the turn of the previous century from their remote site in Western Washington.

The culminating work that he and I set in motion in the College of Education involved a graduate level course that was designed to Connect Neuroscience with Teaching and Learning. Upon John's retirement, I joined the University of Washington School of Nursing and moved across campus to set up shop in adolescent brain science. It was at this National Institutes for Health five-year research project, which we called "How Do I Learn" (HDIL), that the pedagogic model that was first explored at The Boeing Company and the hands-on social and emotional model that was explored at the Elwha Dam Removal project coalesced into a full-blown pedagogic model that was distributive, social, and extensible. I am eternally grateful to JB for his guidance in this work.

This work would not have been possible without the dedicated effort of the authors who carried out the implementation of the pedagogic model and opted to don their neural lenses in the pursuit of excellence. A shout-out to an amazing team: Laurie, Wendi, Mary Catherine, Dani, Stephanie, Valli, Audrey, Paige, Taylor, Gunner, Jeannine, and Michelle. A special thank you to Allison and Lauren for their assistance in writing the Foreword and editing the Introduction. Your effort is truly indispensable. Following are individual acknowledgments from authors who contributed to this publication and in so doing advanced the field. I am deeply grateful.

Laurie Donati: I would like to express my deepest gratitude to my three remarkable children and my supportive and encouraging husband, all sensational humans I am proud to call my family. To my parents, who always pushed me to be the best version of myself (I love you more). A big thank you to my dear friends and family for their constant encouragement and belief in me. To my incredible team at Neural Education, as well as my colleagues, students, and families I have served over the past 19 years in education – all who have helped me to develop into the educator I am today. Dr. Kieran O'Mahony and Dr. Missy Widmann, thank you for your constant positivity, encouragement, and your learner-mindset; you both talk the talk and walk the walk. And finally, to the amazing medical professionals, therapists, and fellow advocates with whom I have been blessed to partner with in the extraordinary work of pediatric stroke rehabilitation and advocacy. Thank you.

Wendi Trummert: I would like to thank my teacher colleagues Amy Gray, Jennifer Dever, Katie Jayakaran, and Janene Jasinski for their collaboration, growth mindset, and a shared passion to think outside the box to implement the very best educational interventions. Thank you Yvonne Swinth and Sheryl Zylstra for your collaborative support in our research process.

Gunner Argo: I would like to thank the district I work in, the administration and staff who trust me as a teacher, and the students who put their faith in me to try. Thank you.

Paige Wescott: I want to express SO much gratitude to Dr. Kieran O'Mahony and Dr. Missy Widmann (Cofounders of NeuralEducation.org) for their roles in inspiring me and empowering me on my educational neuroscience journey! This work is transformational for our own lives, for our schools, our teams, and our students and families! Postdoctoral deep dives with Dr. Lori Desautels at Butler University, while working within her Applied Educational Neuroscience Program, have been an ongoing joy during the past two cohorts! Special thanks, too, go to my mentor, Dr. Kieran O'Mahony, for this incredible opportunity to write and share this chapter.

Michelle Curry: I would like to thank the cast of characters who have walked beside me on the yellow brick road. The Wizard: Kieran O'Mahony, thank you for helping me find my way home with The Brain-Based Classroom Workbook. Special thanks to the Scarecrow, Ray Bolger, for connecting with a little Dorothy by teaching her an impactful and lifelong lesson. Heartfelt gratitude to Vicki and Lloyd Case, my parents, who like Auntie Em and Uncle Henry were responsible for pointing out every Rainbow and believing that someday "Over the Rainbow" I would be an author like my Great (x4) Grandfather Meshach Browning, who wrote *Forty-Four Years of the Life of a Hunter* in 1859. Thank you to the Family of Flying Monkeys – my amazing husband, Mike, and our monkeys Katharyn and Michael Curry, and Mike and Sue Curry, my monkeys-in-law. Special thanks to my brother Norm and his wife Jen Case. Shout out to my monkey nephew Kelly Case and to my Aunt Casey Clutter, who took me on monkey adventures! To Glinda … you, Kelly Hutchison, are my best friend, and my kid's fairy godmother. We wrote our first stories together and my kids always thought you were a *real* fairy godmother! We won't forget the Lollipop Gal: Betsy Seidel, my favorite teacher, who believed I could! Special thank you to The Munchkins: The Neural Education Champions and participants as we co-create Munchkinland together, with our Neural Lens.

Mary Catherine Pilon: Thank you to my husband Christopher Pilon for your endless support in my pursuit of all things brain.

Taylor Cassidy: Thank you to Missy for mentoring me into a teacher who knows better and can do better. Thank you to my students for humbling me and helping me serve them better every day.

Audrey Gallagher: To all the educators, especially my students, who have helped shape me – thank you for honoring our play as we made sense of each growth opportunity. To my neural educators who continue to be my greenhouse to shape, challenge, and expand my thinking; words will never be enough to express my gratitude. Patrick, Niamh, and Danann – thank you for continuing to play and learn with me – being your mom is my greatest joy. Robert – for supporting me always – your love and support help me be my very best self. And finally, to my mom, Celine, you were my first teacher, my confidante, and my biggest cheerleader – thank you for always allowing me to play and explore – I am braver because of you.

Dani Hylton: Thank you to my husband, Russell, who is always my loudest cheerleader.

Stephanie Turcotte: I would like to thank Kieran for giving me the opportunity to share my story and hopefully help others. I would also like to thank my mentor Angela, who has guided me throughout my healing journey. Finally, thank you to my son William. You are my inspiration, my reason to live.

Valli: I am very grateful and special thanks to Mary Snyder, Kieran O'Mahony, and Cumi Ikeda who made significant contributions to this chapter.

Jeannine Medvedich: I would like to thank all of the champions that I've had throughout my educational career for allowing me to do the outside of the box work that helps our children be successful. It is not easy to take risks, and many times putting on those neural lenses can feel pretty uncomfortable. First of all, to one of my favorite bosses who puts up with my daily antics, Marc Brouillet, Superintendent at Chief Leschi Schools. Next, to my partner in crime Binah McCloud, who continuously reminds me that culture is the heart of our school and opens up space for me to learn each and every day. For the support of our Leschi School board, who over the last five years have supported our work to make the impossible possible! To our BIE champions under the leadership of Director Tony Dearman and Dr. Carmelia Becenti, Chief Academic Officer, and Connie Albert for giving us a voice and caring for us so we can support our children. And to our newest partners at WestED, Terry Hofer and Joseph Sassone, who share my love of school improvement and creating equity across this great nation. Special thanks to Lauren Dale for photo credit for the Dopamine Dealer t-shirt pictures.

And finally, we wish to acknowledge you, the reader. We invite you to join us in the emerging market for neuroscience knowledge in learning spaces. We hope you have found something in these pages that continues to inspire you and we wish you the very best in your teaching careers.

Introduction

Kieran O'Mahony

> *Give me a dozen healthy infants, well-formed, and my own specified world to bring them up in and I'll guarantee to take any one at random and train him to become any type of specialist I might select – doctor, lawyer, artist, merchant-chief and, yes, even beggar-man and thief, regardless of his talents, penchants, tendencies, abilities, vocations, and race of his ancestors.*
>
> (John Watson, **Behaviorism**, 1930)

School environments are messy and complicated. Even the best run, tidiest classrooms make it hard to collect data and produce evidence that points to the effectiveness of a teacher's intervention meant to enhance academic performance and quell behavior issues. It is nearly impossible to account for every variable that inevitably affects academic and social-emotional outcomes in classrooms. It can feel virtually insurmountable to draw causative links between an intervention initiated at the beginning of the school year and the results that emerge nine months later. Data collection instruments struggle to account for interruptions, interference, and extraneous variables that rear their ugly heads over the course of a school year. This makes it hard to determine whether the jaw-dropping results demonstrated by a student were due to luck, the choice of breakfast eaten on the day of a big test, a life-changing event outside of the classroom, or the actual intervention introduced by the teacher in the classroom.

Despite the uncertainty teachers face concerning what techniques and interventions produce helpful academic and social-emotional results for their students, they suit up and show up every day. Teachers continue to try new methods. Many are even willing to attempt seemingly crazy, out-of-the-box ideas that are meant to help children struggling with varying challenges. Over time, some teachers become jaded. The *fix-du-jour* too often results in limited and unverifiable outcomes, while proving too big a headache to implement. However, in this book, you will meet teachers who did not give up. These teachers are early adopters of a brand-new pedagogic model that shifts teaching and learning ever so slightly, but with a meaningful and lasting impact. The shift is from a nineteenth century two-dimensional rewards and punishment model to a brain-based cognitive model that is modern and meaningful for the twenty-first century child.

DOI: 10.4324/9781003449683-1

The reason these teachers stuck with this intervention is because it works. They saw results. Within this pedagogic model, teachers learn to trust their instincts and find creative solutions to everyday problems. Moreover, teachers realize that the published scientific literature corroborates their intuitive inclinations toward teaching. When something works, they can see the science behind why it works; when something doesn't work, they can see the science behind why they should never try that again. The shift isn't a big one, but it is incredibly impactful.

Finding solutions to the big crises in education is imperative. Lortie (1) suggested the crisis in education was systemic. Teachers bring their personal experiences of learning from *their* teachers to present-day classrooms. A novice teacher is atypical of any other novice in any other field, for example, riveters who fabricate airplanes, or early career nurses.

> The apprenticeship of observation describes the phenomenon whereby student teachers arrive for their training courses having spent thousands of hours as schoolchildren observing and evaluating professionals in action. This contrasts with novices learning other professions, such as those of lawyers or doctors.
>
> (1)

This apprenticeship, he argued, is largely responsible for the many preconceptions that pre-service student teachers hold about teaching. Many teachers gladly state that they entered education because they wanted to inspire, mentor, and lead children. However, upon further questioning, it becomes clear that teachers inevitably hold deep, sustained, and visceral memories of the several individuals who affected their own school experiences (2). Some memories are traumatic and punishing, resulting in the educator wanting to reverse this experience for future children. Others had the opposite experience, having been warmly influenced by an inspirational mentor who changed their lives for the better. The most common reason why a person becomes an educator is the notion that they can make a difference for countless young people by becoming a role model who can influence the values, attitudes, and behaviors of their students.

While it is wonderful that educators come into the teaching profession with noble intentions, it is also true that many teachers lack pedagogic content knowledge. More often than not, it gets lost in the curriculum. This means that an educator's style of teaching is usually based on what that person observed from their teachers when they were in school. The result is that we have a pedagogic framework that looks very much the same as

Aristotle's Lyceum from Ancient Greece. The pedagogue (teacher) stands in front of a class of students and passes along wisdom pearls of learning to a rapt audience. The only difference is that today's children are not necessarily so rapt to learn from the sage on the stage. We are indeed long overdue for an updated pedagogic framework that can accommodate a fast-paced modern world with technological advancements and increasingly complex social systems.

The crises are made more visible through existential changes that have threatened the foundational pillars of our learning world over the past few years. Teachers continue to leave the profession in large numbers. A recent article from the *Economist* (3) recorded the situation as follows:

> The narrative goes as follows. America is suffering from a nationwide teacher shortage. Teachers have been leaving the profession for years, but recent stresses from the pandemic and the culture war have caused the entire profession to hit a tipping point. Educators are leaving in droves. School leaders are using desperate measures to recruit. Some districts are offering five-figure bonuses. Florida is allowing military veterans without the usually required qualification of a bachelor's degree to teach while taking college classes. Some rural schools are even resorting to four-day school weeks.
> (3)

The crisis continues to loom as year after year, staff and administrators struggle to make sense of, and come to terms with, school shootings, classroom violence, divisive and charged politics, and mental health issues prevalent across stressful learning sites. Chatter from inside school faculty rooms echoes the growing crisis. Post-pandemic hysteria appears in reports from teacher surveys (2022) that indicate a more widespread issue. Evidently, 74% of educators are dissatisfied with their jobs, according to a survey by the American Federation of Teachers, the country's second-largest teachers' union. A survey by the National Education Association, America's largest labor union, estimated that 55% of teachers are considering leaving the profession (3).

The question we must ask ourselves is, can meaningful change take place in such a charged environment? The answer is yes, as evidenced by the recent disruption of traditional learning environments. The catalyst for these immense changes was COVID-19. This life-threatening crisis upended accepted norms and heralded a tech-enabled, muti-verse future made possible by a tsunami of technological wizardry available to us.

Traditional classrooms were disrupted for a few years during the pandemic and have shown real difficulties bouncing back to a pre-pandemic equilibrium (4). Although traditional classrooms face significant challenges in returning to a post-pandemic norm, it is possible that the disequilibrium caused by the global pandemic paved the way for the emergence of fresh thinking.

As previously mentioned, Lortie's apprenticeship model is inescapable – all teachers fit into it. It is easy to fall into the trap of believing, after having been educated by sitting in classrooms and listening to thousands of hours of lectures at higher educational establishments, that "they" must know what teaching is all about. Sadly, the carefully crafted classroom management techniques that are seemingly modern and, therefore, supposedly result in students sparkling with attention and engagement rarely work. It turns out that the reason, while obvious today, didn't seem to make any sense until recently. Robert Sapolsky (5), the Stanford neuroendocrinology researcher and author, offers a solution from history …

> John Watson was one of the founding fathers of the school of psychology called behaviorism. It reached its apogee with B. F. Skinner in the 1950s. The notion that if you could control the rewards, the punishments, the positive and negative reinforcement, you could turn anybody into anything you want whether doctor, lawyer, beggar, thief.
>
> (5)

Sapolsky's work is luminary by way of explaining human behavior. His understanding of educational establishments outside of the university laboratories that he is familiar with in Stanford, however, is a little out of date. To think that behaviorism reached its apogee in the 1950s and that we educators have moved on to a world where rewards and punishments do not exist, where reinforcement schedules are out of favor … is a common and persistent blind spot for people who are not on the front lines of teaching in elementary, middle, and high school every day. To my knowledge, there is not a single school anywhere where children are not rewarded to increase good behavior, or punished to decrease bad behavior. Reinforcement schedules as prescribed by Skinner, including token economies, tickets, clipping, class dojo, and other punishing routines of public shaming, isolation, and even restraints, are liberally used every day with a view to adjusting behavior. A yearlong investigation by Hearst Newspapers reported on a controversial use of restraints and seclusion in schools nationwide (6). Most people do not believe that such punishments are meted out to children in the United States.

> Every day in public and private schools across the country, children are "restrained" – physically held by staff members, pinned to the ground, or bound by mechanical devices such as straps or handcuffs. Other times, students are kept in "seclusion", confined alone in rooms ranging from windowless small supply closets and bathrooms to spaces resembling padded cells.
>
> (6)

Nevertheless, teachers are simply doing what they were taught to do, and what is expected of them based on state law driven by school discipline standards. To make matters worse, many parents agree with this kind of treatment for their children, deeming it as meaningful and righteous in deterring "undesirable" behavior.

And yet, Watson's outrageous claim (which we know is impossible) still persists in schools everywhere and, in addition, Skinner's outmoded thinking is evident in classrooms across the world. People who have never heard of Watson or Skinner are using their outmoded methodologies to raise their kids. Sapolsky, too, is not alone in misinterpreting the advent of the cognitive revolution, which was supposed to have magically replaced Skinnerian thinking on the 11th September 1956 at a meeting at the Massachusetts Institute of Technology (7). In his seminal treatise on the human brain, the eminent neuroscientist V. S. Ramachandran (8) explained it as follows:

> For most of the twentieth century, all we had to offer in the way of explaining human behavior was two theoretical edifices—Freudianism and behaviorism—both of which would be dramatically eclipsed in the 1980s and 1990s, when neuroscience finally managed to advance beyond the bronze age.
>
> (8)

Ramachandran at least brought us to the 1990s, but sadly, he also, appears to not have stepped into a typical American school lately, or one in his homeland India, or any elementary school in Africa[1] since then (9). The reality is much different.

In a modern world that is constantly moving forward with a pace that resembles a whitewater river, it is easy to get confused with the drive for content over person. For instance, in our interminable rush to modernity, Ramachandran is convinced that neuroscience has reached momentum and energy in today's society so that outcomes are progressive and informed (8). Notice that there is no mention of neuroeducation!

> In the last decade we have even seen neuroscience becoming self-confident enough to start offering ideas to disciplines that have traditionally been claimed by the humanities. So we now for instance have neuroeconomics, neuromarketing, neuroarchitecture, neuroarchaeology, neurolaw, neuropolitics, neuroesthetics, and even neurotheology. Some of these are just neurohype, but on the whole they are making real and much-needed contributions to many fields.
> (8)

It turns out that millions of teachers across the globe grew up and were made aware – viscerally and emotionally – of what learning was all about in the same way as our aged household relatives (parents and grandparents). In other words, we were all victims of Lortie's world. We learned from our teachers, from our parents, and from adults who had supped at the same water hole – the dreaded rewards and punishments well.

Some of us survived it, and some ended up in terrible lifelong struggles. It turns out also that those of us who survived the Watson/Skinner psychological experiment can easily be explained by understanding the cognitive world that is so eloquently described by both Sapolsky and Ramachandran. It's simply a matter of understanding our autonomic nervous system (ANS) reactivity score. In other words, how resilient or how sensitive are we with respect to social context? How many teachers do you know who talk about ANS reactivity models?

Today, we understand Watson's dilemma. In 1923, when he published his *Behaviorist Manifesto* (10), the human brain was viewed as a "black box" that was poorly understood. It made sense to theorists in the early years of the last century that a study of what went into the brain (stimulus) and a study of what came out (response) were sufficient for figuring out how children learned. How many of us labored and were trained in Stimulus/Response (S/R) techniques and reinforcement schedules during our teacher preparation courses? Yes, 100% of teachers were immersed in S/R scenarios. It appears, therefore, that the cognitive revolution of the 1950s, outlined by both Sapolsky and Ramachandran, bypassed educators and education. We educators were stuck in an older model. Not anymore.

Today, especially after the decade of the brain (1990–1999), so much new information has emerged about how the human brain works and how children learn that it is easy to bypass both Watson and Skinner. It is easy to understand new constructs like amygdala hijack, long-term potentiation, and play in the phonological loop.

That is to say, for a long time – a very, very long time – education looked the same for each generation. Sure, some change had occurred since Plato and Aristotle introduced the idea that bringing individual learners together into a place of erudite active learning (e.g., the Lyceum) could deliver people who were capable of running city-states, armies, and establishing empires. Interestingly enough, a simple inspection of a black and white photo of classrooms from nineteenth century US or British schools describes modern classrooms in some remote regions of India and Africa today. Take away the smart board, the computer, the iPads – most classrooms will take the same shape as an Aristotelian Lyceum, where the teacher, as a purveyor of knowledge, transmits it to students who sit in seats facing forward. It is easy to see that even in early Greek society, learners must raise their hands to answer questions and respond to teacher's testing questions. Sometimes that is referred to as the Socratic method.

This book is designed to highlight how a cognitive brain-based approach to classroom management and engagement aligns school with the twenty-first century child. It brings simplicity and breadth to difficult behavior issues that teachers solve using a neural lens. Learning is self-evident in every classroom where children and teachers co-create their physical and learning spaces.

All children have brains and all children use them to engage their minds. Each brain is unique. Consciousness is unique to each individual. Mind, brain, and consciousness are in play for each individual separately. Mind is a person's intellect – that is something that enables one to be aware of themselves and their world. It allows us to engage with experiences, especially to think, and to feel. Mind is thus the faculty of consciousness and thought.

The various functions of the mind, like rationalizing and learning, are a set of processes carried out by the brain. Mind capacities are referred to as cognitive ability. The word "cognitive" conjures a rich envelope for concepts that include notions of reasoning, predicting, and thinking.

Without a brain, the mind would not function. Our brains therefore make us who we are. It is because we are able to think, feel, argue, laugh, act, learn, remember, and create that we are who we are. The brain is only roughly three pounds of squishy vesicles, yet it produces our every emotional and intellectual act. It determines our moods. It is also immensely powerful and full of potential – it can endow us with the capability for great joy, terrible fears, real sadness, and awful misery.

The neural lens, which is derived from an understanding of the brain and mind, is critical in classrooms. The child's brain is what makes him or her who he or she is. This transpires into being the genius of a teacher – the facility to manage 20 or more intelligent minds and adjust the environment accordingly so each one can flourish and thrive. The teacher can create a learning space, which fosters a child's personal identity and autonomy. Our biological system is made up of billions of neurons, which form circuits by connecting and communicating with one another. It also includes chemicals in the blood, as well as bacteria in the gut. We recognize a "gut" feeling for a person, place, or thing that sometimes makes all the difference. We are creatures of interaction and reaction. Genetics and epigenetics play their part too. Our school life is affected by where we were born, the parents who raised us, the classes we attended, and the social contexts in which we grew up.

Every day, in schools and homes we see the results of genetics and environment at play. Children either thrive or struggle to learn. Moms and dads anguish over why one of their amazing children cannot compete in academics, or contribute at sports, and will often show up in a negative and reactive way against all expectations and wishes. At the same time, we witness children who used to be dysregulated, disruptive, aggressive, and troubled achieve personal successes in the face of insurmountable odds that ought to incapacitate even the most resilient of our species. What is the difference? How can we explain the connection to the brain, personality, identity, and potential?

In this book, we attempt to draw together strings of neuroscience and learning sciences in order to make sense of children in their social contexts. It comes as a relief to teachers and parents to know that there is a solution to the many distracting and disruptive behaviors that seem to dominate optimal learning scenarios. Teachers explain in these chapters their intimate experiences with commonplace neuronal structures that underlie learning. We accompany these with appropriate pedagogic nuances to illuminate successful learning environments. We begin with the premise that all children are born to learn; we thrive in the knowledge that they are hardwired learning-machines.

In this book, teachers who have embraced a cognitive model and a cognitive pedagogy describe their experiences in their schools and classrooms. Over the past few years (which included a pandemic interruption to normal school life), they implemented a co-created learning environment that was carefully sculpted to follow a brain-based approach.

In order to make neuroscience of learning accessible to non-scientific readers, we view the neuronal structure with the cerebellum and four lobes from a simplistic three-part model. Admittedly viewing the human brain, which is recognized by eminent neuroscientists as the most complex phenomenon in the known universe, through the lens of a simplistic model might prove horrifying to some purists; nevertheless, it serves to make visible and somewhat accessible important techniques and verifiable practices that work in the classroom. And because they work, children and teachers experience a more equitable, fun, and engaging learning space.

The authors who appear here are incumbent, practicing teachers who collectively chose to be "early adopters" in an innovative and groundbreaking educational journey. They sometimes confess that it was an eye-opener to walk through and experience a complex paradigm shift on three planes at the same time. Paradigms included constructs that are in the classroom every day, though usually viewed singularly. The constructs are familiar to educators as mindset (fixed/growth), motivation (extrinsic/intrinsic), and expertise (routine/adaptive). Each, alone, is meaningful in relation to knowledge and method in which teachers are already immersed. When all three are aligned together into a three-dimensional model (7), these constructs coalesce to cause a new view of classroom management in a way they hadn't perceived through novel, goal-directed intentionality.

Over the past five years, teachers represented here have taken personalized training and made exceptional efforts to change their traditional two-dimensional teaching practices by adopting and deeply understanding the shift to cognitive mindsets, motivation, and expertise. It follows that their work has inspired and delivered immense improvement to school systems and classrooms wherever they are invited to speak and teach.

The book is presented in thirteen chapters. Each chapter roughly aligns with lateralized structures that amplify behavior and learning from a specific region of the brain. This notion that a chapter should reside wholly in a region of the brain however is not real. We know that when the cerebellum is active, there are circuits "lighting up" in connected regions as close as the limbic and as far away as the frontal lobes. We know that when learning takes place in classrooms, the occipital visual complexes are usually involved and so also are the temporal hippocampal, amygdala, and speech and understanding regions (Broca's and Wernicke's) and often the fusiform gyrus when children make connections with facial recognition and safety. Similarly, both hemispheres are typically involved in processing and articulating information so that the corpus callosum is doing its extraordinarily intricate diffusion of circuitry to connect parietal and frontal regions on both sides to interpret sensory information and encode it into memory. Author teachers are connecting a neural circuit to create a transformative impact. Other regions are involved also, but we highlight the intentionality of the teacher. For instance, if I want to teach a child what it means to pay attention, I know that large areas of the child's brain will be active, yet I might focus attention on listening and visual processing. Engaging one region of the brain for a child who struggles to sit still has the added effect of mastery and purpose. We know that a sense of mastery coupled with purpose will deliver intrinsic neurotransmitters like serotonin and oxytocin as the child gains confidence in contributing successfully in front of peers. It is our experience that success is contagious and before long we have established a learning space that affords success for a generation of children who are critical thinkers, socially and emotionally capable, and physically and mentally healthy.

The first five teachers focus on knowledge pertaining to involuntary/reactive brain and the reticular formation at the brainstem. These teachers are aware of powerful primal outcomes that are associated with this ancient portion of the human brain – where the medulla, the pons, and the midbrain allow a child to survive and maintain in an unfriendly world, but also where belief systems and implicit bias are put in place.

The next four educators move the reader farther into the brain engaging the emotional limbic areas where a focus on neuronal connections, neural plasticity, and the brain's amazing capacity for rewiring itself based on lived and emerging environmental experiences allows the child blossom in a healthy way.

The final four educators focus on methods and practices that allow children to instantiate and strengthen white matter structures that typically originate in the rear and middle regions of the brain and connect to the higher order prefrontal cortex. These chapters highlight a learner's capacity to predict, plan, and assimilate new information with prior knowledge with fluency that is remarkable.

Chapter 1 is introduced by a teacher whose world dramatically changed because she was brought face to face with the reticular formation in the brainstem. The reticular activating system (RAS) can be a teacher's best friend or worst detractor, depending on how much knowledge and understanding about how it works is available to her and her students. It comes down to mental models that are derived from vocabulary understandings that might seem remote, but, in fact, live in every classroom, playground, and school cafeteria. Teachers learn to manage their classrooms by becoming simple marketing masters. We create opportunities for interest, for attention, and for curiosity in order to activate the RAS and help our students and colleagues create and myelinate new neural pathways.

In Chapter 2, we are honored to witness a truly revolutionary methodology that brings learning sciences and neurosciences into a treasured gift that children recognize and embrace with joy and pleasure. This educator solves a conundrum that has plagued parents and teachers for generations – how could learning be perceived as a gift? She was aware that time spent in occupational therapy was good, but not sufficient, to deliver outcomes that closed the achievement gap for children who arrived at school already lagging behind their classmates. The many skills that children need to be taught by the end of each school year are daunting, especially when they enter with such vastly different ability levels. And yet, identifying the best, most engaging, most equitable, most efficient, and most effective educational strategies to help each student achieve their maximal potential is both the aspiration and struggle of each educator.

Chapter 3 focuses on the teacher. Research has shown that when a teacher changes their mindsets with regard to how they perceive schools, learning systems, and children, amazing change can happen. In this personal account, a simple visit to a hair salon causes a major shift in how the teacher perceives the construct of "perception" and how, when conflated with negative thinking, it can lead to very different realities. The power of the reactive brain is coupled with the reticular activating system to continually look for biases and find "confirmation" anywhere it can. What happens when we find an "implicit" bias that we are not even aware of? It happens to each of us … happens everywhere, including in our classroom environments. What if all that time spent with positive intention on skillfully crafted bulletin boards, classroom posters, announcements, and informational signs … what if that work is sending a negative message? What does brain science tell us?

Chapter 4 has the power and capacity to shake the very foundations of any school and any family. Many teachers are also mothers and fathers. It makes no sense when a teacher's child is not able, is disruptive, is oppositional, and is difficult to teach. But what if that amazing child suddenly and inexplicably becomes non-verbal, immobile, and basically comatose because of seven strokes in the brainstem … this story by a very committed mom and educator delivers information and hope to millions of parents and teachers because of the insights, the calm, and methodical approach to rewiring a young child's brain.

Chapter 5 describes a teacher journey from someone who has worked her way up from bus driving, to para-educator, to classroom teacher. Dani is passionately connected to children whose wiring systems are still making appropriate connections for full engagement in learning environments. Her account of the journey is refreshing and tender. "By the third week the honeymoon was over. It was not only over, but the marriage had crashed and burned. It was a Friday – oddly enough Friday the 13th. Desks were tipped over, counters cleared, books thrown, and some chairs tossed. Students were bodily assisted out of the classroom and taken to quiet rooms to calm down.

These quiet rooms were either in the school or back in the hospital. None of the students were able to return to the classroom. The wheels were off the wagon". Dani's recovery was spectacular and how she took a classroom from utter chaos to solid learning is a must read for all teachers and parents of children who have been institutionalized.

Chapter 6 recounts an incredible story involving neural plasticity and the brain that rewires itself. This account speaks to all teachers and all parents. Their son is born with internal bleeding in the cerebrum that causes both physical and cognitive challenges that are often life-threatening. A teacher, who is a mom, understands the need to deeply grasp that the brain is malleable, that children are incredibly plastic, and that change is possible. More important is that everyone has the ability to learn and develop their potential, regardless of where they begin. The underlying principles and unique techniques used in education therapy are described in this work. This life story is written by a teacher, but especially by a mother. It provides landmark pillars of hope and intention for those wishing to understand the impact of conductive education (CE) for supporting her child who has cerebral palsy. In this life account, you will follow the path of a cerebral palsy child, from birth to school age, who thrived because of the resilience of the parent and educator through conductive education therapy.

Chapter 7 shows us the evaluative healing comfort of art therapy. We explore new research into interdisciplinary relationships between science and art. This chapter looks at how initiatives within the fields of paleoanthropology, neuropsychology, and art therapy complement one another in the search for a better understanding of the nuances of our communication systems within education settings. By considering the biological and cultural evolution of human communication, we gain an understanding of how imagery and creative process contribute to the human ability to "make meaning". Image making contributes to our own emotional and physical self-regulation, consciousness, and broader connection to the community. We show that an understanding of these principles and an engagement in the creative process positively impact brain and body regulatory systems.

Chapter 8 is a heartfelt journey into the joyful world of play when our author teacher takes a risk with a child who is already so traumatized by lived experience that simply engaging in learning systems with his peers is impossible and destructively so. "A ten-year-old boy sits barricaded under a table grunting and growling at me. His face is flushed, his breathing is heavy, I can see the tension in his body … he is watching me carefully. I am told that this is a common occurrence, one of many reasons why he has qualified for extra support in behavior. What actions can I take to help this child feel safe? How can I help him know that he belongs? Deep breath, he needs me to be regulated." "In classrooms across North America, the above is a common scenario … leaving parents, teachers, administrators, mental health professionals, and the community at large wondering how best to respond. What happened to cause this reaction? My neural lens tells me that it is just an evolutionary survival reaction – a reptilian remnant of the survival brain, it is often referred to as the reactive, involuntary brain associated with freeze, fight and flight." Enjoy the playful resolution of this story.

Chapter 9 offers the opportunity to sink into a sea of pain and trauma with the author who explored Dr. Felitti's seminal work on adverse childhood experiences (ACEs). We follow a class of fresh new educators who are new to teaching and are being trained in methods that can change their world. What we didn't expect was the impact of opening Pandora's box for the lead educator who had never before filled out an ACEs scorecard. Great teaching is easier to recognize than to describe. It happens when the teacher is not present as much as when there is a lesson underway. It seems a little non-intuitive, but when the teacher is bored, the students are doing great on their own. It often defies logic to try to make sense of a noisy, animated group of young people arguing, planning, making decisions, and using all their craziest emotional energy to undertake a project that they themselves chose and into which they poured a huge amount of time and effort. Sometimes, intuitively great teachers can get to this place with their students, but when there is a clear science associated with the neuroscience of learning, we can achieve this kind of outcome every time. Teaching teachers is the greatest gift to children because great teachers matter.

Chapter 10 steps us into the higher executive functioning associated with the brain's prefrontal cortex. We follow the journey of a young teacher who is new to the stresses of managing a class and engaging children for outcomes that meet state and societal standards. "I teach third grade in rural Montana. Through my exposure to Neural Education, I wanted to use my neural lens to decrease amygdala hijack in my classroom. I shifted from traditional 'morning work' to a brain-aligned 'soft start' and saw my student's educational experience transform. Instead of greeting my students with a review worksheet when they walked in in the morning, I gave them a self-reflective survey and an opportunity to engage in a variety of interest-based activities." One simple mind shift evolved into a cascade of outcomes that changed the lives of the students and the teacher. This author witnessed how her students had time to regulate before beginning their day and thus were able to access better educational and emotional outcomes. She figured out that by changing the environment instead of the child, good things transpired in their co-created learning space.

Chapter 11 focuses on self-regulation in the high school classroom where sometimes children are old enough but not yet wired enough to be successful. This is an extraordinarily powerful account of one young girl's journey as she finds support and understanding with a teacher who knows the malleability and myelination that occur with cognitive rehearsal and long-term potentiation. The recent pandemic isolation has demonstrated that we have either drastically underestimated student's ability to motivate themselves or drastically overestimated how much impact the structure and placement of a classroom and teacher has on a student's ability to work productively. What we thought was student motivation was actually a product of supports designed to supplement executive function. In this reflection of the process, we learn about co- and self-regulation in the adolescent brain.

Chapter 12 highlights a teacher who has already accomplished in a short few years working with neuroscience, life-changing methods and techniques to impact children's lives and influence systems deeply. This teacher found that school systems were typically built on old practices that punish rather than teach appropriate behaviors. She found that, unfortunately, programs with solution-sounding titles (like PBIS – Positive Behavioral Interventions and Supports) were an unsatisfactory waste of time. They don't work for children with the highest needs and are not needed for our students that know how to "do school". Her work showed that breaking away from a behavior-focused punishment model and moving toward teaching with a Neural Lens helped build a stronger society and broke the "school to prison" pipeline.

Chapter 13 delivers a touch of magic in the classroom together with a yellow brick road and a scarecrow that discovered the power of having a brain. This educator was able to transform her learning space by embracing a new vocabulary. Simple changes in mindset caused huge changes in behavior and academic outcomes. But more importantly, she found that her students were engaging with delight in fun-filled learning environments that highlighted their talents, their appetite over aptitude, and their altruism over fear.

This book is foremost the voice of educators for educators. Teachers teaching teachers is not an easy thing, nor is it welcomed by teachers who have been cut from the same cloth and emerge from similar backgrounds. In this case, however, neural educators are hewn into a different stone, are plowing new furrows in landscapes not frequented by typical education systems, and are breaking new ground in schools, in homes, and in workplaces anywhere in the world where they arrive.

Note

1. Kenya: Mr. Mwangi gets his son to stand and pull up his white vest to reveal a thick, angry scar covering almost the width and length of his back. He says the wounds (caused by his teacher) were so deep the surgeon had to remove large pieces of skin from his thighs to use as skin grafts. https://www.bbc.com/news/world-africa-67229601

References

1. D. Lortie, *Schoolteacher* (University of Chicago Press, Chicago, 1975).
2. K. Fried, *American Teacher: Heroes in the Classroom* (Welcome Books, New York, NY, 2013).
3. The usual suspects: America's new "national teacher shortage" is neither new nor national. The Economist. 2022.
4. T. Morgan, Chief Leschi Schools: Preparing students to walk successfully in "two worlds". Learn to Return, L2R Spotlight. 2021.
5. V, Sapolsky, in *Introduction to Human Behavioral Biology* (Stanford University, 2010). https://www.youtube.com/watch?v=NNnIGh9g6fA&t=1384s
6. E. Munson, M. Rocheleau, A. Putterman, L. Seline, A. Kanik, Controversial and often used, these little-known practices cause harm, even death, among U.S. schoolchildren. 2022. https://www.ctinsider.com/news/article/Controversial-and-often-used-these-little-known-17474949.php
7. K. O'Mahony, *The Brain-Based Classroom: Accessing Every Child's Potential through Educational Neuroscience* (Routledge, Taylor & Francis Group, London, UK and New York, ed. First, 2021).
8. V. S. Ramachandran, *The Tell-Tale Brain: A Neuroscientist's Quest for What Makes Us Human* (W. W. Norton & Co., New York, NY, 2012).
9. T. Odula, T. Ford, Kenya's school floggings: The children suffering from a hidden epidemic. BBC Africa Eye, 2023 (https://www.bbc.com/news/world-africa-67229601).
10. J. B. Watson, Psychology as the behaviorist views it. *Psychological review* **20**, 158–177 (1913).

1

I Can Hear My Baby Across a Noisy Crowded Room!

By Laurie Donati

Emily didn't connect easily. On any given day, she was noticeably "ajar" from the close-knit circle of classmates – as if she were fully prepared for a fast escape. I try to be unobtrusive but cannot fail to note her distance. I felt it deeply. It was not hard to miss the hyper-vigilance and anxious expression (1). I also knew scraps of information related to her history; accounts that were grounded in stress, trauma, and neglect from her home-side caregivers. Consequently, I took care to never "push" her or even suggest she align her chair with the other children.

"Give her time." I thought.

I was prepared to give her all the time she needed in order for her to feel safe in our little group. At 11 years old, she already had learned to not trust.

On this particular day, she sat slightly askew as usual and, also as usual, she mostly hid behind her oversized black hoodie. It was difficult to make eye contact since her long hair covered her face and shoulders. She appeared busy. I noticed the worksheet resting lightly in her lap, but I could see that she was fidgety. At intervals, she was apt to cover her mouth with her hands, which were protected under her long and tattered sweatshirt sleeves. This was an obvious comfort tactic.

I wince to think of how many times teachers "remind" her to take her hood down … and with "good" intentions, warn her to keep "hands away from face."

Connecting with her was a priority for me. I knew that I was making progress – ever so slowly. I also knew that my work was cut out for me – replacing a long entrenched myelinated structure with a new structure that might open her to possibilities (2). I was swimming against the tide since she had already built a robust defense for survival at home and in school.

Our small group was a safe place, but was it safe enough to invite Emily in? Safety and connection would be akin to a "sense of belonging" for her (3). That sense of belonging was more important to me than compliance. So, I allowed her to sit and just listen … while the rest of the children were exploring ideas in deep conversations about school and life.

On this day, I had chosen a difficult topic – the Reticular Activating System (RAS). If I was correct, I judged that RAS would be something that the kids would grasp. I also wanted to approach mindset, since neural substrates to "fixedness" are rooted in the RAS (4).

RAS might be particularly relevant for Emily. This tiny network of neurons sitting askew on the brain stem could explain much about her own "fixedness" and might even open a doorway to a new experience with her home life. She liked novelty. I figured that her curiosity and attention might be tweaked – a fact that would allow her "mirror" neurons to connect with her classmates as they entangled the new construct (5).

I had already introduced this group to the "flight" or "fight" reactive response that is associated with the brain's fear center – the amygdala (6). The kids liked to say "Amygdala Hijack" and were already good at recognizing it in themselves and recovering with some deep breathing when they felt stressed.

Knowing about amygdala hijack, I notice nuances of "comfort seeking" that "sensitive" students tend to need (7). I also understood that if I pushed Emily to "Join the group" or "Take the hood off", she would be triggered into amygdala hijack and unable to access her rational brain in the prefrontal cortex. Inevitably, that would spiral down to negative emotions where she would be unable to learn (8).

They also knew about the hippocampus and the difference between semantic and episodic memories (9). The notion of the hippocampus being a seahorse resonated with the artist in them. Memories and new topics always became grounded in context. That is where we usually begin.

Context is everything when one is stressed (10). And social context defines sensitive children like Emily (11). School in March added a new dimension to social context; it was a little tense – a little testy (12). The imminent "Spring

Assessment" schedule introduced a tangible air of anxiety to the conversations because of "test taking" and "fear of failure" (13).

Indeed, any testing event can be a tense time of anxiety for children. We overhear many intense conversations pertaining to State Assessments. Anxious fear of failure is a tangible taste and worry spreads in contagion across the otherwise boisterous learning spaces. Teachers, too, stress and prep and their students end up feeling the crunch (14).

This rampant dread of not being able to pass the State Test is especially noticeable in my small group of students where they have proven many times already in their short lives that they are not good enough (15).

They have already labeled themselves as "Special Ed" or "IEP" and are very aware that they are not going to do well on any test. This "certitude" has been made abundantly clear each time they are pulled out of Gen Ed for interventions as "struggling" learners. They wear the label with a gravitas that defines and even amplifies their anxiety (16).

So what better time to talk about the RAS and make it a reading lesson! "Reticular time", I thought. I assembled a collection of facts into an article on the RAS that was written with these students in mind. It had the science, examples, and ideas for how to challenge our "self-talk" and ultimately our belief system. I even put together some questions that would help them with depth of knowledge.

I introduced the topic like this. I wanted to get their attention and I wanted to make them think.

Have you ever started thinking about something that you were not happy about? Those thoughts that challenge you from being your best self? Perhaps you are ruminating and obsessing about something someone said to you or a time that you felt they did something that challenges your character, making you question who you are?

We had fun unpacking "ruminating" and "obsessing" until we were ready to move on. A few children were writing notes. But most were just very quiet – uncomfortably quiet. I had their attention and I dived in deeper.

What if you have had these thoughts your entire life because of something someone said to you over and over, even a person that you were wishing and hoping was your strongest ally in life? Perhaps all you know is this trauma. What do we do with this – and how do we change what our brain allows in?

This is the power of the RAS – to learn how to understand these thoughts.

I asked the children to touch the base of their heads at the top of the spine. We looked at a picture that showed where the brain stem is located so we could each visualize our own RAS.

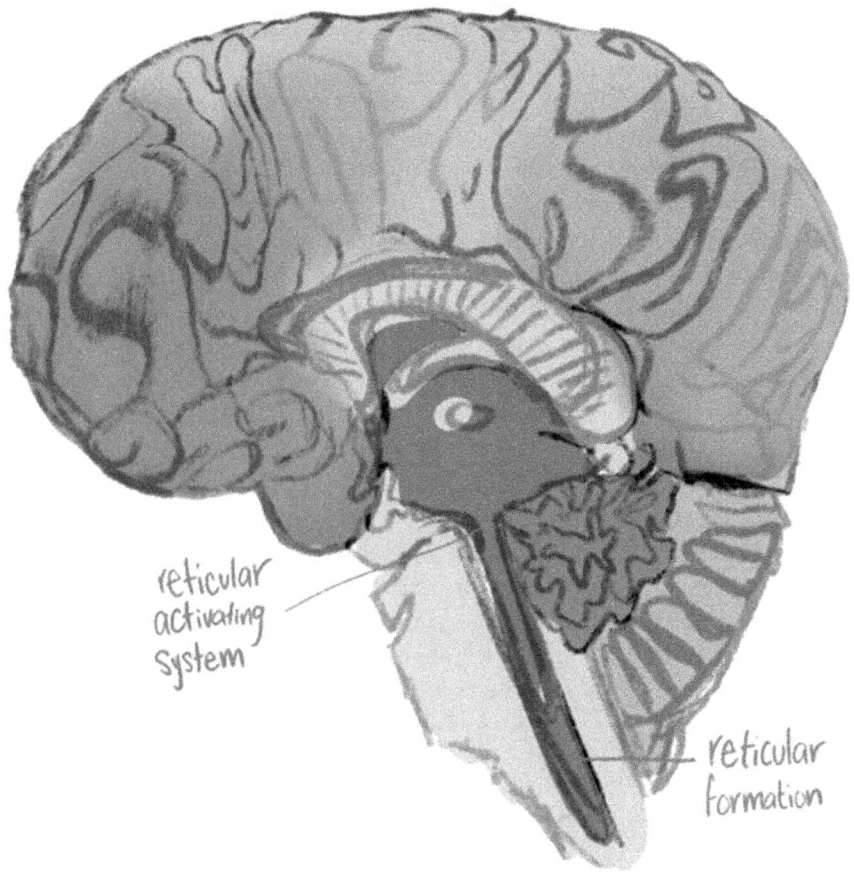

FIGURE 1.1 Reticular Activating System is Attached to the Brain Stem

The children had fun figuring out where eyes and ears should be placed on the accompanying diagram (Figure 1.1). They learned a few simple facts that connected with their knowledge of semantic memory:

RAS comprises a collection of neurons that is located between the brainstem and the cortex

Reticular means network or a net-like structure

This intricate network of neurons within our brainstem is an important filter that impacts our everyday life

Reticular Activating System

So what is the RAS and why is it so important in our daily existence? Studying RAS allows us to look closely at the science behind our beliefs, our self-talk, and our very ability to be present in our lives.

The small bundle of nerves, which we call the RAS, is primarily important because it connects the subconscious part of our brain with the conscious part. For instance, right now, as you read this, you are probably not thinking about the space between your big toe and your sock, but something in your brain is taking care of that reality. If your big toe were in pain, throbbing in inflammatory reaction to a recent injury, you would be thinking about it. In other words, the big toe is either in subconscious awareness or in conscious awareness. You can thank your RAS for that.

The RAS does a lot more; as a complex neural network, it supports our sleep, and our attention, in addition to our conscious awareness. This collection of neurons is known to be quite the sensory wizard, taking in what the brain deems most important for survival.

Take a moment and listen in to what is happening around you. What do you hear? What do you see? What are you tasting, or touching? Can you distinguish the refrigerator motor? Are there birds chirping outside? Notice a passing car, train, or plane? When you turn your attention to your incoming environmental sensory inputs, you begin to realize the conscious from the subconscious brain.

Fun Fact: the RAS does not process smell like it does all other sensory information coming to the brain. The sense of smell bypasses the RAS and goes directly to the olfactory bulb. Smell is too important for our survival – notice how you are protected with a visceral (involuntary) gag from eating a poisonous (icky) substance as soon as your nose gets a whiff of it.

All other incoming sensory information is filtered through our RAS. Our RAS is deciding, based on our own very unique and personal experiences, what it deems to be important to allow through, including sensory input from the environment, our very unique biases, and/or our individual belief systems.

At any given point, we have millions, if not billions, of bits of sensory data coming at us. If we did not have an effectively working RAS, then our brain would be inundated with that overwhelming amount of information and would be unable to perform necessary functions for survival and to preserve energy to reduce neural fatigue. This is why RAS allows roughly 1% of this data into conscious awareness.

When we are working with others ... whether at home, in the classroom, or in the boardroom, knowing about the RAS will help us to empathize and promote progress with ourselves, our families, our students, and our colleagues. When we activate our RAS and look for things that support our growth or well-being, we can begin to notice opportunities around us. If we have been working to meet a goal, journaling about that goal daily, and being fully aware of the solutions that we need to meet the goal, this allows our RAS to pick up on those opportunities.

Alternatively, the RAS can also pull out other things in the environment that remind us of negative belief systems and biases that we may not even know we hold. Perhaps as a child, someone filled our heads with negative belief systems, which we unfortunately believed ... and they continue to be a neural-battle we experience every day.

I am certain we all know of someone who has a difficult time getting past negative self-talk. Perhaps you've observed this with students, friends, or, frankly, most human relationships. An example that will inevitably feel familiar is about a student who struggles with just that.

This Is Emily's Story

I worked with Emily throughout the school year in a small intentional intervention group. Though a sixth grader, she was new to our school and reticent to open up. She gave very little feedback on whether or not she was engaged in a lesson or in building a healthy student-to-teacher relationship. At first, I pictured her being highly introverted.

As an introvert myself, I understood the challenge and tried to make opportunities for connection. I tried to be thoughtful about how I greeted her, engaged her in conversation, and was intentional in lessons and activities that involved her in a way that eased her into comfort. I believe that connections are the name of the game and exactly what makes the difference between helping a child succeed or just getting through the day.

I knew a bit about the history of her home life; most scraps of information being piecemeal as we worked together throughout the school year.

Her talent for drawing was obviously her preferred space, as she was often preoccupied with drawing detailed illustrations in her notebook. I didn't mind. My goal was to connect with her; create a safe space – and not provide any opportunities for an already traumatized brain to withdraw further from school, from her peers, and from trusting adults. As educators, we understand the intricacies of human relationships. We recognize the raw power of building trust with someone we work with.

It was clear to me that trauma darkened Emily's life. She was in another new foster home. I knew she had potential; when she engaged, she was very capable. But could I access that potential? Could I liberate her into her capacity? An average score on standardized assessments should be within her range. This is why she was in my reading group.

When children miss school days, they fall behind fast. Emily had missed hundreds of days of school during the years prior to coming to us. The most distressing deficit sprang from her fifth grade school year when the State finally stepped in. That was when she and her brother were taken from their dad's home. She missed well over half that year.

Of course she was struggling with academics. Not only was she a child in trauma with high ACEs (Adverse Childhood Experiences), but by not attending school, she missed important learning opportunities through several major developmental milestones. I didn't know much more about her history, but was able to connect the dots on these missing links.

I tried to make the human brain fun and accessible. We had a pretty wide text set on the neuroscience of learning developed at this point in the year. My students and I had covered different regions of the brain and colored the lobes together. We knew about neuroplasticity and spoke often about neurotransmitters like dopamine and oxytocin. We talked about cortisol – that icky feeling in the belly that accompanies stress. We explored the science of motivation and switch-tasking and knew the difference between switch- and multitasking. Now we were ready to take on the RAS.

We focused on belief systems – the things I believe. RAS is constantly searching for things it believes. This is what my students and I were discussing. I was hoping to make a big impression on their thinking systems especially as they are entering adolescence and about to move up to middle school.

I was happy with their learning for the week. Students were working on comprehension strategies and using their graphic organizers. The RAS big idea was a concept that I hoped would impact their lives positively going forward. Indeed they were asking amazing questions of each other and really starting to do a deep dive into this incredible part of their self-awareness.

I was also pretty confident that this cohort had co-created a safe place for taking risks; for asking difficult questions. I had worked with many of these children since I started at this school when they were in second grade.

We habituated lively discussions, mainly talking openly about questions that other teachers might shy away from (17). The RAS fixedness question was perfect for such a lively discussion.

This discussion was also timely because we had just wrapped up parent-teacher conferences. A "hot" topic was how some parents were taking ONE NEGATIVE COMMENT a teacher made and making school more difficult for them by focusing on only those negative thoughts.

Marylyn was always quick to jump in. Her mom was a little pushy.

"I know … negative talk," she asserted. "It's awful. In my basketball game yesterday, I started missing shots. Every time I missed I heard this little voice in my head that told me that I was going to miss shots all through the game. That's exactly what happened."

By all accounts, it was a good class. A resounding success if you measured the enthusiasm of the students as they left the room, still carrying on animated conversations about self-talk.

We had ended our class as any other, with a ball-bouncing activity and a one-word/one-concept ending. As we finished and I was saying good-bye to my students, I looked over at Emily. She waited until everyone had left the room. I saw something new in her expression … clear emotions … a hint of tears welling up in her eyes.

"Mrs. Donati," she was definitely struggling to hold back tears. "So … what you are telling me about the RAS makes me wonder … so … you're telling me that when my dad would scream at me … and call me 'no-good', 'stupid', 'loser' … it's my RAS that is showing me proof of those things. And … uh, that those things my mind is constantly thinking … um … are not really true?"

Our students show up at school with stories of things their most trusted allies have poisoned them with – and that they now tell themselves and believe to be true.

Those words and thoughts become who they are!

As educators, the fairest thing we can do is to ensure that we have compassion. But we can do more. Information is freeing.

We can teach about the brain. We can highlight neuroplasticity and RAS (18). We can highlight Mindset and RAS (19). Our students can change thanks to neuroplasticity, mindset, and RAS. We now understand that we indeed have control over our lives!

Think of that little voice in your head that says terrible things to you:

You're such a messy person. You'll never keep this up.

You are always late. People constantly have to wait for you.

You're too dumb to understand this stuff.

The science is clear. When you say things to yourself like this, your RAS confirms your beliefs and continues to search for that proof.

See. Look at this messy kitchen. I can't ever stick to a plan. Proof!

Look at that. Five minutes behind. Everyone else is here and I have to do the walk of shame. Proof!

I can't even pronounce amygdala. See – I will never understand this '*neurosciency*' stuff. Proof!

As a learning specialist, I consistently find myself thinking about solutions to negative thinking that I witness in my older elementary students. What if ... Yes, we can challenge this thinking ... We challenge it first in our own thinking? Because of these words, and these beliefs, many students fail every day ... they fail before they even begin.

I'm a bad reader. I'll never get this.

See. I can't read the words, let alone spell them, so why even try?

This will never work.

Along with teaching students *how to* read, write, or make sense of math problems, these examples were exactly the language I wanted to challenge with my students. And what better way to challenge these thoughts than to teach them the science behind the RAS. Figure 1.2 is a graphic that shows the iterative self-fulfilling nature of the cycle. The brain circles that self-talk, solidifying it into a permanent belief. And, in turn, it searches for proof of that belief whether it is fact or not. Beliefs can be positive or negative – RAS does not care.

Could this be the exact reason why giving positive, specific, and timely feedback to improve student autonomy, mastery, and purpose is so crucial to student achievement?

RAS was important for Emily. She experienced an immediate and permanent mental shift when she learned about the self-fulfilling cycle. For me, it was powerful too. She trusts me today. Connection is central to her life as well.

FIGURE 1.2 Reticular Activating System Confirms Our Beliefs

Admittedly, she was first taken aback, but quickly realized that she was in charge of her thinking. It was possible … and she could override that negative self-talk that was impressed on her by the people who most meant anything to her. Today, she connects with me and eases into schoolwork like other children her age. She has a lot of ground to catch up but she is not alone … and together, we are ok with that.

She has a new belief – the one she calls her main belief. She knows that she has 100 billion neurons and that each neuron has 10,000 connections.

"Same as anyone else," she smiles. "I can learn anything."

Classroom Strategies with RAS

The RAS is a filter that signals the brain – basically telling it what to focus on. Any child could know what and how RAS sifts through important information that is coming into the brain. For this reason, it is important that we understand and optimize a child's connection to his/her own RAS with respect to engaging in schoolwork, sports, any challenges, and homework. The implications between the internal thoughts … "I can do this …" or "I am no good at math …" make all the difference.

When learning about a new structure or function of the brain, it is helpful to think about its simplest functions and how it impacts you on a daily basis. For example, when you get a new car, you might begin seeing that car everywhere and wondering why everyone copied you and your great sense of motor vehicle style. That's your RAS noticing and confirming your selection!

Similarly, when a child learns a new word, new language, or new concept, they will begin to hear and see that word, language segment, or concept everywhere in their life around them. It's not that they weren't in their life all along, but now the RAS is tuned in to confirm the discovery. RAS can be a best friend or, alternatively, a worst naysayer.

Visualization is a very strong supporter for RAS. If the child can visualize getting an "A" in math, then the RAS is alerted to actions and systems that will support the goal.

Parents Use RAS Too

RAS reaches beyond school; it is everywhere and influences everyone. It's just as important that parents know about their RAS also. It's not that they don't already experience RAS; it's that they don't typically learn about it until it hits them in the face. As a new mom, it's the RAS that wakes you up in the middle of the night when you hear your baby cry. Similarly, when your child is playing at the park, you somehow can hear their laughter or cry above all other children. It's the RAS that is responsible for attention, arousal, and focus.

You hear your name called out in the supermarket! That, too, is your RAS attending to the novel or unexpected "survival" information coming in. This is often referred to as the "Cocktail Party Phenomenon". When it is unimportant to your RAS, you will simply habituate to all of the other chatter being spoken around you.

The RAS not only filters sensory information but also learns to identify what is coming in and how to habituate to it. For example, my sister used to live right near a very busy train track. A loud klaxon horn would blare at intervals, warning traffic that a train was coming through. I used to ask her how in the world she and her family slept at night. Dismissively, she smiled at me, "Ah, we are used to it. I don't even hear that train passing by."

Thanks to our RAS, over time we are able to ignore those frequent sounds like trains or planes, refrigerator humming, or even the little fan that is whirring to cool your computer.

Teachers as RAS Instigators

This makes me think of how much we have to keep track of every day as educators. Have you noticed that? We have lesson planning, scaffolding assignments, building rubrics, attending professional developments, collaborating with colleagues, teacher performance evaluations, parent correspondences, counseling students, and lots more. There is evidence that teachers make more decisions a day than brain surgeons do. That is a lot for our RAS to focus on, so much so that it can feel near impossible to do everything (or even anything) well. It becomes easy to miss things or make what feels like simple mistakes (20).

RAS works with habituation also in the classroom. This can be positive or negative – like everything else related to RAS. Think about the classroom from the child's point of view. Has the space been co-created to provide for her to see herself in it?

When she enters through the door, can she find herself in the images on the wall, in the layout of the furniture, and so on? Or is it the most "Pinterest Perfect" and *"visually pleasing"* teacher-created classroom that the teacher worked hard to complete? If the student's RAS doesn't get excited about the room (and in particular if the RAS gets threatened by something in the room), the child will not feel "part of" that learning space.

Inevitably, a negative spiral can occur for that child.

The RAS supports motivation because it constantly searches for things it believes, whether perceived as negative or positive. Some students start to doubt themselves because of life experiences (home or school), no longer the charismatic, engaged, and jubilant child they once were in kindergarten. You might start to hear things like:

I'm a bad reader. I stumble over words.

I'm dumb. I always get bad grades.

I'm always late, so why even try?

No one likes me. I have no friends.

Alternatively, when we focus on consistent affirmations, the opposite can happen. For instance, if the teacher really understands how a growth mindset works and truly believes, RAS does the work for her. This is an expected outcome from the child's point of view.

I'm getting better every day.

I am such a hard worker.

I greet every moment in life with enthusiasm.

Positive words work all day. Affirmations can be statements that help our brain focus on the things we think about. When I challenge my thoughts with positive thinking in my automatic thought processes, it gives me the opportunity to reframe my thinking and in turn myelinate (strengthen) new neural pathways.

We can use positive affirmations that are specific to our situation so they align with what we want in our lives. We won't make a difference for our students unless these affirmations are created individually and with autonomy. In today's world, no one can tell us how and what to think. We like independence. As teachers, we might think like this:

> I know! I will make cute cutouts for my walls or buy posters that say all of these positive phrases … and that'll fix everything.

While this is a valiant idea, this is unfortunately a quick fix that may not make the big impact we are hoping for. So what can we do?

- Avoid putting the child in an amygdala hijack
- Never cold-call students when they haven't had an opportunity to think
- Ensure that all students feel safe and respected in our classroom environments
- Help students "see" themselves in the classroom
- Make sure that students see people who look like them or have families like theirs in the books, art, or even in tangible pictures of them in the classroom

Big Idea – Sense of Belonging: What if the simplest thing we do tomorrow is have our students bring in framed photos of them with their families, friends, and/or during play … together you display them in the classroom?

Teacher Voice

Another way teachers can help is through our voice. When we are teaching in our classrooms, or presenting in staff meetings, the way our voice sounds matters. Adjusting the pitch and the tone or even changing our flow or rhythm can make a big difference on whether or not the RAS of our learners will allow us in. Adjusting our voices or intentionally pausing while moving around the room creates anticipation. When there is anticipation, our RAS is paying attention.

How about novelty? Novelty, or unique experiences activate a child's RAS! When we are creating opportunities to activate the RAS through novelty, we are meeting diverse learning needs in our classrooms.

Novelty can be anything from playing a fun and catchy tune at the end of Centers, to letting your students know it's time to clean up. How about creating novelty by teaching a lesson outdoors and allowing students to respond to their math questions through sidewalk chalk instead of on another worksheet?

Novelty can even be created when allowing more student voices in the classroom. Think of how often our students respond well when we have co-created visuals to support learning. Think about how you can create interest in your lessons through engaging and current illustrations, especially student-made.

Find novelty in visual aids or through a popular TikTok dance or song? What about incorporating photography or cartoons in content slideshows? Co-creating student-made learning charts instead of buying a chart from the teacher store. How many times do you actually refer to the poster that's been on your classroom wall since 2006? Are students referring to it? Probably not, that's due to the RAS's ability to habituate to the environment.

What is new and novel is what the RAS will pay attention to. How about utilizing realia in lessons? Realia is a tried-and-true strategy for multilingual learners. It not only supports our language learners but also creates opportunities for all learners to engage with real-life objects. What will our students remember? Will they remember the lesson that took us hours – working together to create a slideshow about fractions? Or will they remember the time that they helped to measure ingredients for a recipe? Or broke apart a chocolate bar to learn about sixteenths?

Laughter works. When was the last time you laughed with your students? Not only does laughter with others boost our feel-good neurotransmitters like serotonin, oxytocin, and dopamine, but also using humor in lessons creates so many opportunities to jolt the RAS. Creating fun and engaging lessons that create opportunities for joy and connection makes all the difference.

Teachers today are truly marketing masters. We create opportunities for interest, attention, and curiosity in order to activate the RAS and help our students and colleagues create and myelinate new neural pathways.

Call to Action

We end this chapter with an opportunity to help our "Thoughts become things." What are some affirmations that can help you become the person you desire to be? How are you going to use this as a call to action? How do you want to intentionally activate your RAS?

I can't control other people's thoughts, but I can control my own.
I am strong, capable, and brave.
I am connected to my thoughts and how they become things.

References

1. A. C. Graesser, Emotions during the learning of difficult material. *The Psychology of Learning and Motivation* 57, 183–225 (2012).
2. D. Coyle, *The Talent Code. Greatness Isn't Born. It's Grown. Here's How* (Random House, New York, NY, 2009).
3. B. Perry, in *Children, Youth and Violence: The Search for Solutions*, J. Osofsky, Ed. (Guilford Press, New York, NY, 1997), pp. 124–148.
4. C. S. Dweck, E. L. Leggett, A social-cognitive approach to motivation and personality. *Psychological Review* 95, 256–273 (1988).
5. R. Feuerstein, R. S. Feuerstein, L. H. Falik, *Beyond Smarter: Mediated Learning and the Brain's Capacity for Change* (Teachers College Press, New York, 2010).
6. J. Willis, How to teach students about the brain. *Educational Leadership* 67, 2–4 (2009).
7. A. Rattan, C. Good, C. S. Dweck, "It's ok - not everyone can be good at math": Instructors with an entity theory comfort (and demotivate) students. *Journal of Experimental Social Psychology* 48, 731–737 (2012).
8. E. L. Garland et al., Upward spirals of positive emotions counter downward spirals of negativity: Insights from the broaden-and-build theory and affective neuroscience on the treatment of emotion dysfunctions and deficits in psychopathology. *Clinical Psychology Review* 30, 849–864 (2010).
9. M. A. Fernandes, J. D. Wammes, M. E. Meade, The surprisingly powerful influence of drawing on memory. *Current Directions in Psychological Science, SAGE Journals* 27, 302–308 (2018).
10. R. M. Sapolsky, *Why Zebras Don't Get Ulcers* (Henry Holt and Company LLC, New York, NY, 3rd ed., 2004).
11. J. P. Shonkoff, W. T. Boyce, B. S. McEwen, Neuroscience, molecular biology, and the childhood roots of health disparities: building a new framework for health promotion and disease prevention. *JAMA* 301, 2252–2259 (2009).
12. W. T. Boyce, B. J. Ellis, Biological sensitivity to context: An evolutionary-developmental theory of the origins and functions of stress reactivity *Developmental Psychopathology* 17, 271–301 (2005).

13. M. E. Seligman, Learned helplessness. *Annual Review of Medicine* 23, 407–412 (1972).
14. K. D. Vohs, T. F. Heatherton, Self-esteem and threats to self: Implications for self-construals and interpersonal perceptions. *Journal of Personality & Social Psychology* 81, 1103–1118 (2001).
15. S. W. Smith, Individualized education programs (IEPs) in special education—From intent to acquiescence. *Exceptional Children* 57, 6–14 (1990).
16. W. Trummert, Dissertation, University of Puget Sound, Olympia WA (2016).
17. W. Parker, Listening to strangers: Classroom discussion in democratic education. *Teachers College Record* 112, 2815–2832 (2010).
18. T. K. O'Mahony, *The Brain-Based Classroom: Accessing Every Child's Potential through Educational Neuroscience* (Routledge, London, UK, 1st ed., 2021).
19. L. Donati, in *Learning and the Brain* (Institute for Connecting Neuroscience with Teaching and Learning, Neural Education 2.1, 2020), p. 24.
20. C. Chabris, D. Simons, the invisible gorilla. *Viscog Productions*. www.theinvisiblegorrila.com, 2010.

2

Fun in a Box

Purposeful Play

By Wendi Trummert

Introduction

Being an educator brings waves of emotions. Looking at the face of every child who walks in the room stirs a desire to make a difference in their life. Waving goodbye at the end of a school day, knowing that each student inched closer to his/her potential, feels more than just good. It fulfills the WHY for educators. Yet, that same desire can be a source of frustration and discouragement when we don't hit the goal. Mattos, author and advocate for the RtI[1] model, sums it up succinctly for many of us when he compares the educational challenge by using a medical paradigm (1).

> If the medical field worked the way most schools have traditionally worked, you wouldn't get the help for an illness until you were terminal, but at that point it is not help, it is hospice.

> The many skills that children need to be taught by the end of each school year are daunting, especially when they enter with such vastly different

ability levels. And yet, identifying the best, most engaging, most equitable, most efficient, and most effective educational strategies to help each student achieve their maximal potential is both the aspiration and struggle of each educator.

School as Three-Ring Circus

Being an educator is both rewarding and exhausting. Some days, as I look around, I feel as though I am in a three-ring circus, replete with mayhem, confusion, and discouragement. Fourteen years into my career, despite the fact that I love my job, I find myself tired, frustrated, and rethinking everything. I see and feel rewards, but they seem small in comparison to the potential I know exists. Looking back, I realize the disquiet that urged me to make a change.

As a conductor of the circus, I felt responsible. The picture of my life that I imagined didn't correspond with actuality. Where was the happy educator sitting at the end of a day with a coffee in one hand and a colored pencil with which to place an "A" at the top of the pile of work-to-be-graded in the other? I was supposed to cherish the memory of smiling little faces who were excelling … even thriving in school. What I had imagined as I took my first job in a local school district was a far cry from this. I never signed up to be a circus conductor (See Figure 2.1).

The picture was indeed grim. I sat at my desk reflecting on my day; the coffee in my hand was cold. Once again, the assigned work of my students

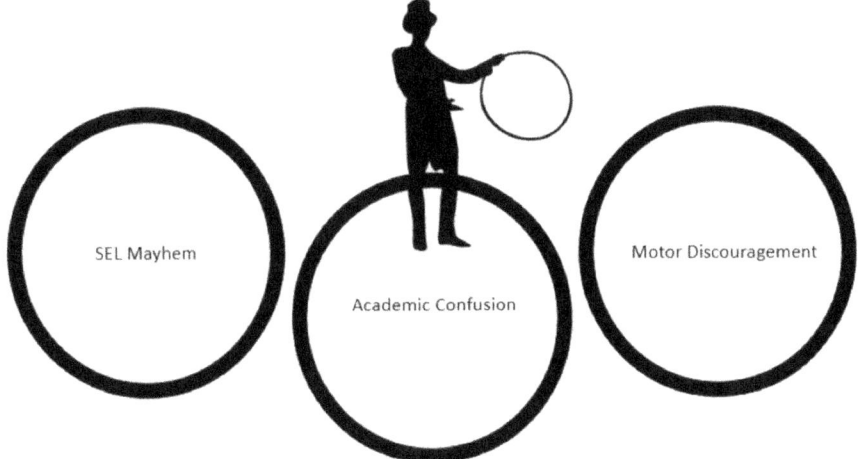

FIGURE 2.1 School as Three-Ring Circus

brought tears streaming down my cheeks. I was looking at one student in particular; I had spent a lot of time with him today.

The work ethic of both myself and the student was strong, and yet the data I was collecting from his work samples did not represent the effort we both were putting in. It was simply defeating.

I did not go into education to simply clock in and out; to simply collect a paycheck. While that was a logistical benefit, it was not what fed my soul as an educator. Impacting students in such a way that they achieve their goals is what fed my soul. It was my why, and I was falling short. Having not achieved the goal I had set out to accomplish with this student crushed me in that moment. Progress had been made, yet I knew in my gut that the highest level of this student's potential was not achieved.

Moments like this can break us or spur us into action. I chose the latter. That decision allowed me the opportunity to go back to square one in my pedagogical thought process and ask myself, "What is my *why* and how can my *why* flourish?"

If I was there to ensure that I provided the amount of instructional time to students as was expected with the tools I was given, then I could proceed as an educator regardless of whether "Johnny" progressed to his maximal potential. After all, he did make some progress. But if my *why* was to find a way to help all students achieve their *maximal* potential, and the mark was repeatedly being missed, then proceeding as normal would not suffice. In this puddle of tears, I found myself at a crossroads.

At this juncture, I determined that simply putting the pieces of my broken heart back together was not going to achieve student goals as I deemed necessary. I had read enough of Carol Dweck's work (2) to know that a "fixed" mindset puts the same broken pieces back together; a "growth" mindset considers if the heart needs some new pieces to work at its maximal capacity.

TTWWADI

Following current educational practices, I realized that I had inadvertently fallen into the murky water of TTWWADI (Tuh-twah-dee), or That's The Way We've Always Done It. At one point in time, that way certainly may have been the best option. As research develops, cultures evolve, and technology advances, systems and processes must also progress. Educational practices certainly are not the same as they were in one-room schoolhouses.

Yet, somewhere along the way, educational practice appeared to have taken a turn away from considering developmental and neurological progression.

My teacher colleagues regularly lamented that "gone were the days" of kindergarteners spending time in play and creative expression; kindergarten was the new first grade. Teachers across all grades began to express the feeling that they had to "teach to the test", and meet a daunting level of district requirements, and there was little or no time for student discovery to ensure developmental progression.

Not only was there pressure for teachers to help their five- and six-year-olds meet state standards, but students were also entering school less and less prepared to meet even basic demands. In fact, research showed that two-thirds of children enter school unprepared to achieve academic standards (3). Some students were able to make adequate progress, while others were left behind. Educators were finding themselves feeling like circus orchestrators, with each subject taught in a ring, and the number of rings just kept growing.

One ring that cannot be ignored is social emotional learning (SEL), which is responsible for increasing amounts of behavioral impacts on learning. Placement of that ring would be vital. Another of the many rings that repeatedly was left sitting outside of the circus tents that we called classrooms was having sufficient fine motor skills that are necessary for academic tools, such as pencils and scissors, and to engage in other tasks relevant to classroom learning.

Fine motor skills comprise both coordinated use of small muscles of your hands and eye-hand coordination. With the push for priority subjects like reading, writing, math, and science, little option was left to secure specific time in any school day to practice motor skills.

This seemed nonsensical! How are children to use their manipulatives for math properly, or coordinate the use of colored pencils to complete their reading assignment without the foundational motor skills necessary to operate them?

Continuing to do things the same way and expecting a different result simply did not make sense. Interventions are historically a reactive response within a failure model. Fine motor interventions that were systematic and proactive were nonexistent.

As a team, our cohort teachers had held many meetings over the years to aid specific struggling students in motor skill acquisition. The big question was this: given the time needed to engage in a rigorous academic curriculum, how can we educators squeeze in sufficient practice activities to provide physical development interventions that are foundational for tool use? Answering this question became my new personal challenge. There had to be a solution, even if it was not immediately obvious.

OT Dilemma

I am an educator, but I do not have a traditional classroom. As a school-based occupational therapist (OT), I serve as a support personnel for all classrooms. I have a role in assisting students who qualify for special education services, as well as supporting teachers with whom, and environments in which, all students receive their education.

The education system is a well-oiled machine that touts decades of practices, which support personnel such as OTs who have been trained to fit within. These decades of practices have, by their own nature, had the unfortunate side effect of pigeonholing the profession's work to be so narrow and prescriptive as to not always allow the true efficacy of the theory by which it was founded to flourish.

Typically, children were pulled out of their classes for focused small motor skill interventions. Assisting with handwriting skills within a 30-minute session, with a splattering of fine motor warm-ups and activities mixed in, was the "go-to" model. Even if the entirety of such a 30-minute session was focused on motor development, there was not a theory on the planet that supported the notion that neurological change could be made in such a setting. This level of support was a mere Band-Aid. The "tried and true" system was our adversary.

Recalling Mattos' comparison to medical systems, I felt backed into a corner. Was this truly the best we could do for our students? I could not accept that I could not continue to wait until students were "terminal" in motor development before I intervened, only to offer a Band-Aid to heal, when what they needed was life support. A passion rose in me to find a way through. How could I fulfill my WHY ... to do what I did daily, better than ever before.

Two educational models of practice permeated the system and were solidly entrenched: Response to Intervention (RtI) and Multi-Tiered Systems of Support (MTSS). These models offered opportunities within the general education classrooms to alter how I thought about our classroom interventions. While some students could be successful with the basic Tier 1 level of instruction, other students needed a little more, called Tier 2, and a select few would need even more, at a Tier 3 level of support. All of these levels could be provided to all students, regardless of whether or not they qualified for special education services. Students who qualify for special education have been identified as needing all three levels of RtI/MTSS support *plus* special education as an additional layer. If I, as a special education provider, could be a part of the underlying tiered support, the students whom I served could then receive OT-designed motor supports at all three levels in addition to the 30 minutes they worked in their unique OT session. This was the quantity and quality of support that research was showing me had the ability to assist students who needed the most support of all, to receive the time and intensity needed to achieve their maximal potential.

A collaborative meeting with the kindergarten teaching team revealed a time of golden opportunity to think outside the box. Analyzing the schedule of the day together, students participated in a daily block called Centers Time. During this time, students were provided with a variety of activities that varied significantly in nature. While one activity was geared toward playful exploration with a doll house, another was a problem-solving puzzle, and yet another was an opportunity to organize letter magnets. Some tasks had a motor element, albeit small; others did not. Wonderful learning moments existed within this time, yet they were not specific in nature, which is precisely what the research indicated was key to motor development. Rightfully so, the teachers indicated that having a time set apart for motor development would not leave enough time to practice other required educational skills.

We had identified a time in the school day that showed its potential to answer our challenge question. So, the next question was, could the activities in this time block be adapted in such a way as to ensure that motor skills as well as academic skills were completed simultaneously?

This challenge took a lot more thought and research. The teachers provided me with the academic standards for kindergarteners, which checked one box of the activity criteria. I engaged in a task analysis of the pros and cons of the existing Centers Time activities. The existing activities were located in various places around the classroom and two or three students were engaged in the same task due to limited numbers of activities. While this allowed for some social interaction, it did not allow for a variety of fine motor experiences.

Motor learning research indicated that a variety of activities would allow for maximal experiences as well as the highest intrinsic motivation and, thus, avoid the typical situation where students lose interest in repetitive uninteresting tasks. Next, we needed to identify motor developmental skills that kindergarteners were lacking, but would nonetheless need … to successfully engage in educational tasks at school. How could we create activities that would allow for their achievement?

Big Idea in a Box

Occupational therapists use big ideas like this as standard practice. In this case, I planned to assemble an activity for children to complete; an activity that was inclusive of manipulative materials and cognitive processing within one container. For instance, I was partial to an activity in which the student would play with theraputty, a comparable material to Silly Putty, and pull out small beads from the putty that had been buried inside. This has always been a "fan favorite" for kids which meant it held its weight in gold on the engagement scale.

Evaluating this activity and the list of academic standards side-by-side, the thought came to replace the standard lacing beads with beads that had letters or numbers on them. If the child was provided with a laminated list of sight words, the beads they found could be placed on the cards to create the words that were to be learned.

Repeatedly finding the buried "treasure" of beads could be fun, allow for fine motor skill building, and allow for practice of a targeted academic standard. All of the materials could be stored in a shoe box for organization and ease.

The beads in the theraputty were just one activity. However, I knew from both experience and research that bored children do not learn. One task would not suffice.

Literature Search

I wanted to know a little more detail regarding exactly what the goal post needed to be in terms of activity design and time in practice. Karen on social media was not going to be my go-to source for such an important explanation of the data. Research-based interventions are critical to success. So, I hit the web hard for journal articles that would provide me with the best and most current information. The results of my search were more helpful to the construction of my design than I could have imagined. Here is what I found:

> Motor skill acquisition is best improved with specifically designed tasks that are completed regularly to allow for sufficient time in practice (4, 5).
> Poole (6) explained that motor skill acquisition "involves more than mere repetition of a movement." Whiting (7) indicates that it also requires

the creation of "new plans of action to solve motor problems posed by the environment" (p. 545).

Random practice in which each trial is different shows significantly greater gains in skill acquisition, as opposed to blocked practice where the same pattern of movement is repeated (6).

Rule and Stewart (5) found that "…although most kindergarten classrooms are rich with fine motor activities, results underscore the need for carefully constructed and coached activities."

Bhatia, Davis, and Shamas-Brandt (4) found that kindergartners who engaged in Montessori practical life activities showed improvements in fine motor accuracy, speed, and established hand dominance.

Fine motor skills were found to be significantly predictive of reading and math achievement (8, 9).

Higher levels of student engagement improve academic outcomes in reading, math, and science (10–12). More is learned when learning is FUN!!

And with that, I had a formula for success.

$$\text{Fun} + \text{Fine Motor} + \text{Academics} + \text{Collaboration} + \text{One box}$$
$$= \text{Maximal Motor} + \text{Academic Progress}$$

Circus rings no more. We educators were making ourselves dizzy attempting to fit meaningful activities side-by-side. Rings that we deemed necessary need not be pushed out of the tent; they could overlap. My model shifted. Instead of circus rings, my new image became Olympic rings. Olympic rings represent the union. Uniting elements of academics, motor skills, collaboration, and engagement into a single box became my new goal.

My work was not yet done. I needed more activities. The fine motor ring had its own set of criteria I needed to abide by, if I wanted to ensure the formula would work. Fine motor skill acquisition is most effectively developed through completing tasks that require the individual to engage in thoughtful exploration rather than rote motor repetition. Creating a variety of activities would be essential.

I went about the creative process in a couple of ways. I looked at other activities that I regularly use as a fine motor intervention. They needed to be engaging to children by nature. How could I add the criteria of academics?

Fun Characters

Mr. Tennis Ball Guy was my First Character. To create it, do the following:

1. Take any tennis ball
2. Cut a one-inch incision in it
3. Draw a face on the ball with a marker, using the slit as the mouth…

As explained to the students who I engaged in this activity, Mr. Tennis Ball Guy gets very hungry. He typically eats small objects such as beads. The child would hold the ball in one hand and squeeze it such that the hole (mouth) opened. With the mouth agape, the child's other hand was free to pick up beads to feed him.

This activity could be altered to the child's ability level in many ways. For example, the slit in the ball could be made larger or smaller. If the hole was smaller, the child would need to squeeze harder, thus working on hand strength at greater resistance, than if the hole was cut larger and the resistance was less.

The child was encouraged to trade which hand was in charge of feeding him versus opening Mr. Tennis Ball Guy's mouth, so each hand had equal opportunity to focus on elements of strength (squeezing) and dexterity (manipulating the beads, see Figure 2.2.). Typically, the beads I would choose

FIGURE 2.2 Voila – Mr. Tennis Ball Guy

had no rhyme or reason for their use. Beads that were in the shape of circles could be "donuts" and beads that were shaped like stars or hearts could be Lucky Charms in the imagination of the child.

What if the circles, stars, and hearts could be organized in a unique fashion to connect with and advance an academic standard?

I went back to the list the teachers had given me and found that one goal for kindergarteners is to learn patterns such as ABA, ABC, ABBA, etc. I created cards that had horizontal lines of pictures of the beads, with each line having a different pattern. One line would be star, circle, star, circle. While the next line was circle, heart, star, circle heart, star. The children were taught to feed Mr. Tennis Ball Guy the beads using the cards. In fact, Mr. Tennis Ball Guy would "ONLY eat his lunch if he was fed in the correct pattern order."

When trialed with a few students, the students found the stubborn Mr. Tennis Ball Guy to be quite amusing and engaged in the task happily. The Mr. Tennis Ball Guy Activity could be adapted not only for grip strength but also in regard to dexterity. And, in addition, each child had opportunities for autonomy, immediate feedback for mastery, and guaranteed purpose associated with each box.

Motivation: Autonomy Mastery and Purpose

The child could pick up beads one at a time to feed him. They could use small tongs or tweezers (included in the box) to feed him, or they could hold five beads in the palm and practice moving one bead at a time from their palm to their fingertips. The latter option of engaging the small muscles of the hand to move the bead to the fingers is called "translation" and is a fine motor skill that aids children in tasks such as writing and drawing.

Coercing the stubborn Mr. Tennis Ball Guy to eat his lunch was simply fun as the children saw it, and yet it allowed students to work on their fine motor and academic skills simultaneously. Work disguised as fun in a box. So far, the kids were sold, and so was I.

I needed to continue to build my repertoire of fun in a box. This time, I worked backward with academic standards in mind. How could I take an academic standard and design an activity around it?

Letter Recognition Automaticity was next on the list of standards. Wanting to ensure that each activity was unique, I trekked myself to the local Dollar Store for materials. It was a personal game of Eye Spy and the "something" I was searching for needed to have a fine motor component. And there it was! I spied a toy dinosaur. Not just any toy dinosaur, but a dinosaur that, if you held his body in your hand and pulled on his short arms with your index finger like a trigger, the resulting action was – dino closing his mouth. Engaging the trigger finger repeatedly would allow the dino to pick up and release a variety of small objects.

The question was, what would the dino pick up? When entering a toy aisle, it is vital to wear your best imagination hat. I spied a variety of other small toys in the aisle, but one item stood out as having notable potential. On the bottom shelf was a bag of traditional glass marbles with an intricate swirl vein down the center. While this type of marble is technically called a Toothpaste or Cats Eye Marble, I saw the imaginative potential for it to be a dinosaur egg. The swirly vein down the center could easily be thought of as a developing baby dino embryo.

Since my goal was to create an activity in which kids could practice letter recognition that would develop automaticity, I also purchased a permanent marker with which to assign a letter to each "egg". Mommy or daddy dinosaur, whichever the child wished to call it, could protect its eggs by organizing and storing them safely in a designated location. I left the toy aisle in search of this egg organizer. A traditional egg carton was a bit too large and soft for this task. The kitchen aisle supplied me with a small ice tray that would work perfectly for the job.

As I took all my materials home, I pondered how the students would know which hole of the tray to place each marble. Placing them in ABC order down to Z was certainly an option. This is a method that other activities and worksheets tend to require. Yet, teachers indicated that many children have to start at /A/ when they are asked what comes after /R/.

A novel task was far more desirable to meet the criteria for our project. Instead of the marbles being placed in A-Z rows, I pulled a picture of the same marble from the web, pasted it three times in a series, and wrote a letter on just two of them, leaving the third one blank. For example, one marble contained a /J/, the next a /K/, and the third remained blank. I continued to make these three-marble series, printed them to size, until all 12 holes of the ice tray could each have a paper lining at the bottom containing one of the marble picture series. The child was asked to use the "mommy" or "daddy" dinosaur to pick up one marble egg in its mouth at a time and then place it in the correct space of the ice tray to complete the series. If the ice tray hole had the paper letters /S/, /T/, blank, then the child would place the marble egg with the letter /U/ in that hole.

After collaboration with the teachers to ensure that the academic component was up to par with their academic requirement needs, the activity

FIGURE 2.3 Dino Alphabet Pattern Game

was trialed with a few kids. Directions were given to take turns with both the right and the left hand using the "mommy" or "daddy" dino (see Figure 2.3). The idea of "mommy" dino being protective of her eggs and organizing them carefully to ensure none were lost was taken to heart by the five-year-olds. This was certainly an important job, and they were the "mommy" dino's number one helper!

I had started the task creation from two different angles. They were unique tasks, which took a bit of thinking on my part. But research showed that with novelty comes both engagement and efficient motor acquisition. So, variety in the activities was not an area that could be sacrificed.

I forged on with the creation of tasks. With about 20 students in each kindergarten classroom on average, ensuring very little repetition of the same task would entail the creation of about 40–60 different activities. I decided to "go big or go home" and settled on 60.

Not every task required a trip to the store. Items from around the house or school also could make a great option in some cases, so long as I followed my formula. An upside-down used egg carton was painted with a bird face, a construction paper beak added, and a mini hole punch placed under the beak just large enough to insert a small piece of pipe cleaner.

The egg carton was transformed into a flock of birds each had a math problem to be solved (see Figure 2.4). Small, brown pipe cleaners were transformed into worms, each of which had a laminated paper number affixed to it as a possible "solution" to the math problem. The "worm" could be fed (inserted into the hole) to the bird whose problem matched the solution. The worms could be fed with the child's fingers or using a tool such as tweezers or tongs. Each hand was given a turn to feed the bird, ensuring that each hand received motor practice. At this point, the academic criterion was met (math), the fine motor criterion was met (pincer grasp of pipe cleaners and tweezers), it was a fun and engaging task that all children would enjoy, the OT/teacher team had collaborated on the skills involved, and it all fit in a box.

Check. Check. Check. Check. Check.

To ensure we knew at the end of the school year that our new intervention had the desired effect, data was collected on student scores for (i) academics and (ii) motor skills. The research design was carefully scripted. Not all kindergarten students would use the new activities. Two kindergarten classrooms used the new activities and two used the old activities. After

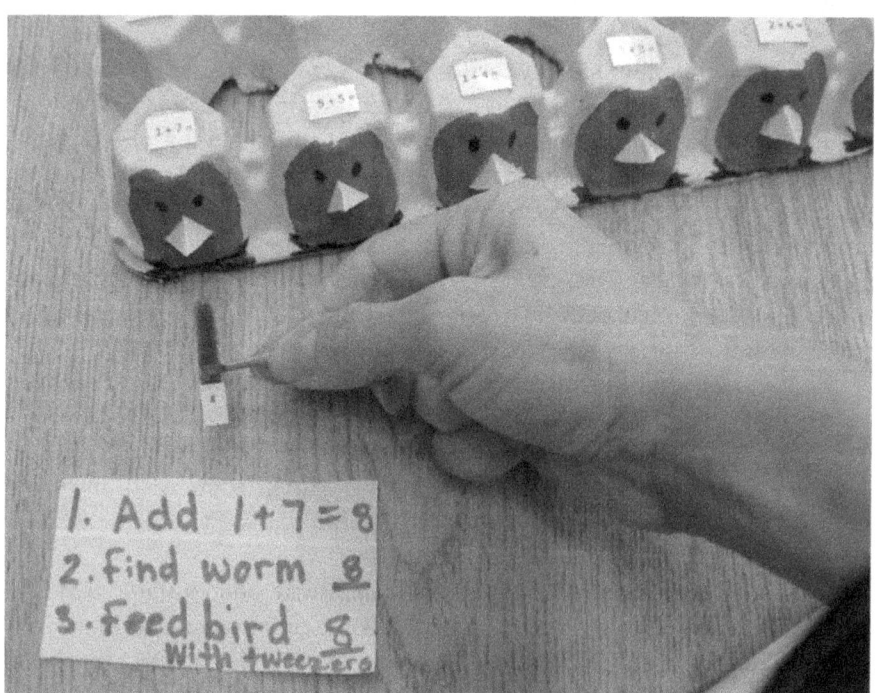

FIGURE 2.4 Bird Feeding Math Game

all, in order to know if the activities did what we hoped they would do, we knew we would need something to compare to, which would be the pre-existing activities in the Centers Time. The number of activities climbed until I reached the goal of 60 unique activities for the two classrooms that would try out the activities. A pilot study was born.

Motor learning research was clear. Poole's research (6) showed that it was essential for the student to first and foremost understand what the goal was, particularly in the beginning stages of learning a task. Thus, it was an important part of our planning to include 3 days of instruction during that 30-minute block to demonstrate activities prior to allowing students to engage with them physically. This would ensure each student understood the directions for each activity.

I sat at the front of each classroom, opened one box at a time, and modeled for the students as I played with each task in front of them. I channeled my inner child in this process. Instead of the message being, "Kids, we do not use the tools this way, we use them that way." The words used were, "Daddy Dino, I know you want to keep your little eggs safe, I will help you," as I spoke in a whimsical tone talking directly to the dino toy.

Similarly, with the "flock of birds" math task, I would change my voice tone to emulate a mama bird and say, "Baby birds, I know you are hungry, let's get some yummy worms to eat, we can find the right size worm just for you." The key to success was focusing on fun. The natural offshoot of the fun was learning. Step-by-step pictures were also placed on the lid of each task so that if the child forgot how to use a task, they could use the pictures as one means of remembering.

Following the demonstrations, day four of our process was the full implementation of activities. All activities were organized on shelves on one side of the room. At the scheduled time, the children were told to choose one box and sit at their table in groups of five or six. While seated, the children opened the box they chose and found an activity. The joy in the classroom was palpable.

It's like Christmas!

This game is my favorite.

The students were genuinely enjoying learning. They played with the activity they chose for about seven or eight minutes, at which time the teacher rang a bell. Upon hearing the bell, the children knew it was their cue to put the materials back in the box, close the lid, and pass the box to the student on their left side.

This routine allowed the child to engage in a second activity for another 7–8 minutes, and the bell rang a second time. On the last rotation, they had an opportunity to play with a third activity until the bell rang, concluding this block of time. The boxes were returned to the shelf until the following day, when the 30-minute block of time with the boxes was repeated for each school day that followed.

It stood to reason that the school schedule would not always allow for the center's time to take place. The day came when there was a field trip for the kindergarteners. Upon returning from their field trip, there was just one hour left in the school day, and other tasks needed to be attended to besides centers.

To the teacher's surprise, when they explained to the students that the center's time would be missed, the students expressed their extreme discontent.

But we love Game Box time! Can't we just do them for a little bit?

The students had fondly named this time on their own. To them, the activities did not mean "work". We knew they were learning, but to them, they were games. And the students in unison explained to their teachers how disappointed they were to miss out on this time of the day. We looked at one another with a smile. Nailed it! Engagement and fun were confirmed through their enthusiasm to participate in these activities.

And there we had it. As a team, we had come up with a way to engage children in rigorous academics at the same time as they built upon their fine motor skills, all in a fun and engaging way that had them yearning for the next time they were able to participate.

The collaborative process boasted many benefits that were not anticipated. As a special education provider, I served a group of students across the school who showed delays in their fine motor development.

- These students needed additional support and accommodations to be successful with many educational tasks.
- These students needed more time to practice tasks that were difficult for them.
- These students received weekly time in occupational therapy sessions with me; however, this time was limited in comparison to what would aid in neurological change needed for skill attainment.

With their teacher and I working together to ensure that both academic and motor skills were practiced simultaneously on a daily basis, these students were able to receive interventions developed by an occupational therapist more frequently than just one time per week. We could work together to ensure that students who needed more support could utilize these games as a Tier 2 or Tier 3 intervention. The potential for developmental and neurological growth was increased, thereby increasing their opportunity for success.

In addition to needing more time, often the students whom I served needed interventions to be different in order to achieve success. While the majority of students in any given classroom were able to utilize tweezers to feed the baby birds their numeric "food", students with fine motor delays at times needed to use their fingers because the tool use was too challenging. Children who were struggling with holding their pencil and writing their name may have had an underlying fine motor deficit that impacted their ability to use the pencil correctly. Ensuring that these children practiced with activities that would strengthen the underlying fine motor deficits daily, and scaffolding or differentiating the activity up or down in motor skills to be tailored to the child's ability level, allowed us as a teacher-therapist team to guarantee that the students with special needs received the unique support they required to be successful.

In other ways, such as with academics, for the baby birds tasks, the activity could be graded up or down to the child's unique math level of skill. Collaborating with the teacher, we were able to modify and even specifically design some of the activities in a way that would support the unique needs of the student who was in need of both fine motor and academic tasks. While this was incredibly encouraging, we could not officially call it success yet, not without the final data. So, the activities continued until the end of the year. Eighteen weeks passed and the numbers were crunched once again.

Results

Results showed that greater gains were made for those who completed "Game Box" time, as compared to those who completed "existing" centers activities in the areas of fine motor skills with the non-dominant hand, and reading skills – Whole Words Read and Letter Naming Fluency (13).

The data demonstrated that children's academic and motor skills could simultaneously be strengthened more with specifically designed activities than with standard classroom tasks.

There are multiple factors that we believe made this project successful. Because each activity included both academic and fine motor components, one theory is that the regular participation in, and practice of, fine motor activities yielded significant, positive improvements in fine skills, while participation in academic activities resulted in significant, positive improvements in academic skills as separate entities. This theory supports a task-specific approach to intervention that has been previously supported in literature (14). In this way, the simple fact that each skill was practiced yielded positive improvements. Yet, if this were the case, why didn't we see the same rate of growth in the classrooms that did not have the new activities? We looked further.

An alternative theory is that participation in both academic and fine motor activities simultaneously provides for an increase in outcomes through their shared neurological processes. This theory would be consistent with previous research findings that the use of hands-on manipulatives, activities, and interventions are positively correlated with improvements in academic skills and learning (15–19).

Brain research supports the theory that simultaneous participation in motor and academic activities promotes the greatest motor and academic outcomes. The cerebellum is active during both academic and motor activities (20). There is a growing body of evidence that suggests that regions of the brain responsible for motor functioning, such as the basal cortex and cerebellum, are coactivated with the prefrontal cortex during cognitive tasks (4, 20).

The fact that children in this pilot study participated in simultaneous fine motor and early reading activities with the Game Boxes and the result was an improvement in early reading skills may support the theory that improving fine motor skills not only predicts academic success (21) but may, in fact, support academic success. The question of the correlation of motor and academic outcomes and causation requires additional research to understand, but the growing evidence is promising. For our group of students, playing with "Game Boxes" supported their learning in a multifaceted way. Co-activation of the brain was successful.

One question we asked ourselves was, why was fine motor growth in their non-dominant hand even greater than in their dominant hand?

As a team, we used this program as a Tier 1 intervention for all students on the continuum of RtI/MTSS models. Based on scores, "Game Box" activities appeared to be effective at assisting students who, at the start of the school year, had scored below average in motor coordination skills for their non-dominant hand to improve their fine motor skills even more so than those who used traditional classroom activities.

Looking closely at the old activities was instructive. Tasks that required putting together a puzzle were like most of the other tasks that existed. These tasks could be completed by using only the dominant hand. By contrast, activities that were intentionally created for this pilot intervention required the use of both hands to be successful. One consideration we believe occurred was that because the activities implemented in the intervention group primarily required bilateral hand use, cognitive and fine motor skills improved. Thus, requiring students to use their non-dominant hand more frequently increases reading, writing, and math skills. This intervention turned out to be a win-win learning experience in more ways than we had anticipated.

The inclusion of bilateral coordination tasks in activity development was an important criterion of the activity development process for this study because of its link to academic potential (22). Therefore, because the students who played with the "Game Boxes" contained general education students as well as students who received special education services, the intervention demonstrated its ability to offer tiered levels of support for general education students, and special education students within their general education time. Students who qualified for occupational therapy services were able to benefit from additional OT designed motor activities throughout their educational week in addition to their assigned OT session.

The activities in this "Game Box" pilot program provided motor activities that were varied in nature, with no two activities being the same, thus requiring the child to problem-solve solutions with each new task, as well as maintain engagement. Some literature suggests that motor skill development and transference to other tasks are enhanced with variation, as compared to rote repetition, thus providing another possible rationale for the positive results we obtained (23). The findings may provide support for use of this program as a Tier 1 and Tier 2 RtI program to support students within the general education classroom who demonstrate below average fine motor coordination or bilateral integration skills, which both teachers and occupational therapists have vested interest in improving.

Fun should not be underestimated. As the children opened each box, the expressions heard were as if it were a birthday gift. "It is my dream come true". The gift of fun in a box that replaced the paper and pencil activities but was nonetheless successful at demonstrating its worth as hard work was immeasurable. Kids who are having fun have minds that are wide open for learning. Fun is associated with neurotransmitters like serotonin, oxytocin, and norepinephrine.

Collaborative Team Effort

We learned too the significance of the collaborative process. Each professional on an educational team brings a different perspective and training to the table. We have all heard the popular saying, "Two heads are better than one". At the end of the school year, a time of reflection revealed that teachers believed the collaboration process with the occupational therapist helped them to learn more about the full scope of occupational therapy practice. Indeed, it appears that a synergistic professional learning community emerged that was successful in supporting each other as well as student learning.

This is noteworthy in that if teachers have a better understanding of occupational therapy's scope of practice, they will be able to more effectively access the support and expertise of the profession. This, in turn, may have the effect of furthering the collaborative process the teachers have with the occupational therapist that the teachers indicated helped them to learn more child-individualized strategies and increase progress of student educational goals, a concept highly supported by literature (24–30). Similarly, when occupational therapists better understand the skill sets and academic standards with which teachers work and which students are held to account, they can help the therapist to better support the needs of students in special education as well as the classroom as a whole through the RtI/MTSS process.

Remember how we discussed that one of the elements of critical importance was social learning opportunities? It was evident that as students were happily "working" on their academics through this playful means, they would talk among one another about the process and results of their work. They would boastfully exclaim to one another when they achieved a goal of the task or request help from one another if the task was not going as planned. The opportunities for social interaction were more defined by the structure of the program than they were by the pre-existing activities, but they were nonetheless powerful. This was yet another unexpected but exciting result of Game Box activities. The vital circus ring of SEL could remain in the ring as an essential influence after all.

Replication

Could it have been that our exciting results were just a fluke? There was only one way to find out. The following school year, we did it all again. Instead of just two classrooms having Game Boxes, all four kindergarten classrooms at this school were given the boxes, and the results were compared with a nearby school of four classrooms with similar demographics.

Year number two gave us the *same* exciting results, plus more. Students at both schools made significant progress just like the first year. But students who used Game Boxes made significantly more progress than those who did not (i) in reading (nonsense word fluency and letter naming scores), (ii) fine motor skills of non-dominant hands like the first year, and (iii) reading phoneme segmentation and handwriting skills (uppercase and lowercase letter formation), which were not identified the first year. Two school years in succession, Game Boxes demonstrated powerful and significant effects.

As a team, we recognized that this daily 30-minute block of time we had designed did not solve all of our educational problems. However, what it did do was give us reassurance. Reassurance that, given a collaborative, evidence-based intervention that encouraged co-activation of multiple centers of the brain, we could improve student educational outcomes in a more effective way than ever before. This reassurance brought us one step closer to fulfilling our WHY. Our WHY wasn't to merely satisfy contractual hours of the school day; to place in front of the children a curriculum set in place by the school district. Our WHY was to help each student achieve their maximal potential, and we had found a more effective and efficient way to achieve our mission.

As educators, we walk into our buildings daily with a choice. We can do things the same… or we can do them better. But better will always be better. My mission, my WHY, as an occupational therapist is to help children, staff, and families improve their social, emotional, and physical quality of life through collaboration, compassion, devotion, and skilled intervention. I achieve my mission when I use a research-based neurological lens to approach my daily work, and through this means my teams and the students I serve can thrive.

Our circus, with rings side-by-side and ever-growing in number, struggled to fit all the rings of student success under the same tent. This method of overlapping rings appeared to be not only stronger but also more efficient than any side-by-side method (see Figure 2.5). The evidence continues to grow indicating that connectivity across the brain is stronger and more efficient when academics and motor tasks are completed concurrently. As one student remarked, "It's like Christmas!" The fondly termed Game Boxes offered the academic and motor gift of maximal progress toward potential. The games were a gift in a box.

FIGURE 2.5 Overlapping Olympic Rings

Reflection Questions

As a team we sat down and tried to make sense of the outcomes so that we could (i) better understand what we had accomplished and (ii) make adjustments that were needed in order to push the envelope and improve where possible. We used the same three cognitive questions that are part of the neuroscience of learning program that we loved.

What was surprising?

- It was surprising that kids can view their work as play if designed intentionally. Providing rigorous academics has been drilled into me as an educator, and somehow, I rarely felt that rigor could be fun. The picture of rigor meant that all students were focused, sitting still, and producing a product. I tried to fit in some fun activities in between the hard work just to keep the kids motivated. I am surprised at the immense potential and powerful effectiveness of fun activities. In fact, I was very surprised that combining motor tasks with academics produced the greatest outcomes in academics.

What did you know, but now see in a new way?

- I knew motor skills were important to children's growth and development. But setting aside a specific time for it was impossible in the short time we have in the school day. I hoped that the minimal amount of physical education they got would be enough. I also knew that kids needed to learn academics to be successful in their communities. But now I see that combining motor and academic tasks actually gives me the biggest bang for my buck as an educator. Using motor skills as the medium through which to teach academics is more effective and efficient than the massive amounts of paper and pencil work that is usually used.
- I knew that students who qualified for special education needed extra help, but I thought just going to OT once a week would do the trick. I assumed that because it had always been that I did my job and they did theirs, we were just doing the best we could with what we had. I had no idea I was actually stuck in a system of TTWWADI and that other options could give us better results. General and special educators teaming up to share expertise and increase the tiered support for kids who struggle the most as well as all students in the classroom is not only genius, but clearly best practice. I won't be going back to the ways of TTWWADI.

What do you want help with?

- I need help figuring out how this kindergarten example can be expanded or modified to other grade levels and other activity options.
- How can motor activities be used to teach or reinforce learning in lieu of paper and pencil worksheets?

Summary

The formula for success for our team was clear. We worked together, identified fun activities that incorporated academics as well as fine motor skills, and fit it all in compact packages that students named Game Boxes. Combining motor activities with academics allowed us to not only cut down the time to provide motor activities in isolation but also allow multiple areas of the brain to work together to achieve stronger results for all students (31). The children who needed additional support in areas of motor or academics benefitted from the additional time spent than they otherwise would have received with only the OT or only the teacher providing interventions individually. And, best of all, the children did not have to be coerced into engaging in the intervention because it was uniquely designed as play.

Note

1. RTI stands for *Response to Intervention*, a model that highlights how children make progress as a result of programs that are designed to help them.

References

1. Knowledge Delivery Systems, Pyramid response to intervention: How to respond when kids don't learn (2011). https://www.youtube.com/watch?v=ApzX15USq2w
2. C. S. Dweck, *Mindset: The New Psychology of Success* (Random House, New York, NY, 2006).
3. C. Kenning, in Courier Journal (USA Today Network, News Education, 2014).
4. P. Bhatia, L. Davis, E. Shamas-Brandt, Educational gymnastics: The effectiveness of Montessori practical life activities in developing fine motor skills in kindergartners. *Early Education and Development* **26**, 594–607 (2015).
5. A. Rule, R. Stewart, Effects of practical life materials on kindergartners' fine motor skills. *Early Childhood Education Journal* **30**, 9–13 (2002).
6. J. Poole, Application of motor learning principles in occupational therapy. *American Journal of Occupational Therapy* **45**, 531–537 (1991).
7. H. Whiting, 33 dimensions of control in motor learning. *Advances in Psychology* **1**, 537–550 (1980).
8. K. MacDonald, N. Milne, R. Orr, R. Pope, Relationships between motor proficiency and academic performance in mathematics and reading in school-aged children and adolescents: A systematic review. *International Journal of Environmental Research and Public Health* **15**, 1603 (2018).
9. D. Grissmer, K. Grimm, S. Aiyer, W. Murrah, J. Steele, Fine motor skills and early comprehension of the world: Two new school readiness indicators. *Developmental Psychology* **46**, 1008–1017 (2010).
10. M. Kirby, M. DiPaola, Academic optimism and community engagement in urban schools. *Journal of Educational Administration* **49**, 542–562 (2011).

11. M. Reyes, M. Brackett, S. Rivers, M. White, P. Salovey, Classroom emotional climate, student engagement, and academic achievement. *Journal of Educational Psychology* **104**, 700–712 (2012).
12. K. Singh, M. Granville, S. Dika, Mathematics and science achievement: Effects of motivation, interest and academic engagement. *Journal of Educational Research* **95**, 323–332 (2002).
13. W. Trummert, Effects of a Collaborative RtI Based Integrated Kindergarten Motor and Academic Program, PhD Dissertation, School of Occupational Therapy, University of Puget Sound, 2016.
14. M. Hamilton, T. Liu, The effects of an intervention on the gross and fine motor skills of Hispanic pre-K children from low SES backgrounds. *Early Childhood Education Journal* **46**, 223–230 (2018).
15. M. Boggan, S. Harper, A. Whitmire, Using manipulatives to teach elementary mathematics. *Journal of Instructional Pedagogies* **3**, 1–6 (2010).
16. S. Botha, E. Africa, The effect of a perceptual-motor intervention on the relationship between motor proficiency and letter knowledge. *Early Childhood Education Journal* **48**, 727–737 (2020).
17. D. Groouws, K. Cebulla, Improving student achievement in mathematics. Part 1: Research findings, International Bureau of Education (IBE), P.O. Box 199, 1211 Geneva 20, Switzerland. Web site: http://www.ibe.unesco.org.
18. M. Lienenbach, A. Raymond, A Two-Year Collaborative Action Research Study on the Effects of a "Hands-On" Approach to Learning Algebra. Eric Clearinghouse, 1996.
19. H. Li *et al.*, Decoding the role of the cerebellum in the early stages of reading acquisition. *Cortex* **141**, 262–279 (2021).
20. S. Marek, J. S. Siegel, E. M. Gordon, S. E. Petersen, D. J. Greene, Spatial and temporal organization of the individual human cerebellum. *Neuron, Elsevier* **100**, 977–993 (2018).
21. C. Roebers *et al.*, The relation between cognitive and motor performance and their relevance for children's transition to school: A latent variable approach. *Human Movement Science* **33**, 284–297 (2014).
22. S. da Silva Pacheco, C. Gabard, L. Gerdi Kittel Ries, T. Bobbio, Interlimb coordination and academic performance in elementary school children. *Pediatrics International* **58**, 967–973 (2016).
23. T. D. Lee, L. R. Swanson, A. L. Hall, What is repeated in a repetition? Effects of practice conditions on motor skill acquisition. *Physical Therapy* **71**, 150–156 (1991).
24. K. Barnes, K. Turner, Team collaborative practices between teachers and occupational therapists. *American Journal of Occupational Therapy* **55**, 83089 (2001).
25. S. Nochajski, Collaboration between team members in inclusive educational settings. *Occupational Therapy Health Care* **15**, 101–112 (2002).
26. C. L. Bayona, J. McDougall, M. A. Tucker, M. Michols, A. Mandich, School-based occupational therapy for children with fine motor difficulties: Evaluating

functional outcomes and fidelity of services. *Physical & Occupational Therapy in Pediatrics* **26**, 89–110 (2006).
27. B. Hanft, J. Shepherd, in *Collaborating for Student Success: A Guide for School-Based Occupational Therapy*, B. Hanft, J. Shepherd, Eds. (American Occupational Therapy Association, Inc., Bethesda, MD, 2008), pp. 73–104.
28. D. Casillas, in *Early Intervention & School Special Interest Section Quarterly* (The American Occupational Therapy Association, Inc., 2010), vol. 17, pp. 1–4.
29. B. R. Sayers, Collaboration in school settings: A critical appraisal of the topic. *Journal of Occupational Therapy, Schools, & Early Intervention* **1**, 170–179 (2008).
30. D. Reeder, S. Arnold, L. Jeffries, I. McEwen, The role of occupational therapists and physical therapists in elementary school system early intervening services and response to intervention: A case report. *Physical & Occupational Therapy in Pediatrics* **31**, 44–57 (2011).
31. K. O'Mahony, *The Brain-Based Classroom: Accessing Every Child's Potential through Educational Neuroscience* (Routledge, Taylor & Francis Group, London, UK and New York, ed. First, 2021).

3

YOU LOOK GOOD

By Mary Catherine Pilon

Introduction

The Reticular Activating System (RAS): Don't go into your classroom without knowing about it!

MC loves this two hours of pampering by Jose. She has been going to this hair salon for eight years. Everyone in her family knows that this is mom's time and short of a hospitalization, they do not interrupt it. Yet, every time she sits in the chair, and José leaves to mix his miracle hair potions, MC looks in the mirror to see the word "UGLY" appear over her shoulder and quickly looks down, knowing that it is true, and longing for José to hurry up so he can fix it (see Figure 3.1).

This occurred for eight years until one day, MC turned around and looked. What she saw did not match what she thought she saw. The sign was square, black, with white block lettering, intentionally hung there by April and José the salon owners, to encourage their clients…

YOU LOOK GOOD

So why? Why did MC see UGLY? There is no way that April or Jose would intentionally put up anything that would cause their clients grief during a

FIGURE 3.1 The Sign That Appeared to Lie

visit, yet there it was a sign that told MC that she was ugly for eight years. How did this happen? What is going on?

Simply, MC's Reticular Activating System was the cause of her interpretation (see Figure 3.2). The RAS is the system that continually looks for biases and finds confirmation of them anywhere it can (1). Could it have found a bias that MC was not even aware of? What happened to MC in a beauty salon, happens everywhere to all of us, including in our classroom environments (2). What if all that time spent with positive intention on skillfully crafted bulletin boards, classroom posters, announcements, and informational signs is sending a negative message? What does brain science tell us?

From the moment you take your first breath, your RAS is filtering and sorting millions of bits of sensory information each second, most of which

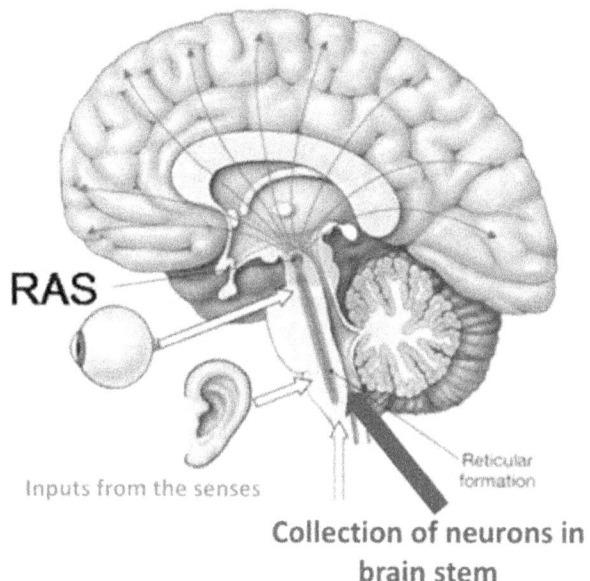

FIGURE 3.2 The RAS Confirms Your Beliefs

are carried out in unconscious processing. Around 60 bits per second get to conscious awareness (3). All of the experiences of childhood, safe or unsafe environments, words, physical experiences, and emotional experiences are recorded and logged in the RAS. They impact and influence how we navigate and respond to sensory input until we take our last breath (4). Your RAS takes instructions from your conscious mind, which becomes diligent and alert to your intention, and gives you more of what you focus on. The RAS seeks the data that validate your beliefs. It screens the world through the parameters you give it and using generalization, distortion, and deletion it gives you a re-personalization of your beliefs from those parameters (5).

The RAS has important jobs to do so that we can live our daily existence. Attentional arousal is one of them. The RAS sharpens our attention by filtering millions of bits of information coming into the brain each second and selectively settling on what we have told it to pay attention to. The RAS also works to keep us safe. This safety function is constantly looking for anything out of the ordinary and unpredictable in order to survive. The RAS learns what keeps us safe, so it is honed to the environments we operate in. What keeps you safe may not be what keeps your students safe. The RAS works with a sense of efficiency as well. It quickly makes sense of input, seeking patterns, stereotyping, and shortcuts based on our limited view of the world.

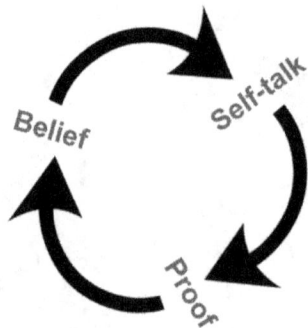

FIGURE 3.3 The RAS Acts Like a Self-Fulfilling Prophecy

The RAS contributes to our Confirmation and Negativity Biases. We filter incoming sensory information based on our beliefs. The more confirmation we receive, the stronger our beliefs become and the more difficult it is to change. This sets up a self-fulfilling prophecy (see Figure 3.3). From an evolutionary/survival perspective, we are wired to perceive negative in order to avoid it. Indeed, the number one job of the RAS is Safety.

Anyone working with humans but especially educators, should know about the RAS, and its role in keeping us safe. How can we use this information to help our students? Knowing what the RAS is looking for helps us to set our own, and our students' brains, up for success.

Since the number one job of the RAS is Safety, we can use that information by connecting with the brains need to live with regard to "Me Here Now" (6). Me Here Now is about connecting new information to students where they are right now so they see value in the information. We can use Novelty to alert the brain to incoming new information and get the brain ready. Giving students options in study and presentation of what has been learned is key to addressing the element of Self-interest. Providing autonomy and choice keeps the model intrinsic with opportunity for mastery (7). Using the elements of Suspense and Color grabs the attention of the RAS, builds anticipation, and provides a release of neurotransmitters. The last aspect is Surprise! Wearing a costume, sharing a bizarre factoid, suddenly singing, and doing the unexpected are definitely a treat for the RAS.

Classroom Setup

To ensure your environment is the safe place you want it to be, co-create the learning space with the children. A motivational poster you want to put up, flags, whatever it is, put it up together. Talk about it with your students;

engage in discussion that provides space for all voices to be heard, so all the students know the reason for the item. Then it can be a safe place.

How to influence RAS in the classroom:

Avoid amygdala hijack.

Use your voice

- Speak in a different cadence
- Adjust voice, tone, and inflection
- Intentional pauses to increase novelty
- Suspenseful pausing: builds anticipation
- Use gestures while talking

Use movement

- Use your space!
- Making an important point? Stand still.
- Conducting questioning or discussion? Move all around

Become a storyteller

- Illustrate important concepts through storytelling
- Use visual aids
- Photographs
- Cartoons
- Charts
- Realia (real-life objects)

Use humor

- Humor is a jolt to the RAS
- When classrooms are fun and engaging, there is great potential for learning to occur

Involve the group

- Involve students to participate in short review activities
- Stand and stretch opportunities

- Power-ups (brain breaks)
- Have students draw simple diagrams to represent learning
- Create interest, attention, and curiosity to activate the RAS and strengthen existent and new neural pathways

Parents

You are the most powerful investors in your child's RAS. The environment you set up, the words spoken, and the safety you provide all have a huge impact on how your child perceives the world as they grow.

Parents who are aware of the power of the RAS can support their children by modeling positive self-talk, verbalizing or picturing with their child a positive focus goal to support the RAS. Intentional practice will support a filter for goals and intentions modeled and verbalized. Parents can have success in setting appropriate filters for whatever success looks like for their child. Henry Ford was correct, "If you think you can, or you can't, you are right."

Students

Students who acquire a mental model about the brain that includes RAS are easily persuaded to self-regulate. Students who do not have a good mental model about RAS can easily be persuaded that they are inadequate, not good enough, and so on. If you are a student reading this book, you are awesome! You are learning important information about the human brain and how your own brain works. You can use this knowledge for emotional, physical, educational, and relational life success. I would encourage you to challenge the negative thoughts you experience with mindfulness, and intentionality. Check for data to find the opposite. There is a fun lyric I tell my students, "Check yourself before you rickety wreck yourself"? There is some truth to it. Interrogate the biases that you live with, especially the ones about yourself. "I'm always late," "I am not good at math!" Then focus on positive truths. "I can be early if I plan ahead." "I can be good at math if I take my time." your brain will begin to focus on the new belief and you will find a bigger world that you are a part of. Pushing back on the RAS purposefully means the more frequent and intentional we are about producing a desired change, the stronger our new pathways become.

Being a Neural Educator who was lied to by my own RAS in a salon chair, I immediately think about all the time and energy we educators spend each year on bulletin boards, classroom environments, classroom doors... the list goes on! I think about intention. The intention of the salon was to affirm to their clients that they look good. Of course that was their intention! But for me, yes I am MC, for eight years I have gotten a different message - a subconscious message "UGLY". Thinking back to my students, what messages were they getting from the classroom spaces I managed all these years? What has been confirmed, in error of any intentions meant, by the students in my environment? YIKES! Knowing what I know now, I absolutely will be using co-creation in my classroom environment. How fun is that?! Ok, I know how fun it is as I have been doing it. The students and I walk into a "clean slate" fresh off of summer, and begin to get to know each other. Happily, and with intention we invest together in our shared spaces. I teach the brain to all my students, yet this co-creation is vital for the RAS to install its filters about co-created fun learning environments that are safe. Together we invest in an inclusive opportunity to allow all voices to flourish. Will you join me?

References

1. D. Kahneman, *Thinking fast and slow* (MacMillan, New York, 2011).
2. S. Sleek, The Bias Beneath: Two Decades of Measuring Implicit Associations. *Association for Psychological Science.* https://www.psychologicalscience.org/observer/the-bias-beneath-two-decades-of-measuring-implicit-associations (2018).
3. J. Medina, *Brain Rules: 12 principles for surviving and thriving at work, home and school* (Pear Press, San Francisco, 2008).
4. L. Squire, S. Zola, Structure and function of declarative and nondeclarative memory systems. *Proceedings of the National Academy of Science* **93**, 13515–13522 (1996).
5. S. Quasim, U. Mohan, J. Stein, J. Jacobs, Neuronal activity in the human amygdala and hippocampus enhances emotional memory encoding. *Nature Human Behavior* Pub Med., DOI: 10.1038/s41562-022-01502-8, (2023).
6. J. Willis, Three brain-based teaching strategies to build executive function in students. Brain Based Learning. George Lucas Education Foundation, Edutopia, 2011.
7. D. Pink, *Drive* (Riverhead Books, New York, NY, 2009).

4

Our Stroke of Enlightenment

Neuroplasticity and Resiliency in Action

By Laurie Donati

Introduction

September started just like any other month. My family was in full swing of the new school year and fall was in the air. I was getting into the routine of another year of teaching – and my two older kids were settling into their new classes. My husband and I were doing our very best to keep our 9-year-old, 7-year-old, and 18-month-old healthy, happy, and involved. We were busy just like any other family. My husband was leading our oldest child in Cub Scouts and his Puget Sound select basketball team in Washington State. My daughter was starting her second-grade year and was so excited to be back in school with her friends. Our 18-month-old was toddling around and keeping us on our toes (see Figure 4.1)!

Life was busy, but stable and relatively predictable until our 9-year-old started to complain of headaches. He was a healthy child with no prior medical needs, so we questioned the reason for his headaches which were severe enough to send him to the nurse's office at the worst times for a young athletic kid, including PE and recess.

FIGURE 4.1 Happy Family in Seattle

We hypothesized that the headaches could be from the bright overhead school lights, or perhaps fourth grade was becoming increasingly difficult for him. He then began to be dysregulated at home and we noticed his behavior begin to revert to a toddler when upset, throwing out-of-character tantrums. This was startling to us, as our oldest was mostly a cool, calm, and collected kid. We feared that something could be very wrong.

Concerned, we brought him to our pediatrician. Our regular pediatrician retired that week, so we saw a new doctor. She checked him out, evaluated his temperature, checked his pupils, and assessed his reflexes. After ruling out something major, she let us know that he was checking out normal and sent us home with a prescription to give him Tylenol at school for headaches.

As parents we both left feeling uncertain and fearful for the future, while still trusting the medical professional who assured us everything was fine.

That night all our lives were changed forever. Several hours after going to the doctor, the date of September 27, 2017, will forever be ingrained in our minds. This was the day our son was unable to get out of bed, wake up or move his body, and unable to respond or open his eyes.

Overnight our oldest experienced what we thought were night terrors saying his eyes were burning and attempting to explain his dreams and thoughts through tears and scrambled words. This was something new he had never experienced before. We comforted him and he finally fell asleep in our bed for the rest of the night while my husband and I lay worried and concerned.

We started the morning as usual while we let our son sleep in. We parents were up as regular, getting ready for the day. There were the usual rushed routines like feeding the dogs and getting our daughter and baby son fed and dressed. We let the oldest boy sleep till the last minute. He looked so peaceful in bed. I went to him to get him up but he didn't rouse.

"Time to get up, my love…" I began to say his name. Nothing! My voice started to tremble with urgency as my greatest fears began to increase. My hand was on his shoulder, still asking him to wake. All he could do was moan. I called for my husband, who was about to step out of the house for work. He came running and I called 911.

The medics arrived after my husband assisted our son to walk to our bathroom floor. He was lying on the floor, unable to talk, move functionally, or respond to us other than moaning. The medics were talking, trying to get him to respond while checking his pulse and oxygen levels. His vitals checked out "normal". After the medics had completed their evaluation, I worked on getting new pajamas on him. It wasn't easy. While attempting to pull his sleeves on his body, I noticed that his right arm was not moving typically. It felt more like a newborn baby's arms. I mentioned that to the medics, but they didn't seem concerned.

> "You can either drive him yourself to the hospital, or you can have us call an ambulance". The head medic didn't seem as panicked as we were. "What do you prefer?"
>
> "This is not normal!" I reiterated to the medic. "We are not driving him. What if he has a big episode in the car and I'm driving? We want an ambulance."

They called an ambulance. We were headed to the nearest major hospital. Prior to leaving the house, one of the medics took me aside and told me bluntly, "Do not take no for an answer with the doctors. You make sure they do a brain scan."

This terrified me. I could see the growing severity of what was happening right in front of us. His words meant something and I felt his anxiety. I took his advice and was prepared to advocate.

My husband rode with our son in the ambulance while I safely deposited our two younger kids at my brother's place next door. Then I drove right behind the ambulance. The ambulance drove without lights on for most of the trip. I was wondering why. Just then, my husband called me from inside the ambulance. He told me that the medics just noticed that our son was unable to move the right side of his body. This concerned them. "They are needing to turn their lights on to get ahead of the traffic." He was letting me know that the pace was quickening.

That was the longest drive of my life.

I parked my car and ran to the ER. One of the medics who had been at our house stuck around to check in with me. He let me know that our son was getting a CT scan and that my husband was with him. The look of concern on his face was unnerving.

After the CT scan, we were sent back to a room in the ER where we met nurses, ER doctors, and a pediatric seizure specialist. We spent several hours getting to know these folks as they checked on our son's vitals and hypothesized that he had a seizure overnight. They were trying to make sense of it since his CT scans looked clear.

"He never had a seizure before." I offered.

When a doctor lifted his eyelids to check for dilation, his eyes would roll and be unable to track.

Our family members were called, and we had quite a supportive group gathering in the waiting room, coming in and out of the ER room to check on him and us (see Figure 4.2).

The seizure specialist informed us that they were considering sending our son home. "We don't know what's wrong. It might be better to care for him at home."

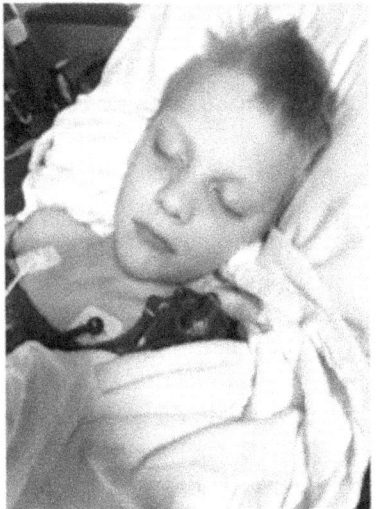

FIGURE 4.2 Waiting in ER

My husband looked at me and we both were not ready to accept that he was ready to go home.

"This is not normal behavior." I could barely find words. "There is something seriously wrong with our son. There must be something else to be done?"

The specialist then made a plan to give our son an MRI.

Shortly after the MRI, my husband and I sat beside our son on his bed. Holding his hands, he felt so feeble and lost.

The ER doctor entered the room. His tone was matter-of-fact. He said to us, "I am so sorry to tell you this, but your son has had multiple strokes."

"Strokes!" Again there were no words. He's only a child. It never dawned on me that kids could have strokes.

"He's going to get better, right?" I felt a huge weight on my being.

"No. He is not going to get better." The doctor's response came in like a dream. "This is as good as it's going to get for him." I looked at my son. I looked at the doctor.

He was already turned to leave the room.

I didn't want our son to have heard those empty words. I am a person who believes deeply in positivity … positive self-talk and affirming messages to improve and uplift mindset. I was also convinced that our son could still hear us.

I leaned over him and whispered into his ear.

"That doctor is wrong." I repeated it and added. "You **are** going to get better. We will help you every step of the way."

Now, that I knew it was a stroke, I was aware of the small window of opportunity and the danger of doing nothing. Time is the big issue. Time is Brain.

Seattle has a very competent children's hospital and thankfully the ER staff reached out for us. One of the doctors we were working with came back to our room and informed us that they were receiving guidance from a pediatric stroke specialist from their ranks. She was a top specialist in the Pacific Northwest. She was making all the decisions for him going forward until we could be transferred to their hospital.

We were soon back in the ambulance and were transferred to Seattle Children's Hospital. We were brought directly to the Pediatric Intensive Care Unit (PICU). Here they began a barrage of tests to determine why our son had these strokes and what the team could do to prevent any recurrent strokes.

All this testing wasn't completed for a few days and we lived on the edge. Finally, our new medical team went over the results with us. It was the best feeling in the world. Our son was in competent, safe hands. Talk about a true Professional Learning Community. Twice a day the medical team made their "Rounds" to evaluate his condition and provide us with updates. We would discuss his progress including his medical data, rehabilitation goals, his schedule for the day, and what we were noticing as his parents.

During one of these official meetings with the team, we were shown our son's test results. This is when we began to get real familiar with images and vocabulary that is deep inside the human brain. It's hard to think that a child of this size brain could have seven strokes. We were shown in detail where the seven strokes occurred in his brain. Three strokes were in the occipital lobe, three strokes in the cerebellum, and one larger stroke in the pons.

We were also shown an updated scan of what actually happened to our son. We will never know how or why, but our son had an arterial dissection in his vertebral artery. Many things could have caused this trauma including something as simple as a sneeze. Something unexpected was also discovered in those scans. Our son was born with additional collateral blood flow, something only 30% of the population has. Had he not had this additional collateral blood flow, other people with the same severity of strokes wouldn't typically survive. He is a miracle.

Seattle Children's Hospital is a teaching hospital and is also open to other doctors from local hospitals to come and learn from them how to best care for young patients. Early in our stay at Children's, we were asked if it would be alright for our doctor to do a check-in with our son along with medical students and medical staff from other local hospitals. After our original experience in the hospital, we knew we wanted as many medical staff as possible to get to know and understand stroke in children to help other children and families in similar situations. Our response was: "Of course, the more brilliant minds on our son, the better."

In his PICU room we had at least 20 brilliant minds surrounding our son's bed. Our doctor was asking him questions to see his response. Things like: What is your name? How old are you? No verbal response. And then the doctor had a moment of wonder.

"Is he left- or right-side dominant?" He was looking at us.

"Left." We said.

Since his strokes were affecting his right side, the doctor had an idea. He addressed our son again.

"I am going to put this pen in your left hand. Here's some paper. Can you write something for me?"

Our son slowly grasped the pen with his left hand. He put the pen to the pad of paper and wrote slowly, but surely "Hi" and spelled out his name.

The brain is a miracle.

The cheering in the room and the collective breath of relief is a moment I will never forget. Still, six years later, it brings tears to my eyes. Our son was able to understand and respond to a simple question. He knew who he was and could communicate with us!

We spent 31 days in the hospital, a week of that in intensive care. This is where we truly understood what it means when we say – the brain is plastic.

Our son had to relearn everything from scratch. They had to rewire his brain with him so that he could open his eyes, smile, get into a sitting position, brush his teeth, talk, and walk. I'm talking about everything! It all had to be learned as if he were an infant again. When we were in the hospital, our doctors, nurses, and rehabilitation therapists constantly talked about how the brain is "plastic" and how kids are resilient. We loved that talk. We lived those words.

I am a teacher, but I learned so much about teaching from these doctors. When the speech and language pathologist was doing a word recall activity with our son, I got to see how the brain connects with phonemes and language encoding. At first, he was unable to recall most words such as apple, pencil, or dog. He had aphasia. I remember reading about aphasia and the fact that it happens to a lot of elderly people when their language processing centers get damaged through aging or disease.

Our son was relearning how to use and comprehend language and we were along for the ride. I asked why he was having difficulty remembering words such as apple. The speech pathologist drew a picture of a brain. She drew an "x" as an example of where the word apple was once located in the brain. She explained that the neural pathway he originally used to find the word "apple" was no longer there due to his strokes. His brain had to rewire itself. Once his new neural pathway was myelinated, he would be able to access the word again. And he would be able to do it quicker and more efficiently.

She also explained that the reason they are so intentional about early intervention was because the brain matter around the seven strokes was "stunned" and if we don't work quickly at reconnecting the pathways, the stunned material will further atrophy and die, and he would have a more difficult time recovering. This lit a fire under us to keep pushing forward, no matter how difficult, because NOW was the time for recovery. And recovery is hard work.

They were right about the brain's plasticity. We could see the connections being made right in front of us. With repetition, practice, focus, an amazing medical team, and an incredible support system of friends and family, he turned a corner. Amazingly, a whole raft of new folk joined our lives to cheer him on constantly and fill his heart with a true belief that he could recover. He had to believe that he could.

That is exactly what he did.

Without our son's personal trust that he could improve, I truly believe that we would not be where we are today. Six years later, there are lingering effects of his strokes. He has to make a concerted choice to work hard every day to continue to rehabilitate. He is never alone. With thousands of rehabilitation hours over the past six years and the help of the best and most brilliant minds in the medical industry, he has made incredible progress.

I am told that if you didn't know our son almost lost his life six years ago, you would not notice the ongoing symptoms of his strokes. His brain has completely rewired itself and he inspires me every day to tell his story and do the work that I am destined to do with other families and educators. The brain is truly plastic!

Leaving the safety of the hospital and moving onto our own medical care at home as well as driving him to and from rehab for Occupational Therapy, Physical Therapy, and Speech Therapy, I was reintroduced to the school system that I understood from a teacher's perspective and felt it to my core from the parent perspective (see Figure 4.3).

FIGURE 4.3 Relearning to Live

There are many misunderstandings of brain injury. Brain injury can occur and is medically distinguished in two ways. First, traumatic brain injuries can result from external factors like falls, sports injuries, motor vehicle accidents, and such. Second, acquired brain injuries occur due to an injury coming from within. These can include aneurysm, tumor, or stroke. All brain injuries look different. No brain is the same, and no brain injury and recovery is the same. Because every brain and potential injury varies, so do the recoveries and the outcomes.

I have connected with many families through organizations both locally and internationally thanks to organizations like the Pediatric Stroke Warriors who are now partnered with the International Alliance for Pediatric Stroke, as well as partnered work of Seattle Children's Hospital, the Brain Injury Alliance, Camp Korey, and Outdoors for All. These incredible organizations expanded our awareness of the support in our community for children with brain injury and disabilities and provided an opportunity for much needed fellowship for our children and our family.

Stroke is often missed in infants, children, and teens because of a lack of understanding that stroke can happen in pediatrics and a proper awareness of the signs. The American Stroke Association and the International Alliance for Pediatric Stroke co-wrote an infographic (https://iapediatricstroke.org/fact-sheets/) that showcases how to "Spot a Stroke F.A.S.T." In children and teens, look for **F**ace drooping, **A**rm weakness, **S**peech difficulty, and **T**ime to call 911. There are several warning signs typically seen in children including:

- Sudden severe headache
- Sudden weakness or numbness on one side of the body
- Sudden confusion, a difficulty producing or understanding language
- Sudden difficulty with vision in one or both eyes
- Sudden difficulty with balance, coordination, walking, or dizziness
- New onset of seizures, usually on one side of the body

Some typical post-stroke effects include cognitive fatigue, changes in motor coordination, short-term and/or long-term memory deficits, as well as changes to executive functioning. Also, watch for high or low muscle tone, slowed processing speed, changes in communication skills, as well as changes in vision or hearing, etc. Mood swings can be very typical post stroke, as well as Post Traumatic Stress Disorder for the child and the whole family. Each survivor is affected by stroke differently. No recovery is the same. The thing that is the same is that our children are amazing examples of resiliency. My son specifically has reframed my mindset on plasticity and the ever-changing brain, especially post stroke (see Figure 4.4).

Knowing this information, it's crucial that we as educators are brain-aware and equip ourselves as best we can to positively support our students. Knowing this information can greatly impact our students and families through awareness and allows us, as educators, to work forward with compassion and a powerful understanding of the plasticity of the brain ... both for us as the caretakers and educators and especially for our brain injury survivors.

FIGURE 4.4 Back on the Team

Educators will likely see children with an Individualized Education Plan (IEP), a Section 504 Plan, and/or an Individualized Health Plan (IHP). These plans are made with a whole team of people and are so powerful when they are based on extensive neuropsychological exams. I say this because brain injury can often be "invisible" for many, including educators. The physical, cognitive, emotional, and social needs of a child are extensive and must be taken seriously by our educational teams. There are several amazing organizations that have taken this work to partner with schools and families for the best outcomes for our survivors. Check out: www.chasa.org/schools; https://iapediatricstroke.org/; https://community.internationalpediatricstroke.org/return-to-school-after-young-stroke/

With the knowledge we have on neuroplasticity, we can now move forward with a mindset of improvement. I think back to the ER doctor who misinformed us that our son would never get better. Then I watch him running, jumping for the basketball, and tossing a shot at the hoop and marvel at the miracle. He is happily playing with his friends like any other child – but he is the one who taught us about child stroke and collateral blood flow.

Every day I marvel at the amazing work accomplished by the dedicated medical staff who use phrases like "kids are resilient" and "the brain is plastic…", I recognize the great progress that they believed he would make. Every chance we get to practice shifting our mindset and recognize the power of neuroplasticity gives us countless opportunities for personal growth and a stroke of enlightenment.

5

Leave with Dignity!

By Dani Hylton

Introduction

I was so excited to have my first permanent teaching position. I did not care where it was. I graduated with my teaching degree in December 2009 and accepted that first teaching position on January 15, 2010.

I was to teach special education in a self-contained room for kindergarten through sixth grade in a hospital setting. My first three students were in a classroom located in the high school building. They were older in elementary fourth and fifth grade. At that time there were not enough admissions to the elementary cottage to support a second elementary classroom.

I started with three students – one girl and two boys. They were not exactly excited to meet me and pretty much ignored me or seemed annoyed if I tried to interact. I spent a few days getting to know them or at least being in the room with them. After a few days, I was told we would be moving to the elementary wing the following week. I was given a few days to set up a classroom.

To get to my new classroom, I would exit the high school building, cross a small courtyard, enter another building, and then walk down a long hallway. This part of the school looked as if the 1970s were alive and well. There were lots of browns and golds mixed with the smell of an old building.

I soon discovered that the staff did not seem to believe in purging things. The classroom was piled high with old curricular materials and an assortment of random "teacher" and school things. Some things were simply standard for classrooms at that time. When entered, the whiteboard was to the right and students' desks were to the left facing the whiteboard. Beyond the teacher area was a tiled section that included a large conference table. Standing there, I was happy to be looking out at the playground.

There were standard built-in cubbies for student's stuff, with open storage above. At the back of the classroom were built-in bookshelves for a student library. I loved every inch of this – my first classroom. I soon got over the musty smell and the strange 70s color scheme. Avocado, I reminded myself – think avocado – a little harvest gold with some obnoxious orange thrown in. But it was my classroom. After driving a school bus for 16 years while raising a family and going to school, I felt as though I had been handed the keys to my castle.

The children, being patients of a hospital, lived in one of three cottages. Each cottage served a different range of ages. My students lived in the elementary cottage, which served students aged 5–11 or roughly kindergarten through sixth grade. I visited the cottage soon after my employment, as I was curious to learn about the setting my students lived in outside of school.

The front doors led into a large mostly circular room, which was a shared space for the students. Looking around this room, one's eyes were steered to hallways that lead to the students' bedrooms. These were aptly called pods. All pods looked the same. Each student had a similar bedroom that included a built-in bed, a built-in nightstand, and several shelves. Each pod had its own bathroom.

Most students brought very little in the way of personal belongings with them. They had clothes and maybe a few toys or books in their room. The cottage stood back a ways from the school – separated by a large sometimes muddy field. The students would have to walk across this field to get to school. Each day they were accompanied by hospital staff and they walked together as a little group.

It took me four days to purge and arrange. Excitement rose with each day's cleaning and adjusting. At last, I welcomed my students to their new class. It was a Monday morning in September. I ignored the fact that I was clearly more excited than were they.

Mary, my para-educator, seemed happy to be here also. She was assigned to my room by the school district. In addition, the hospital sent anywhere from one to four counselors to support the classroom depending on the student's needs.

Within two weeks my little classroom had grown. Four boys and another girl were added, bringing the total to eight. The school, in conjunction with the hospital, used a passport system for students. I recognized this "token economy" as a Skinnerian design for primitive behavior modification (1). I didn't necessarily like it that much, because it didn't work very effectively as a deterrent and in some ways seemed to contribute to a sense of impending doom and learned helplessness (2). But I was driven by and obliged to implement system norms. Each student had a chart with their name attached and their subjects displayed on it. At the end of every subject, I would ask each student to rate themselves on a simple scale: zero being a student had great difficulties; three meaning they were a rockstar. Simplicity was key; I tried to avoid confusing instructions and cognitive overload (3). Together, the student and I would come to a mutual agreement on the score. Higher scores on their passport meant more privileges at the cottage. Notwithstanding the obvious doubts about the reward system based on token economies,[1] we were off to a happy marriage.

By the third week, the honeymoon was over. It was not only over, but the marriage had crashed and burned. It was a Friday – oddly enough Friday the 13th. Desks were tipped over, counters cleared, books thrown, and some chairs tossed. Students were bodily assisted out of the classroom and taken to quiet rooms to calm down. These quiet rooms were either in the school or back at the cottage. None of the students were able to return to the classroom. The wheels were off the wagon. I was in serious burnout (4).

Feelings of despondency overwhelmed me as I finished the day with only two students. When they too had finally returned to their cottage rooms, I sat on the floor in the middle of my classroom wondering just what I had gotten myself into. I questioned if I was any good at this task. After that day's events, I felt like a complete failure. I was not sure if I wanted this job after all.

Monday arrived much sooner than I wanted. My students arrived and settled in even if they appeared somewhat subdued. We began as usual with an opening task. As usual, I was busy, circulating – helping students where they needed assistance. At one point I was standing by my desk surveying the children and wondering, rather apprehensively, what the day might bring.

One of the counselors came over, put her arm around my shoulders, and said, "I just wanted to tell you that you are doing a fantastic job."

I looked at her dubiously. "Are you kidding … you were here on Friday when almost my whole class was bodily removed."

At that point she shared that these new students were being weaned off medications. This contributed to and partially explained why they were struggling to control themselves on Friday. Disruption, like fun, is contagious.

Other children just joined in. Contagion is contagion – they are beyond self-regulating. I came to understand that in this classroom there would be good days, in between days, and just plain bad days.

I assumed, as a new teacher does, that I would find a way to decrease the number of escalations. After all, I had some tools in my toolbox. I made sure we had daily routines and clear expectations for every lesson (5). I worked hard to build relationships with each student, individually (6).

It wasn't working. No matter how hard I tried, there were multiple escalations every week. I followed without question school/hospital protocols regarding passport scoring schemes. Still, escalations happened. I could see patterns associated with the escalations; patterns that disturbed me. I watched in dismay how, even if just one student escalated, all instruction and all student work stopped. Depending on the day and the overriding mood of the students, a quick contagion typically overtook the learning space. Contagion being contagion didn't mean it was always the same for all children. Some children would cheer on the instigator and some would join in and escalate themselves.

Nothing I tried seemed to diminish or extinguish escalations. One other thing showed up after a few weeks. I could tell that the children were often embarrassed later about the escalation tantrums that had ended class activities.

It was one of those early spring days that remind a weary winter traveler that summer is on its way. It should have been a bountiful day, but I was in the middle of what had become a particularly rough week. There were lots of escalations and debris of halted instruction. Yet again, a student was escalating, and others had decided to join in.

I am almost three months into this career and feeling very frustrated with the drama that accompanied these escalations. Once again I stand in pain, watching hospital staff haul most of my class out of our room.

Words scream in my head, "This rollercoaster needs to stop."

It appeared to me that if I could halt the contagion, then there might be a semblance of order and progress. It was a lot of emotional drama. Drama is contagious. How could I change the dynamic of one child "going off" without classmates cheering and/or joining?

I had already given up thinking that escalations wouldn't happen. It was obvious that it was beyond my power to prevent all escalations. But maybe I could modify the escalation scenario and achieve a better outcome. What if the escalating child could leave without drama – without requiring adult supervision and hospital staff hauling them out? It occurred to me that what I really wanted was, when they became upset, for them to exit on their own volition and without contagion. Could this be taught to the children?

I knew about brain plasticity (7) – but would it work? I certainly hadn't taught them how to leave without drama and, clearly, no one else had either. I and everyone else expected that when they were upset, they could leave without hysterical tantrums. Impossible! They had not been taught how to do this.

The idea had been brought up at staff meetings – we talked about it, attended lectures about it – but never explicitly taught the children and gave them time for practice (8).

Staying true to Miller's Law (9) and simplicity, I decided I needed a catchphrase to remind them of the solution – a prompt to guide the activity that I wanted them to try. Perhaps I could tie emerging positive outcomes to existing passport expectations that were experiencing some successes (10) and aligned with hospital requirements. I mulled it over for the weekend and resolved to try it out.

Monday morning, I got in early. I wrote the words **"Leave with Dignity"** at the top of the whiteboard. When students settled in, I asked them to help me define dignity. Together, we defined that new construct – dignity – and grounded the definition in the context of our classroom; these were activities and ideas that they already understood. We could be in control of ourselves; we could avoid putting on a show; and we could stop doing things we might be embarrassed about, later.

I then explained what "leaving with dignity" meant in our classroom. "If you have to leave, try leaving the room without yelling, screaming, calling names, throwing things, and needing physical assistance."

This was a new concept for everyone.

I then demonstrated it. I left the room quietly, alone, and without any drama. Dignity.

We then discussed how **"Leaving Without Dignity"** was the opposite. I demonstrated what that might look like.

They watched as I screamed and yelled and made a fuss as I left the class. No dignity. I could tell that it was getting through to an emotional part of their being. They sat quietly and kind of squirmed as I "acted out" leaving without dignity.

We created a simple rule associated with the new learning. Here's how it was proposed. When you are frustrated and need to leave...

- Breathe
- Get yourself together
- If you leave with dignity, you earn a two on your passport

A two was considered good – way better than zero. It meant you would not lose all privileges on the cottage. If they chose to leave without dignity, it could be a zero. I also explained if peers chose to join in or encourage another person to escalate more, they would also earn a zero on their passport.

We practiced. I asked for a volunteer to demonstrate leaving with dignity. Calmly and with great presence, a student went through the motions, just like I had shown earlier. Next, another student demonstrated leaving without dignity. Again, it was obvious that these demonstrations were meaningful to each individual and spoke to a place of honesty and decorum.

It was decided that on Monday mornings we would create a new routine. Children would volunteer to demonstrate each skill. We decided that more practice would be better. In retrospect now, I realize that this practice was in fact myelinating new neural pathways (11).

There was a perceptible change taking place in the classroom. The first thing I noticed was a new sense of play (12). Students loved acting out the demonstrations, although leaving without dignity was the favorite. In retrospect, and with my new neural lens, this is to be expected – leaving with drama, chaos, noise, and fuss was what every child understood at a molecular level. They had been building neural structures that strengthened these pathways for all the years of their existence (13).

That first week, a couple of students did leave with dignity. It was extraordinarily vindicating to witness. A measurable beginning! Not everyone was able to overcome the reactive rage and so a few reverted to the familiar chaotic exit (14). But a new almost tangible feeling made itself available. The children who had already left with dignity at least once and who had practiced leaving with dignity reacted differently when other children were not yet at a place of dignity. They hesitated and then plainly refused to give in to the contagion of jeering and egging on as their classmates struggled while leaving. Insightful jeering and raucous cheering for escalation began to decrease in volume and enthusiasm. This, I considered a huge win.

Things got better every day. Leaving with dignity became a "thing" in the children's vocabulary. Within about three weeks, students were mastering the new lesson (15) and could leave without the usual screaming and ugly display of fear and pain. This changed the dynamics of the classroom in several long-lasting ways. First, the children began to feel better about leaving with dignity. Second, we got to spend more valuable time on tasks, doing school projects and learning, as there were far fewer interruptions. Finally, life at the cottage also improved because there was a transfer of dignity feeling wherever the children went (16).

Yes, there was still some escalation. The exigencies of each day introduced trauma and triggers that caused outbursts and dysregulated reactions. However, because of the more mature attitude to both escalation and exit, we were able to resume instruction much more quickly. Around the fourth week, something happened that made my heart melt.

It had been a rough day for one of my students. It was during normal instruction time. Suddenly, he stood up, let out a yell, and placed his hands on his desk. Everything screeched to a halt. I reminded him to leave with dignity. He just stared, slowly computing what that meant. I could see he was contemplating his next move. I held my breath. It looked like he was going to knock his desk over. It was a long pregnant moment.

He straightened up and started to walk toward the door. It was clear to everyone that he was struggling to maintain control. This was self-regulation in real life. Then the miracle happened. One of his peers whispered to him as he passed by. "Just leave with dignity… you can do it." The whisper was as audible as a loud scream. Others joined in. They whispered this until he was out the door.

There was a visceral sigh of relief in the class. You could see he was struggling, yet he managed to leave without a scene. I could barely hold back tears. Sure he had made it happen. But there was more – much more. These were the same students who rarely said anything kind to one another. And here they were supporting a classmate by encouraging him to leave with dignity. Had we just set up an environment where it was possible to be gracious, kind, and helpful?

We had been on a perilous journey together. At the beginning of the year, we went from escalations that stopped all instruction with students either joining in or cheering on the escalated person … to a class where students supported one another to leave with dignity.

That moment cemented my decision to be intentional about teaching students how to leave with dignity. I was beginning to see past behavior into brain structures that were meaningful.

While I loved working in this setting, I decided at the end of the school year that I wanted to work in a more traditional school setting. I accepted a position in a kindergarten through third grade self-contained classroom. This elementary served approximately 350 students. It was quite a contrast. The building was bright and cheery; the floorplan a modern H pattern, with each leg of the H a different color.

Third grade hall was a soft orange; second grade a pale shade of green; kindergarten, where I set up shop, and first grade were a bright yellow; and the last hallway across from us was a deeper yellow in the kitchen and back end of the gym. The library and office joined the two sides of the H together.

I felt like I had moved into a more expansive world far removed from the drab "seventies". I loved that my room had windows along one wall looking out over a fresh green courtyard. Once more, I seemed to have followed a teacher who was a secret hoarder. There was not much storage, but it was stuffed brimful of school paraphernalia. I spent a happy time cleaning out and cleaning up.

My thinking about the "leave with dignity" solution began to evolve in the new setting and with new situations. Student demographics were different and I had to adjust my thinking to accommodate. I now had children with Down syndrome, autism, and a few students with some poor regulation skills. After my first meeting with them, I realized that the phrase "leave with dignity" was too many words. They were not able to connect with the construct.

That's how it got shortened to "RESET". We did the usual demonstrations and we practiced it frequently. If a student became upset, one of us (I or a Para-educator) would accompany the child to a designated reset area. We were able to abandon Skinner and never punished. Instead, we were intentional about supporting the child with praise and love (17). We were careful to not get in their space; we could stay near but let them have time to de-escalate, calm down, and breathe.

One child, in particular, threw lots of tantrums. Initially, we would help him to the reset area and then just be in that space with him. I loved the day that I found him in the reset area by himself. I had to make a visit to the office and when I returned, he was already in the reset area. I asked my paras if they had sent him there. They had not. He went there by himself. Here was a clear case of moving from co- to self-regulation (18).

I approached and asked if he was ok.

"I need reset," he responded almost matter-of-fact like an adult.

I said OK and since he seemed to be calming down, I asked if he was ready to come back.

He looked at me and said, "I not resetted."

I stayed near and when he was ready and was reset, he returned and joined his classmates.

The experience of mastery in the classroom with regard to self-regulation reaffirmed for me that when I was working with students who struggled to regulate emotions, I could teach them a strategy that would work across settings.

After two years in that self-contained kindergarten through third grade, I decided to make a move to developmental preschool. My students were now three to five years old, and they could begin school on their third birthday – if their IEP was in place. Many of these students exhibited language delays and they did not seem to connect or understand reset, so I had to switch again. It came down to a choice of two titles – "Time Out" or "Take a Break".

Take a Break won out.

Many students were familiar with the concept of "time out". However, this reprimand is often used in the context of punishment. I had come to dislike the idea of time out because I witnessed how it impacted most children – especially the children described by Bruce Perry (19) and Thomas Boyce (20) in their child research studies. If an adult directs a child to take a time out, the child has no power over it and reduced autonomy (10). The adult determined they needed the time out and essentially the adult determines when the time out is over. I now also feel that if I tell a child to take a time out, I own it. I determined and told them they needed a time out – therefore, I must determine when the time out ends.

Why not instead teach children to simply "take a break"? The reason is clear. We want our children to maintain a sense of control over their emotions and their consequences.

Also looking forward I wanted to equip my students with a phrase that was easily understood across settings and would not feel "babyish" as they aged. In hindsight, I should have used the phrase "take a break" over "reset" in my previous position.

I continue to teach my students and families about taking a break when they are upset or have very strong emotions. If a student rejoins the class and they are not quite ready, I might gently encourage them to go finish their break. Sometimes parents will point out to me that if they send their child to their room to take a break, they often start to play. I explain that it is fine that they play. They are free to rejoin when they are calm.

Breathe.

Everyone has strong emotions at one time or another; those of us who can manage them are often more successful in the world at large.

Note

1. Even Skinner himself maintained that token economies would only be a temporary solution for self-regulation and that building strong relationships and a sense of trust should replace that method.

References

1. B. F. Skinner, *Walden two*. (Macmillan, ed. 1, 1948).
2. M. E. Seligman, Learned helplessness. *Annual Review of Medicine* **23**, 407–412 (1972).

3. A. D. Baddeley, *Working memory* (Oxford University Press, New York, 1986).
4. N. Ziaian-Ghafari, D. H. Berg, Compassion fatigue: The experiences of teachers working with students with exceptionalities. *Exceptionality Education International* **29**, 32–53 (2019).
5. J. Willis, *Research-based strategies to ignite student learning: Insights from a neurologist and classroom teacher* (Association for Supervision and Curriculum Development, Alexandria, VA, 2006).
6. I. Jones, Social relationships, peer collaboration and children's oral language. *Educational Psychology* **22**, 63–73 (2002).
7. D. Linden, *The accidental mind: How brain evolution has given us love, memory, dreams, and God* (Harvard University Press, Boston, MA, 2007).
8. D. Hebb, *The organization of behavior* (Wiley & Sons, New York, 1949).
9. N. Cowan, The magical number 4 in short-term memory: A reconsideration of mental storage capacity. *Behavioral and Brain Sciences* **24**, 87–114 (2001).
10. D. Pink, *Drive* (Riverhead Books, New York, NY, 2009).
11. S. Bunge, Structural Connectivity Sets the Stage for Later Reasoning Ability. *Building Blocks of Cognition Laboratory, Berkeley, CA in The DANA Foundation study.* https://doi.org/10.1523/JNEUROSCI.3726-16.2017, 2017.
12. S. L. Brown, C. C. Vaughan, *Play: How it shapes the brain, opens the imagination and invigorates the soul* (Avery, New York, 2009).
13. D. Coyle, *The talent code. Greatness isn't born. It's grown. Here's how* (Random House, New York, NY, 2009).
14. M. Richey, T. K. O'Mahony, M. Prince, F. Zender, B. MacPherson, Revert to default - Insights on transfer of expertise in a complex competitive workplace paper presented at the American Society of Engineering Education, Seattle WA, 2015.
15. A. Gallagher, T. K. O'Mahony, in *Learning and the brain conference*, K. O'Mahony, Ed. (Neural Education, San Francisco, CA, 2023).
16. C. Bereiter, M. Scardamalia, in *Knowing, learning and instruction: Essays in honor of Robert Glaser*, L. B. Resnick, Ed. (Lawrence Erlbaum Associates, Hillsdale, NJ, 1989), pp. 361–392.
17. T. Boyce, The lifelong effects of early childhood adversity and toxic stress. *Pediatric Dentistry* **36**, 102–108 (2014).
18. L. Corno, R. Kanfer, The role of volition in learning and performance, in *Review of research in education*, L. Darling-Hammond, Ed. (American Educational Research Association, Washington, DC, 1993), pp. 301–341.
19. B. Perry, *The boy who was raised as a dog: What traumatized children can teach us about loss, love and healing* (Basic Books, New York, NY, 2006).
20. T. Boyce, Differential susceptibility of the developing brain to contextual adversity and stress. *Neuropsychopharmacology* **41**, 142–162 (2016).

6

We Are Hardwired Learners No Matter What

By Stephanie Turcotte

Introduction

I always dreamed of having a perfect life. A perfect house, a perfect marriage, a perfect family with perfect children. This was what I perceived from the families who attended the school where I had been teaching for a few years. I studied to become a special education teacher and then completed my bachelor's degree in Education. At 34, I was determined to achieve perfection like others. Little did I know at that time that perfection is just an illusion…

On the first of December 2010, I gave birth to my first child by emergency cesarean due to alarming symptoms indicating that my fetus' life was in danger. William, my newborn child, then spent three weeks in the Neonatal Intensive Care Unit at Gray Nuns Hospital in Edmonton, Alberta, before being able to return home.

It was during this time that his dad and I learned that our son had suffered two major hemorrhagic strokes during pregnancy. The extent of the damage extended over more than half of his brain and was irreversible.

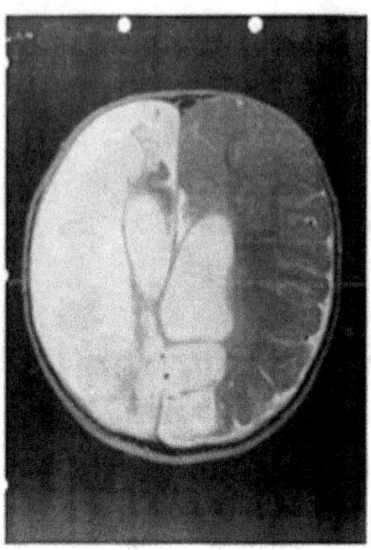

FIGURE 6.1 MRI of William's Brain at Birth Shows Bleeding Internally to 50% of His Brain

Overnight, we found ourselves "parents of a severely disabled child" who would have considerable needs throughout his life. The medical specialists told us that William would never walk, or talk, and that he would have a severe intellectual disability. Like a hunted and injured animal, I picked up my newborn baby and we huddled together, crying for a long time. Never could I have imagined that my dream of perfection would be so different from the reality that was manifesting.

From birth, I knew that William had cerebral palsy, even though he did not receive his official diagnosis (hemiplegic cerebral palsy affected more on the right side than the left side) until he was two years old (see Figure 6.1). Thanks to my training in special education and as a teacher, I had a lot of experience and knowledge about this condition.

The brain damage that affected my son resulted from a stroke that occurred before birth. Two major veins that carry blood from the heart to the brain burst, creating internal bleeding in the brain. Even though William and I underwent several tests to try to determine the cause of the stroke, it still remains unknown to this day.

Here is part of the result of the second magnetic resonance imaging (MRI) test of William's brain, produced on November 18, 2011:

> The encephalomalacia observed is of the same magnitude as during the previous examination (Dec. 8, 2010). Fluid replaces essentially all

the cells in the left hemisphere, except for a few in the occipital lobe and in the posterior temporal lobe.
>> University of Alberta Hospital, Edmonton, Alberta, Canada

The hospital discharge summary of December 18, 2010 reports the first facts observed:

A cesarean section was performed on the mother after 38 weeks of gestation due to the baby's low heartbeat and a declining biophysical profile. The Apgar score was 2, 6 and 7 after one, five and ten minutes of life. The baby was cyanotic (blue in color), apneic (not breathing well) and apathetic (without tone) with a heartbeat below 100. He received positive pressure ventilation for 3 minutes 30 seconds.
>> Neonatal-Perinatal Care (NICU) Pediatrics, Gray Nuns Hospital, Edmonton, Alberta, Canada

I naively believed that once I got my son out of the hospital, everything would get better. William came home for the first time at 18 days old. This is when the challenges really began. Our newborn was not feeding well and was visibly losing weight. He cried day and night, with a particularly high-pitched, unbearable, and very disturbing cry. He slept for a very short time and he was such a light sleeper that he would wake up at the tiniest amount of noise. When he managed to feed, he would quickly projectile vomit, everything he had swallowed. This lasted three months.

Meanwhile, post-traumatic stress disorder and depression was settling in. My husband and I were exhausted and we had to take turns taking care of our baby to get some rest.

We eventually discovered that William's cerebral palsy had also affected his facial muscles, which made sucking milk extremely difficult. The problem was simple. He was hungry, but unable to feed. We had no choice but to administer him a gastric nasal tube. Thanks to this new way of nourishing him, it was only then that he stopped screaming, started to sleep, gained weight, and calmed down.

His oral-motor and oral-sensory problems would continue until much later. Until the age of two and a half years old, we had to mash everything he ingested. William was unable to chew and swallow solid food. Furthermore, the food's different textures or the simple fact of having a utensil in his mouth would inevitably cause him to gag and regurgitate … again, whatever he had swallowed.

During this period, we also discovered that William suffered from sensory overload problems. After a brain injury, sensory filters no longer work properly and cannot identify and filter out irrelevant or unnecessary sensory information. When he would be in a social setting and people would applaud, he would be terrified and have a full blown meltdown.

Other times, he would show a reduced sensitivity to the various sensory stimuli of the environment. The only way to calm him down was to hold him tight in our arms while bouncing on a large exercise ball. His brain was asking for more intense sensory experiences of touch and/or movement, since the information he was receiving was not getting to its destination well or fast enough.

At six months, William began to have epileptic seizures. The brain damage caused by the strokes had created an imbalance in the networks of the brain, leading to abnormal neuronal activity. His seizures started at the age of six months, requiring daily medication.

My husband and I had chosen to take up this challenge with a lot of love for our son. There was no doubt in our minds that we were going to be able to raise him so that he would reach his full potential, whatever that might be. I also knew that timing was critical. The faster we could stimulate his brain, the more and better results we would get. From then on, our motto was to be proactive – we would undertake the treatment and therapy opportunities ourselves. We wasted no time and began our research to find out which therapy would offer him the best chance of psychomotor improvement.

At first, we tried all the alternative therapies we found or that were recommended to us: craniosacral, reiki, massage, energy treatments, and so on. Subsequently, we discovered Conductive Education (CE). From that moment on, we worked tirelessly. All of our resources – time, money, and energy – were devoted to improving our son's quality of life.

William took his first CE class at the age of 21 months. A group of parents that we were part of hired a conductor from Hungary who had a university degree in the field. We rented a space in a nearby school, and we bought the necessary equipment. Due to his young age, William participated in the program for a total of 130 hours as follows: ten hours per week (two hours a day) for 13 weeks.

During this first CE session, William was unable to speak (or stammer), to sit cross-legged, and to walk upright or crawl on all fours. Here is the conductor's note during the evaluation meeting at the beginning of the program.

> William can be easily motivated by toys. He resists cooperating in new tasks, usually crying to show his unwillingness. His muscle tone is spastic, his joints are especially stiff on the right side. His lower limbs are hypertensive, the ankles turn inside. It is extremely

difficult to bend his right leg, even manually. Walking and supporting one's own weight, barefoot is recommended for both legs. He is able to walk with his left leg. His right arm is in flexion, his right hand is closed in a fist. He can open his right hand by himself, but he is not able to grasp objects with it. He can sit with straight legs on the ground independently. His game mainly consists of putting toys in his mouth and throwing them. He makes sounds, but cannot speak. He is not potty trained. He suffers from epilepsy.

Chief Conductor, Rehabilitation Expert, September 10, 2012,
Edmonton, Alberta, Canada

Following are the educational objectives of CE that Katalin worked on throughout the session:

- Adapt to the program.
- Strengthen the muscles in general.
- Stretch the muscles and joints.
- Learn to bend both legs.
- Learn to hold furniture with two hands.
- Learn to walk with his right leg.
- Learn to get up from the floor while holding a piece of furniture.
- Extending his right hand and using it in his daily life.
- Learn to grasp and hold objects with the right hand.
- Develop speech by pronouncing short words.
- Improve attention-concentration.
- Improve hand-eye coordination.
- Learn to use the potty.

When this first CE session was over, the expectation was that parents were to continue the training at home, on a daily basis. However, my husband and I worked full time and unfortunately no daycare had agreed to take care of our child. Thus, we decided to hire a nanny and offered her training in CE. That way, William's brain kept on being stimulated. Here is the list of exercises that William had to execute at home, on a daily basis.

- Roll in both directions.
- Roll over onto the stomach on the right side.
- Stand on all fours with the brace on the right arm and play in this position, pushing a ball forward.
- Crawl with splint.

- Kneel on a chair.
- Crouch down.
- Make the wheelbarrow using the straps.
- Sit cross-legged.
- Sit on a stool and lift objects off the floor.
- Stand up with one foot flat and hold on to a piece of furniture.
- Sitting to stand with and without support.
- Stand straight at the wall.
- Walk between parallel bars, between two tables.
- Walk with two chairs.
- Take care of yourself; get dressed and eat.
- Play with modeling clay, reading books, doing puzzles.
- Blow feathers and bubbles.
- Repeat short words and animal sounds.
- Learn to use the toilet.

The key to success for us was the daily application of these therapeutic movements. Every day, William repeated his series of exercises to accustom his brain to these new movements. The muscles that he wasn't using before began to grow stronger and he started to improve his endurance and his muscle strength. Slowly but surely, William could carry out daily activities with greater ease and energy and his posture and balance were strengthening.

Here is the report at the end of the program to describe William's progress:

- William quickly adapted to the program.
- He has become stronger – learned to roll independently in both directions.
- He is able to stand on his hands and knees (on all fours) for a short time, when wearing a right arm support brace.
- He crawls, and he can move his arms and left leg forward.
- He is able to get up with or without the help of furniture.
- He can stand on his own, clinging to furniture with both hands for a longer time.
- He is able to stand independently (without help) for a short time.
- He is able to step forward to walk with his right leg.
- He can take a few steps on his own (supervision is necessary).
- He can hold objects with his right hand.
- His attention-concentration has developed a lot.
- He plays with more adequate toys.
- He is sometimes successful on the potty.

One month later, William received his second CE session. Two conductors offered the course in Picton, Ontario. My husband took his vacation time early and in January 2013, father and son took off for an adventure that would last five weeks – five hours a day, five days a week. This time, the programming was much more intense.

After the second session, we observed considerable changes in William's skills. Suddenly, he had way more balance, he was able to walk with a walker, and he was moving his right arm and right hand by himself a lot more. He was even able to say one- and two-word sentences! At this time, William was three years old.

The ultimate goal of this strict and intense routine was to create new synaptic connections between the neurons of his brain. We had undertaken a colossal workload and nothing could stop us in our mission. Gradually, William's physical abilities evolved. He could perform certain movements on his own that were impossible for him to do in the past. His progress gave us the courage and the strength to keep going.

However, time was pressing. We knew that the majority of brain development takes place at a young age and we wanted to take full advantage of this opportunity. Every time we had put aside enough money, we would enroll him in a new session of CE. At the time, this therapy was only available in the private sector, outside of our province, and cost around 6000 Canadian dollars. That didn't include the expense of travel, meals, and accommodation.

We quickly came to the conclusion that we were going to run out of funds to finance this type of therapy. No organization or government had agreed to reimburse the cost of the therapy which, even today, is controversial due to a lack of evidence regarding its effectiveness. Consequently, we decided to hold a benefit evening that would bring our community together: a spaghetti dinner and silent auction for William. It was a great success! We raised $12,000 in one evening (see Figure 6.2). It gave us the opportunity to enroll William in two CE sessions (one per year, for two years).

Subsequently, we repeated the evening on two other occasions and we were able to offer a total of eight CE sessions to William between the ages of 12 months and six years.

In August 2015, our family traveled to Grand Rapids, Michigan (US). The Conductive Learning Center (CLC) was, at the time, CE's only training center in North America and they offered summer camps. William was then four years old and he was about to start his sixth CE session.

Throughout his first six years, our son took part in multiple initiatives that aimed to stimulate his brain in every way possible. Stollery Children's Hospital (Edmonton), Glenrose Rehabilitation Hospital (Edmonton), Early

FIGURE 6.2 Fundraising with Spaghetti Dinner Was a Great Success

Intervention and Home Care programs (Alberta Health Service), Ability Society of Alberta (now, Ability 4 Good), and the Shriners Hospital for Children were all involved. William had multiple weekly therapeutic appointments. Sometimes, these consultations were to execute Constraint Induced Movement Therapy (CIMT), bi-manual training, to receive botox, or to participate in different studies, i.e., Lokomat (see Figure 6.3).

Every month, William met with his general pediatrician, neurologist, neurodevelopmental pediatrician, occupational therapist, physiotherapist, nurse, nutritionist, behavioral specialist, psychologist, and speech therapist.

The main goal was to stimulate William's brain on all fronts: physical, psychological, emotional, and social. In addition, since birth, our son has been wearing different splints on his right hand, ankles, and feet. He also used several types of walkers or supports to help him move around or to help him with his daily functions, such as getting on his bed or using the toilet.

The original lesion that leads to cerebral palsy (CP) cannot be cured. There is no cure for CP. However, there are many therapies, surgeries, medications, equipment, and technology that can help reduce CP symptoms. Thus, its impact on the body can be moderate and by the same token, it is possible to improve the quality of life of the individuals who suffer from it (1). However, none of these treatments have a **permanent positive** impact on the brain.

When he started full-time kindergarten at the age of four and a half, William could no longer dedicate so much time to CE. We had to be creative to

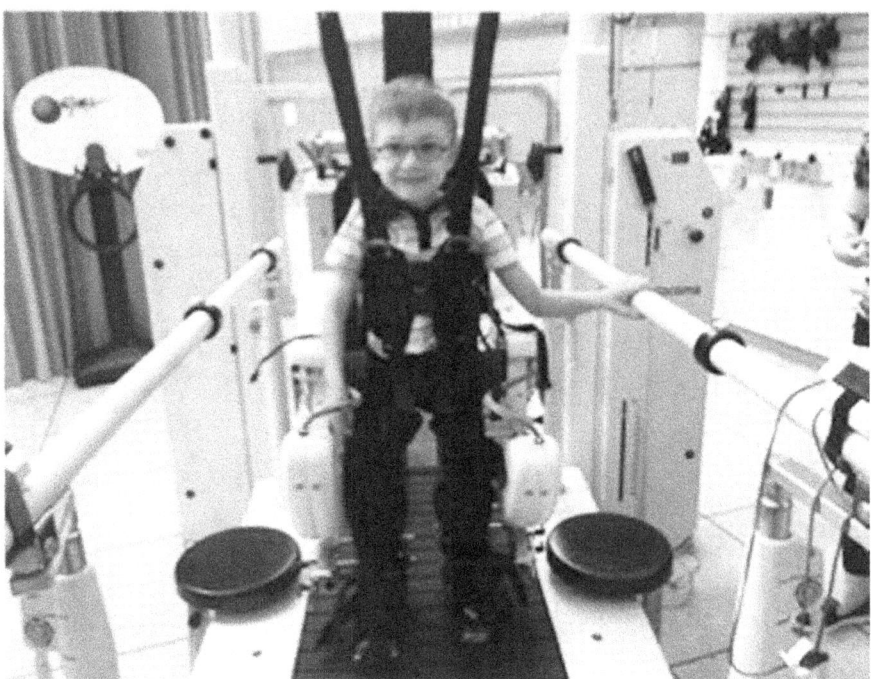

FIGURE 6.3 William Having Fun at Lokomat Activities

keep developing his physical skills. We then turned to sports. Therefore, evenings and weekends were dedicated to movement, in order to stimulate his brain: training at Free2BMe (physical activity and fitness center for children with disabilities), hippotherapy, swimming, alpine skiing, ice skating, cycling, and more (see Figure 6.4). William even took Spanish lessons, dance lessons, and piano lessons in order to develop different areas of his brain. This is how we spent the first six years of the life of our precious boy. We were intensely committed and dedicated to developing his full potential, whatever that meant.

These sports complement the exercises that are done every day at school and help him to perfect his physical skills. For us, these sports have become the therapy that William does since he is in school full time and he no longer has time during the school year to do CE.

By this time, the newborn baby that was threatened with a debilitating handicap had evolved in his development and he had made progress beyond what science and medicine had initially anticipated.

Today, the severity of William's cerebral palsy is level II according to the Gross Movement Function Classification System (GMFCS) (2). He walks

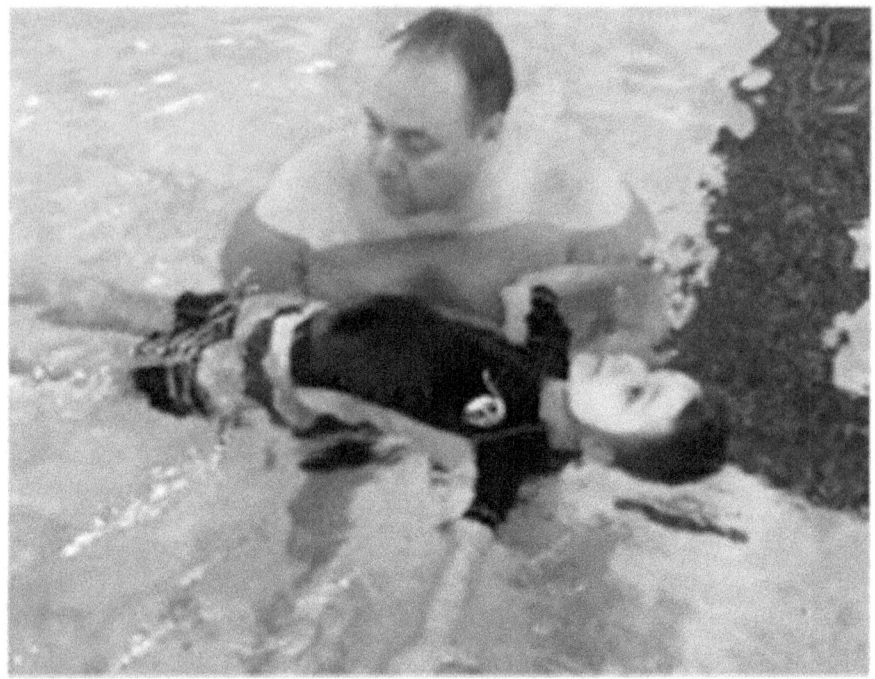

FIGURE 6.4 William Gaining Physical Mobility Strength through Swim Exercise

with certain limitations but he can walk, despite a lack of balance. The limits of his gross motor skills generally require some adaptations to enable participation in physical activities or sports. William's type of cerebral palsy is hemiplegic, although he is affected on both sides of his body with the right side being more afflicted. His motor function is a combination of spastic and floppy movements (mixed). He can control some muscles like his left hand, but as soon as he concentrates on a task, his whole right side becomes tense (spastic). On the other hand, the muscle tone in his pelvis is so flexible that he can sleep (non-spastic) head on feet (see Figure 6.5).

The neurologists and other medical specialists who have worked with William have all told us about the positive effects of neuroplasticity. Neuroplasticity is defined as the ability of the brain to create, undo, or rearrange networks of neurons and the connections of those neurons. The brain is thus described as "plastic" or malleable (3). This information is still recent in the medical community, but it has already proven itself. As parents, we decided to stimulate our child's brain using this knowledge and every approach available. It was the best decision we have ever made.

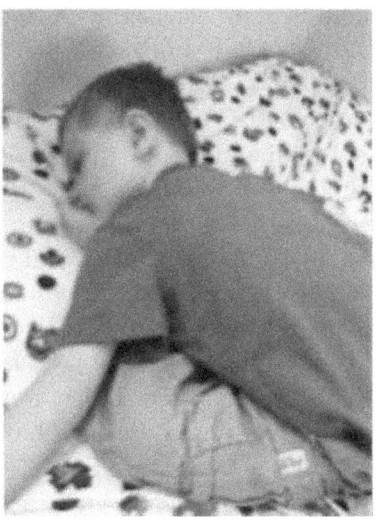

FIGURE 6.5 William Can Sleep Head on Feet

The activities that William was asked to do had to be of great intensity; they had to be repeated several times in a short period of time and they had to take place over a long period of time. The goal was to train the body, using movement, and force the brain to create new links between neurons (neural circuits). We know that high-intensity physical exercise enhances connectivity between the two cerebral hemispheres, as the complex movements engage different motor, sensory, and cognitive areas of the brain (4).

CE met these criteria perfectly. CE is an intensive training and holistic approach to educating people with physical disabilities that recognizes that teaching and learning are linked to emotions and cognitive and physical aspects of individuals. Andras Peto developed this approach in Hungary after World War II. His method aimed to help children acquire new skills, in different social environments integrated into daily life, both in terms of communication and in terms of motor activities (5). Activities were designed to be carried out in a structured environment, such as a classroom, for several hours a day (6). The approach is intense and it offers repetitions of complex movement, which stimulate the two hemispheres of the brain over a long period of time. It was just what our boy needed; repetitive movement created new connections in his brain that amplified his abilities.

Programs based on CE principles have been implemented in mainstream and specialized schools, in hospitals, in early intervention settings, in independent clinical settings, in after-school programs, and in summer camps.

CE programs can also take the form of a parent-child group program. It aims above all to educate and provide resources for the development of motor skills that proceed in stages (5).

The conductor is responsible for creating a stimulating environment and a supportive atmosphere that promotes fun, participation, and learning. The motivating environment is created by the group, by the use of specific techniques, and by the routine that structures the program. Ideally, children are grouped according to age and ability, need, and rate of progression (7). The group provides a source of motivation, support, camaraderie, and challenge for every individual. Children learn from each other by imitating strategies that others use to accomplish the same task. In the group, the child learns that he can have a positive impact on his environment and achieve the desired objective. CE develops a sense of responsibility for action and with that action comes the ability to care for oneself (5).

One of the principles of CE is that children take personal responsibility and engage themselves in their learning. Problem solving, active participation, perseverance, and a positive attitude are required. The conductor must also demonstrate a positive attitude, expect the success and progress of children, and create learning opportunities that promote their development (5). The conductor reinforces what the child must do and avoids scolding unsuccessful attempts.

According to experts of this methodology (5), other CE teaching strategies include that the children:

- Be as active as possible throughout the day.
- Know the purpose of the activity and that this purpose is related to their personal needs.
- Perform the tasks requested in an optimal way (to allow a clear intention and the success of the child).
- Use the time and have the opportunity to practice and repeat important tasks.
- Have the opportunity to participate in both challenging and new tasks, to maintain students' attention and motivation.

On the other hand, the conductor:

- Gradually removes supports from the child when they reach a certain level.
- Avoid fatigue or loss of attention, otherwise learning will no longer occur.

In the groups in which William took part, several children improved significantly at the psychomotor level from the beginning to the end of the program. The improvements were more noticeable in some children. I remember a little girl entering the session on crutches and leaving by walking without any support. Other times, the improvements were more subtle, but all children improved on something, according to their parents. Here is how William evolved during his six years of therapy.

After three CE sessions in 2014, on a cold February morning, three-year-old William got up from his bed, by himself, and joined his father in the kitchen. We were amazed! This had never happened before. William had walked alone, without our help, standing from time to time by the wall. Before long, he was using complete sentences of three to four words, using stairs to go up and down, and he could walk on unstable surfaces, like snow or sand, without falling. Even the epileptic seizures ceased. His progress didn't happen overnight. It happened gradually. However, for us, it was obvious that there was a direct link between our knowledge and application of neuroplasticity and our son's progress. We were a far cry from the child described by the doctors after his birth.

Today, William can walk (limping on the right side), run (not very fast), and jump on two feet. He is now learning to lift his right knee when walking, instead of dragging his leg, and to use his right hand during bimanual tasks. His sense of balance is always to be reworked when he grows since the brain must readjust his cerebral landmarks. Nevertheless, William has succeeded in meeting several major challenges that allow him to participate in many activities like other children his age.

In our experience, CE has been instrumental in our son's progress. This therapy gave us a structure and clear goals to achieve. It was about relearning all the movements that a newborn baby does until he can walk. We simplified and reproduced them until William mastered each step along the way. This therapy offered us a way forward and a concrete means to achieve our goals. We can never be one hundred percent certain that all the results obtained stemmed exclusively from this method of stimulation, but we firmly believe that it had a major impact on William's psychomotor development.

William is a miracle. Who would have thought that he would develop so much in such a short time? He is a being of love, hope, and inspiration to others. He never gives up, he never stops, and we all learn from him. We've always believed in him and were faithful that he could become way more than he was originally predicted to be. We have nicknamed him "Rocky" like the boxer popularized by Sylvester Stallone. We even credited him with the theme song to one of the movies, Survivor's "Eye of the Tiger". Since birth, William has worked tirelessly to develop his physical, psychological, and social skills. He had to become a fighter to learn to walk, to eat, to dress, to speak, or to perform other simple everyday life tasks – simple and natural tasks that we all take for granted. Because of William's journey, I have the privilege of reminding people every day that everyone has the ability to learn and reach their full potential, regardless of life's inherent obstacles.

Appendix I – Resources

Here is a list of websites that offer various resources.

Cerebral Palsy
Cerebral Palsy Association in Alberta https://www.cpalberta.com/
CP Canada Network http://www.cpcanadanetwork.com
The Canadian Cerebral Palsy Registry https://kidsbrainhealth.ca/portfolio-items/the-canadian-cerebral-palsy-registry/

Conductive Education
Association for Conductive Education in North America (ACENA) https://www.acena.org/
Conductive Learning Centre (Grand Rapids, Michigan, É.-U.) https://conductivelearningcenter.org/
Families of Alberta for Conductive Education https://facealberta.ca/
March of Dimes Canada https://www.marchofdimes.ca/EN/programs/CE/Pages/ConductiveEducation.aspx
András Pető Faculty – Semmelweis University https://semmelweis.hu/pak/en

Appendix II – Videos

Physical skills before conductive education https://www.youtube.com/watch?v=50ZEXCTlWnY
William in conductive education (first two sessions) https://www.youtube.com/watch?v=yZDyn8opF38
The evolution of William, to conductive education (one year later) https://www.youtube.com/watch?v=v29dDh6PONU
The video that was presented during the 2nd spaghetti dinner https://www.youtube.com/watch?v=OiTY7fHoFSo&feature=youtu.be
William goes downhill skiing https://www.youtube.com/watch?v=8jJ5JsNZ4TU

William talks to his friends https://www.youtube.com/watch?v=V6C8px9IMgY&feature=youtu.be

One year of therapy, other than school https://www.youtube.com/watch?v=dbbyF-M4EcE&t=2s

References

1. CNFS, in *National Health Training Consortium (CNFS) University of Ottawa component* (CNFS, University of Ottawa, Canada, Ottawa, 2019).
2. R. Palisano, P. Rosenbaum, D. Bartlett, M. Livingston, in *GMFCS - E&R* (CanChild Centre for Childhood Disability Research, McMaster University, 2007). Developmental Medicine & Child Neurology, **39**, 214–223 (1997).
3. F. Martin-Vallas, Y aurait-il des bases neurophysiologiques au transfert? *Cahiers jungiens de psychanalyse* **3**, 93–112 (2009).
4. Y. Sun, N. Ledwell, L. Boyd, P. Zehr, Unilateral wrist extension training after stroke improves strength and neural plasticity in both arms. *Experimental Brain Research* **236**, 2009–2021 (2009).
5. H. Bourke-Taylor, R. O'Shea, D. Gaebler-Spira, Conductive education: A functional skills program for children with cerebral palsy. *Physical Occupational Therapy Pediatrics* **27**, 45–62 (2007).
6. K. Ratliffe, C. Sanekane, Conductive education: Benefits and challenges. *TEACHING Exceptional Children* **41**, 66–72 (2009).
7. P. Bairstow, R. Cochrane, J. Hur, Evaluation of conductive education for children with cerebral palsy: final report, (Office for Standards in Education, Great Britain, 1993).

7

Creativity, Brain, Response Art, and the Making of Community

By Valli Rebsamen

Introduction

Eddie was lonely. It was easy to see why! He hadn't had a play date for months. We were in the middle of a pandemic where homebound isolation, social distancing, and face masks caused children to be alone and were wearing down patience for many of us. This new way of living was an uninvited instability for him, when the daily anchors of his routines were loosed so that he found himself cast adrift in a turbulent sea of disquiet, confusion, and uncertainty.

I created this sketch ... *What Does Lonely Look Like?* (see Figure 7.1). Using color crayons and sharing it with Eddie – he was in the fourth grade – the image was in response to his efforts to express his feelings of isolation due to COVID-19 quarantine. I shared the image with Eddie and also explained the visual symbolism that I suspected would resonate with him. The disproportionately small heart in the insurmountable ravine between two mountains symbolized his capacity and desire to connect with others and the obstacles in his way. Additionally, a cloud blocked

FIGURE 7.1 What Does Lonely Look Like? (Valli Rebsaman, 2020 with 4th Grader)

the nourishing rays of the sun that he very much longed for. This visual representation added an additional dimension to our verbal conversation and demonstrated that I heard his words and could empathize with the overwhelming sense of isolation that he felt and struggled to articulate. We were able to explore a shared recognition of how barriers to connection with his friends and greater community had accompanied this new reality in a Zoom-driven school experience.

This drawing was emergent "response art" that was made during a discussion with Eddie via Zoom; we were each in our respective homes. The invitation to jointly and independently each draw a response to a specific prompt is a variation of a technique that art therapists sometimes use called response art. In this instance, our shared prompt was, "What does Lonely Look Like?" We each took about five minutes to simultaneously draw while still on Zoom. His sense of isolation and aloneness loomed overwhelming as he tried to make sense of the strange new world that included lockdown, online classes, cameras on or off, limited bandwidth, social distancing, being away from friends and extended family, wearing face masks ... and other scary things like quarantine, vaccinations, sickness, and death. I shared this drawing to mirror what I heard as we engaged in conversation.

Response Art

A working definition of response art is as follows: "... creation of a visual art piece with focused intention to increase awareness on a situation, experience, dynamic or concern" (1).

Response art is a concept that art therapists are trained to use in response to interactions they experience related to their clinical work and professional development. Art therapists use response art in their interactions to (i) make visible and (ii) name enduring ideas and important thought processes that emerge prevalent through the art making process. It is highly useful to manage evolving ideas in order to:

- Frame difficult subject matter
- Express latent emotions
- Examine experiences that are meaningful
- Explore symbolism and find common vocabulary
- Gain insight into situations that might not be self-evident
- Express emotions and feelings such as empathy, fear, worry, hope, relief, and anger

Art therapists use artwork in this manner as a practice to help manage and understand their clinical sessions with clients and supervisees, as well as personal and professional reflection. The method and practice of using response art is useful in post-session processing and expression and can serve as a protective wellness strategy to mitigate vicarious trauma. Response art can be kept private or shared with peers or even clients such as the abbreviated example with student Eddie. Barbara Fish, an industry leader, prolific art therapist, and educator (1), has demonstrated effective use of response art in interdisciplinary educational settings. In particular, she introduced nursing students to the response art process and effectively facilitated the practice as part of supervision seminars during their initial clinical experiences (1, p. 181). The phrase *response art* may have been coined from within the discipline of art therapy; however, the process is one in which the artist/creator has a great deal of autonomy and is not necessarily always considered "clinical therapy". In this respect, the effectiveness in eliciting reflection and new ways of thinking invites further development of the practice outside of art therapy settings – we'll return to this idea later.

My work with Eddie was part of a school district initiative to support students and families. As a licensed Marriage & Family Therapist (LMFT) and Art Therapist (ATR-BC), I provided short-term support as requested. The idea of "community" in school initiatives has exponentially ballooned, as a direct result of social awareness of family needs and prevention initiatives from public health agencies. External programs now co-located within school districts are very common today and have a complementary focus on social and emotional competencies that many districts have in addition to academic goals that formerly might have been a school's leading objective. Programs include food backpack supplies (2) and healthcare schemes where community-based mobile teams provide regular wellness check-up visits (3) for students and families. Students are better prepared to learn when their sense of safety and basic needs are met and families are better equipped to support/encourage their students when they have access to necessary resources and healthcare (less fight, flight, or freeze responses in classrooms and at home).

External behavioral health providers are, also, commonly available in school-based settings. In addition, districts are increasingly hiring community engagement coordinators and social workers to better connect families with supports to positively affect community well-being. This expansion of social awareness into school systems coincides with the emphasis on trauma-informed healthcare settings, where school communities are also now trauma informed (4).

Educators, like therapists and counselors, are now beginning to understand the need and accept encouragement to use strategies to manage how they are affected by their work. As stressors increase with seemingly unobtainable academic benchmarks, disconnected students, and competitive work environments, teachers experience burnout (5) and compassion fatigue (6) at alarming rates. More and more educators are leaving the profession as a result. Intrinsically this can leave educators feeling helpless, powerless, and despondent. In reality, supports like the continuum of "hub resources" varies from district to district, state to state, so that often teachers are compelled to contribute their free time and personal money to their professional work (7).

What has been missing in this educational equation of co-located resource hubs is that educators have not been systemically encouraged to self-reflect on their personal responses to the work with provided tools for self-reflection and processing.

The COVID-19 pandemic offered me a fortunate opportunity where I was asked to create a creative arts workshop for the Neuroscience of Learning pedagogies that invited teachers to experience art making in a non-judgmental setting. Given the tumultuous state of the world, I hoped to offer teachers a Zoom-based opportunity to self-reflect while exploring whatever creative material they had on hand at home. Response art seemed like the natural fit.

De-stigmatize Art Making

Transitioning to a more introspective activity, we consider our own relationship with creative processes. For some readers, this is a welcome invitation and for others – you know who you are – it immediately has elicited a degree of stress.

I recognize that art, or image making, does not feel comfortable for everyone. Like many things in life, our response to art is a learned experience. Many of us have undergone social conditioning and experiences that have left us feeling vulnerable when we judge our images to be inadequate. Such experiences have already programmed our reticular activating systems so that we are prone to amygdala hijack when the mention or the idea of art is suggested.

In this setting, "art" could most simply translate into image making using color and shape. This exercise is not capital "A" fine art. A primary objective is to invite you to reflect on the "process" rather than on the "finished" product. In doing so, you are engaging and honoring multiple senses of your highly evolved self to enhance and solidify your learning and understanding.

Sometimes, teenage children, parents, or adults say, "I'm not an artist", and it reminds me of how I would say, "I'm not a math person" or "I'm no good at French language". This kind of pre-programmed thinking displays a fixedness that is not aware of the science behind neural plasticity (8) and mindset (9) or mental models. As educators, we are only too familiar with the child who is convinced that other people in the classroom are smarter, more intelligent, and more talented. The widespread misunderstanding of growth versus fixed mindset is often propagated unwittingly by teachers who are unaware of the nuanced approach of plasticity and synaptogenesis and ensures a learning experience that sends children on a downhill trajectory through life (10).

Just as I do when facilitating an art therapy group, when facilitating a community creative arts activity in a non-therapy setting, I invite hesitant participants to de-stigmatize the concept of image making. If you have ever uttered the words, "I am not an artist" or "I'm not artistic", I invite you to be curious about this thought process and suspend judgment on yourself. For centuries, going back through human history *Homo sapiens* has had the capacity to make meaning by expression and interpretation of life, in mediums that were available at the time (plant-based dyes, textiles, bones, shells, and so on). This coincided with the evolution of a powerful brain that had a cerebral capacity for spatial conceptualization, meaning making, and expression. It was, and is, a primal extension of our expressive selves.

Historically our ancestral neighbors created art, interpretive, utilitarian, useful, aesthetically pleasing, and novel. The latter, novel pieces, likely represented collective "shared" beliefs in a social community (e.g., shells for Neanderthal burials, handprints on cave walls). This shared meaning is also found in language – stories passed down over generations prior to written language (11). This concept of attributing meaning to shapes and images has become seamless in our daily lives – national flags, religious symbols, family crests, images on currency, emojis, and, of course, the industrialization and monetization of symbolism – advertising. We continue to communicate and rely on a world of image, shape, and color. It is in this exploration that we come to realize that historically, in culturally diverse societies, humans did not separate artistic disciplines; visual art, song, and dance were integrated into ceremony to acknowledge what had shared importance (12).

Prepare a Creative Scaffolding

In the following invitations, I encourage you to slow down and notice your relationship with the creative process. Before even creating a response art image, let's first explore what art therapist and educator Cathy Malchiodi referred to as … *Your Personal Art History* (13). This perspective offers a framework for developing a timeline for your relationship with creative arts and exploring your personal history of experience with creativity.

This timeline can include what we typically define arts to include: visual arts, music, writing, theatre. However, I invite you to consider art much more broadly. Perhaps include martial arts, handiwork, craftsmanship, woodwork, knitting, sewing, gardening, and even cooking, activities that involve using materials to create something or alter our spaces. By broadening our definition of art and considering our personal engagements with creating, we can lower our defenses and calm our threat response.

Whether you're comfortable with art materials or hesitant to engage, it can be helpful to be aware of your "personal" art history. This exercise supports breaking down internal barriers around art making and supports identifying spaces in our lives where we are creative. These skills contribute to expanding problem-solving and resourcefulness. Participants are invited to pause and write down responses to the bullet points below. This process is based on Malchiodi's extensive work in the field of art therapy. She summarizes the outcomes as communication in a stressful world:

> Art is a powerful tool in communication. It is now widely acknowledged that art expression is a way to visually communicate thoughts and feelings that are too painful to put into words. Creative activity has also been used in psychotherapy and counseling not only because it serves (as) another language but also because of its inherent ability to help people of all ages explore emotions and beliefs, reduce stress, resolve problems and conflicts, and enhance their sense of well-being (13).

On a separate piece of paper, take a few minutes to jot down your thoughts to the following prompts.

Your Personal Art History[1]

- What was art in your life growing up? Was it, for example, drawing and coloring, crafts, museum or gallery trips, learning handiwork from a relative, or pictures on the living room wall? Write down some notes about what you remember.
- What kind of beliefs did your family have about art?
- When you were young, did you have a favorite art or craft activity, such as coloring, painting by number, embroidering, knitting, or building things? What do you remember about it?
- Did you ever have a negative experience with art when you were a child? Were you told, for example, that you were not artistic, that your older sibling was the artist in the family, or that your art expressions were not good enough?

Reflective Questions
Now reflect on your responses to **Your Personal Art History** above.

- What stood out to you?
- What surprised you?

- What memories surfaced that you hadn't anticipated?
- What feelings and thoughts are associated with some of the memories?

Create Response Art!

If you've made it this far, you are well prepared to begin your own creative exploration!

Reminder – response art is "the creation of a visual art piece with focused intention to increase awareness on a situation, experience, dynamic or concern" (1). The subject of your response art is up to you. The materials you choose are up to you. They may be supplies you're comfortable with or ones you're curious to explore. The piece can be literal, abstract, two- or three-dimensional. There's no wrong medium. Here are some suggestions: collage, paint, crayon, pencil, natural materials, found objects, sculpture, sewing, yarn, wood, clay, etc.

Identify a Topic or Intention to Focus on. Tips to Consider

- Notice your experience objectively – is your "inner critic" being noisy? Put them in time out; let them wait it out.
- What is the momentum of the situation that you're contemplating? Is there a push and pull? An element of stalling or avoiding? Is there a student who you consider too loud or too fast? What is the student's experience like?
- What is your point of view? Are you outside looking in; are you inside looking out? Is it a collaborative or isolated experience?
- Does the piece need to be created from someone else's point of view?

Consider a Share Out

You're in a unique position with this activity in that you're likely working independently. Or maybe I'm wrong and you're reading this book in tandem with others – and can each create response art and then share it with each other – I love that idea! Regardless, consider sharing your piece with a trusted colleague. Beforehand, let them know they don't need to "approve" of your piece, like it, or even understand it. You're not eliciting their opinion or feedback. If you choose to share out, the goal is to be witnessed, not evaluated or interpreted through someone else's lens. It is very important that the sharing process remain non-judgmental. Perhaps later down the road, you consider facilitating a similar response art process in your classroom.

Please be very mindful of the potential for students to evaluate each other's work and make comments.

It is entirely okay to allow the visual piece to stand alone and be the "share out". And it is also entirely okay not to share and contain the process within your own experience – choice is the priority when it comes to sharing.

Educator Response Art (Shared in 2020)

Below are images (7.2–7.7) shared by the educators who participated in a remote Zoom-based response art workshop. They were offered the same prompts above. A majority of folks created their piece in response to the pandemic as we were still navigating stay-at-home life and school had not yet resumed in-person. The experiences with the cohorts of educators validated

FIGURE 7.2 Balloon Limits (Brooke Huddleston, 2020)

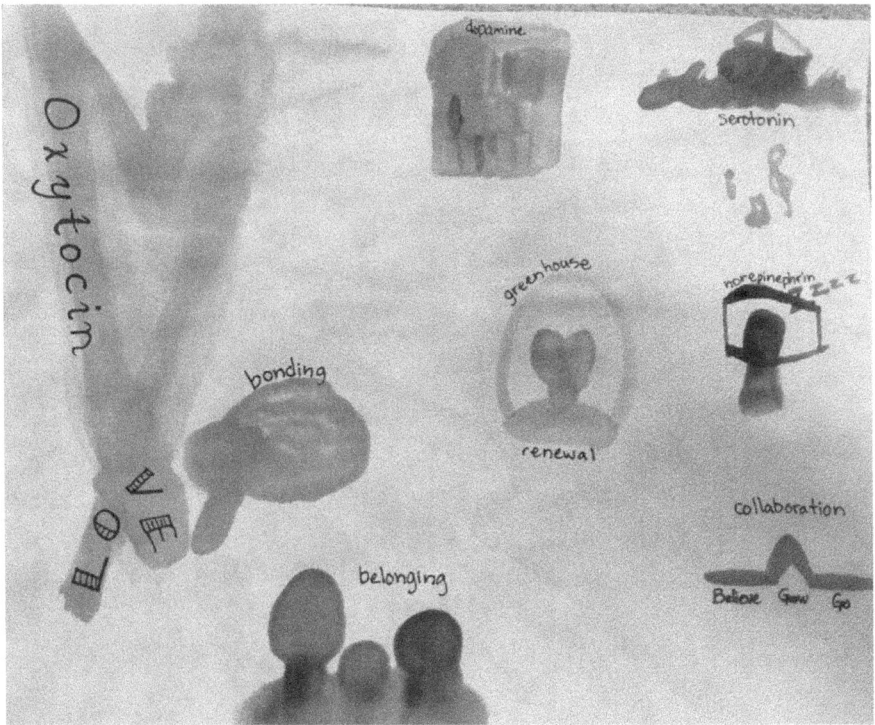

FIGURE 7.3 My Neuro Needs (Alyssa Benham, 2020)

my observations that educators are not routinely invited to reflect on their experiences in a wellness or stress management capacity. The feedback and engagement were considerable. Participants added their images and short descriptions to a shared drive "gallery walk" document that we viewed together and also independently of one another. This format offered a sense of visual community and shared experience where dozens of teachers had contributed – the visual gallery enabled each person to contribute in a way that a verbal discussion could not have afforded. Many contributors also included a short paragraph describing or reflecting on the experience.

> Sacred work of developing minds
> Carefully tending to our garden
> Straight to the prefrontal cortex
> The interplay of nature and nurture
> Carefully tending to our garden
> Dismantling bias

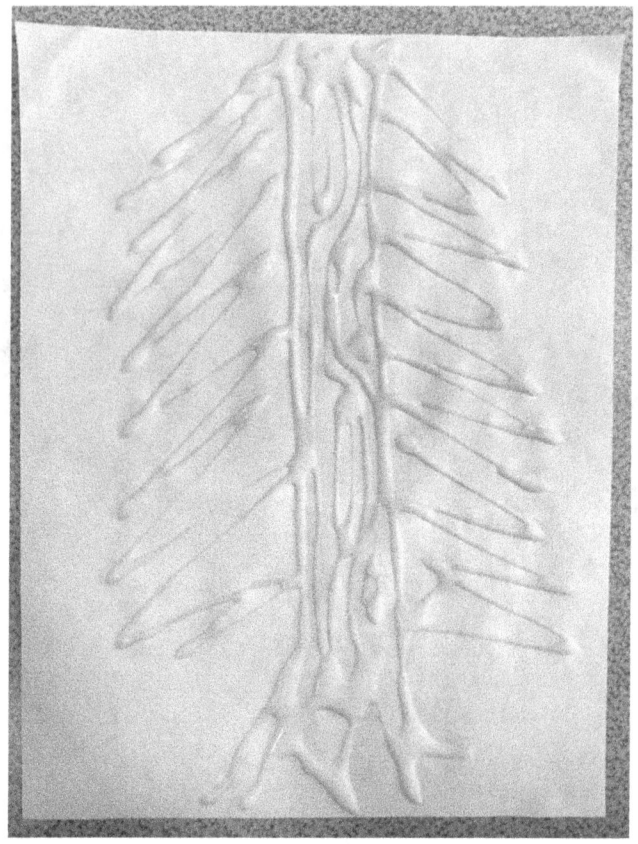

FIGURE 7.4 Tears (Dakota Heilborn, 2020)

>The interplay of nature and nurture
>Building myelinated connections
>Dismantling bias
>Finding new pathways
>Building myelinated connections
>Spiraling through infinity

Art Therapy

While we've explored how the process of response art is a technique that has the capacity to be adapted for interdisciplinary, non-clinical settings to increase participant self-reflection and community connections, it is

FIGURE 7.5 Still Processing (Laura Mercier, 2020)

important to maintain awareness of the boundaries of clinical art therapy. Obviously, art therapists do not hold a trademark on art making or creativity. Humans have been generating creative works since we developed the capacity for abstract thought and dexterity to manipulate objects with tools. My community-based workshops and even some of my school-based support with students, family, and staff have often taken place under non-clinical interactions. However, my approach has been informed by my experience and education in art therapy.

Art therapists are formally trained, master's level behavioral health clinicians who incorporate art making into the therapeutic process. They don't judge client art or try to explain what it means or even prioritize clients who are learning "correct" artistic skills – in this way, art therapy differs from art classes. Art therapists are not necessarily focused on a final artistic product. Instead, they are focused on facilitating the client's experience via art techniques that make visible social and emotional experiences in a person's life. They use art to help clients of all ages (individuals, families, groups) improve their mental, physical, and emotional well-being by using creative tools like

FIGURE 7.6 Sacred Work of Developing Minds (Jodi Franks, 2020)

FIGURE 7.7 The Forest for the Trees Needs (Allison Burch, 2020)

drawing, painting, and sculpting to help people express themselves. Art therapy is a mental health discipline and can further develop a client's sense of creativity. Creativity is part of our human drive (14). It can foster resilience, spark joy, and provide opportunities for self-actualization. In schools, creativity is seen as both utilitarian and non-utilitarian, including writing, thinking, and expression. Creativity can be intangible, such as an idea, scientific theory, musical composition, or a joke. It can also be a physical object, such as an invention, printed literary work, or a painting.

Training in art therapy includes both traditional counseling pedagogy and integrated concepts specific to art therapy that have roots in arts education and psychotherapy and established itself as a professional certified discipline primarily throughout Europe and North America in the 20th century. Art therapists are able to make meaningful contributions to the welfare of a community and especially to individual children who require mental and social interventions by providing a broad range of support in clinical and learning sites. As a result, art therapists are in schools, medical hospitals, psychiatric facilities, military-connected treatment centers for Post-Traumatic Stress and Traumatic Brain Injury, community counseling clinics, prisons, and assisted living facilities. Art therapists diagnose and treat conditions found in the Diagnostic Statistical Manual (DSM), common conditions addressed include: depression, anxiety, and ADHD, and encourage clients to meet their self-directed goals and grow into their full potential like any other counseling profession. Art therapy can be a rewarding career that integrates a variety of disciplines while adhering to discipline-specific tenets. I'm fortunate to have found this calling and over the years have reflected on how my journey to becoming an art therapist based in schools came to fruition.

My Creative Roots

I grew up in a house my parents built in the mid-1970s. It's a barn-shaped log house situated on five wooded acres in rural South Puget Sound of Washington State. The house sits among a variety of second growth maple, cedar, and fir. An organic playground filled with Salal, Sword Ferns, Oregon Grape, and even a few moss-covered old growth stumps provided coverage for rust-colored salamanders. The summers revealed a smattering of wild strawberries and, later, thimbleberries and huckleberries. The land offered a sensory paradise. I was often building forts and haphazardly weaving bundles of cedar boughs together to serve as roofing, or collecting bird feathers to use as quills; discarded oyster shells could be strung together where Sea Stars had left a hole; nimbly splicing buttercup chains together left green stains under the fingernails. Evidence of a productive day!

While I had free reign of the outside, inside the house also held a creative outlet. My dad encouraged me and my friends to use the entire surface area of a staircase of unfinished sheetrock as our canvas. My friends and I stood tiered along the stairs for hours, equipped with crayons, chalk, and markers adding whatever shapes, images, and words we felt inspired to contribute to the corridor walls. Initially, I think he assumed he'd get around to texturing and painting the sheetrock. However, this graffiti decorated chamber accumulated nearly 20 years' worth of scribbles, drawings, and images. It became visual documentation of my life-stage transitions and reflected a continuum of communication skills and social and emotional development – all through visual expression that had been created both individually and in community with others.

Creative problem-solving and hand building were also encouraged at school. I was fortunate to attend a small, community Waldorf School from kindergarten through sixth grade. In lieu of tuition, my parents often traded their construction and facility maintenance skills for their respective careers as a general contractor and musician who maintained a lower middle class income. Waldorf curriculum often integrates a variety of subjects, which provide hands-on learning that offers a broad range of kinesthetic and sensory learning experiences. Classrooms are furnished with natural fibers, organic shapes, with considerations to minimize artificial lights. Kindergartners make bread from scratch, use beeswax block crayons, and are provided with often simple, sensory-rich materials that encourage imaginative play – log rounds, carded wool, silk, or gauze "capes", and nature tables are standard, offering walnut shells, curved rounds of textured tree bark, moss, sea shells, and smooth beach stones. In reflecting on these experiences, I now see how they contributed to a lifelong search and appreciation for human's need for creative expression.

The Search

I think about my own childhood when I encounter children in various settings who may not have been exposed to an environment or settings that encourage the creative instinct. There are numerous accounts of individuals who after engaging in art therapy go on to hone their fine art skills – this is of course not a primary goal of AT; however, it indicates a profound joy and latent innate talent that has so far not been incubated or supported. Genes are only part of the answer; epigenetic environmental provision and upkeep are also necessary. It has been shown that following a child's appetite is more important than following their aptitude (15). Are some of us just naturally inclined to enjoy working with our hands? Is the degree of joy and satisfaction experienced in being creative due to the opportunities and invitations from caregivers, parents, and teachers to engage with creative materials? I am convinced that there's strong evidence that humans lean toward creativity and that it is the seed of culture and community (16–18).

Along the Northwest coast of Washington State, at a site called Ozette, rocks along the coast reveal petroglyphs made by members of the Makah Tribe hundreds of years ago that made a significant impression on my adolescent brain and scheme of cultural traditions. My eight-year-old fingers traced these indented lines and shapes. What story does the whale tell? Later in my twenties, I explored Anasazi ruins throughout the Southwest and marveled at the petroglyphs along the Colorado River. In 2009, I explored a variety of caves throughout Southwest France that demonstrate a range of petroglyphs (carving method) and pictographs (painting method). The images that remain in some of the sites are thought to be up to 37,000 years old (19). Petroglyphs, which are carved into stone, generally outlast the weathering and erosion of time that the painted techniques in pictographs undergo.

The Modern Mind, Neural Historical Considerations

What had to be in place for our brains to coordinate spatial awareness, dexterity, concept of tools, shared meaning with community, conceptualizing the past, present, and future. How are these questions relevant to creativity and art making? And how can exploring these questions inform educators today and make a positive impact in their classrooms?

Answers begin to unfold within a milieu of disciplines. These include paleoanthropology, neurosciences, evolutionary psychology, and cognitive pedagogies. Art therapy is a lens that enables a connection to each of these disciplines and, in particular, offers a window into the developmental world of participants.

Researchers highlight a statistically significant percentage of participants experienced reduced cortisol levels after 45 minutes of art making (20). The reductions were consistent for both individuals familiar and unfamiliar with art materials. Art therapist and psychologist Hass-Cohen pointed out the evolutionary journey of *Homo sapiens* and neurosensory activations. "The development of the neocortex … enabled sensory perception, precise motor control, spatial reasoning, abstract and rational thought, and in humans, the capacity for developing language" (21). These qualities enable a broad range of cultural activities, the evidence of which is still being discovered and explored to this day. Anthropologists note early signs of human burial as markers for abstract thought and culturally shared meaning (22). Objects made from carved stone and shells without any obvious utilitarian (or survival) purpose are also indicators of abstract thought, humans' ability to ascribe meaning, or to engage in novel (creative) behaviors (23). Collectively this trajectory of development leads to cultural identities, images, shapes, symbols, spoken language, and the need humans have to connect with one another and to share meaning. In essence, the cultural anthropological evidence of human behavior is a stronger indicator of their capacity for higher order thinking than skeletal remains can reveal.

My work in community and school-based programs has only solidified my earlier experiences and intuition – humans are hardwired to create (24). In one way or another, we have an inherent aesthetic sense to create, organize, assign meaning, to share our space and ideas with others, to live in the community. It's all tied up together – the petroglyphs, the pictographs, oral traditions, written language, and spoken language – we create images, shapes, and sounds that symbolize a shared meaning. As scholar Ellen Dissanayake describes, humans have an innate need to "make special" through ritual, ceremony, and tradition (12).

In the present day we may take some of these routines for granted or simply appreciate the comfort of traditions; however, what are our brains and bodies experiencing during these interactions? As educators we can introduce children to their physiological response to shared meaning, group cohesion, unison, rhythm, predictability, trust, the ability to positively navigate threat responses, manage cortisol, feel attunement, and a sense of belonging with neurotransmitters like oxytocin. These concepts belong to us all and are not unique to the clinical realm; they are part of our human experience and deserve attention to further strengthen as they contribute to protective social and biophysical factors.

In seminal research, Magsamen notes the connection between primal survival characteristics associated with the human brain and mental health, mood, and creative art practice.

> Neuro-aesthetic researchers are also studying the activation of reward systems and the default mode network when viewing or creating art. The reward system releases feel-good brain chemicals like dopamine, serotonin, and oxytocin that trigger sensations of

pleasure and positive emotions. We see these pleasure centers light up in the brain when we are both creating and beholding the arts or engaged in aesthetic experiences.

The default mode network, once associated solely with daydreaming, is now linked to many different functions core to human connection and well-being. These include personal identity, sense of meaning, empathy, imagination, and creativity as well as embodied cognition, which allows us to place ourselves in a piece of artwork and make us *feel* what the artist was feeling (25).

In essence, *Homo sapiens* grew into our abilities to transfer information through shared meaning – especially through visual means whether it is artwork, symbols, shapes, or some of these cave images with the dots. There is meaningful relevance related to even the topography of the selected spot in a cave where an image is added. This, in itself, is a primitive form of language and a form of communication that extends beyond time. Hominid cave art has produced images that can be viewed year after year over a multitude of generations. Their timeless art demonstrates their understanding of continuity of present, future, and past and their capacity for abstract thought.

I've come to accept that I'm an educator. I don't have a certified teaching certificate and despite being a credentialed family therapist and art therapist who has worked in schools for over a decade, in my roles I have not had to labor for hours over the nuances of IEPs, 504 plans or navigate the ever-changing requirements of a standardized curriculum. To some extent I'm grateful for bypassing these facets of the education system, and sometimes I feel like an outsider. Approaching my work with students and through the lens of a family therapist and art therapist has afforded me a systemic perspective separate from some of the typical administrative or bureaucratic educator stressors. Too often I encounter teachers who express hesitation, avoidance, or insecurity when it comes to integrating art making in their classrooms. We are all creative beings who often lack the invitation to flex our imaginative muscles. Our education systems minimize or neglect the health (and educational) benefits that creativity and art making contribute to an individual's sense of self and connection to community. My hope is that you'll take away at least one spark of opportunity for a child in a classroom to experience the continuum of wonder, problem-solving, and joy that our creative history has passed down. We have a shared responsibility to contribute to students' enthusiasm for knowledge, relationships, sense of self, safety, autonomy, and belonging.

Note

1. This process is from Cathy Malchiodi's work of 2006.

References

1. B. Fish. Mildred Chapin, The therapist as artist, in *Approaches to Art Therapy: Theory and Technique*, Judith Aron Rubin, Eds (Routledge, New York, NY, 2016).
2. M. Fram, E. Frongillo, Backpack programs and the crisis narrative of child hunger—A critical review of the rationale, targeting, and potential benefits and harms of an expanding but untested model of practice. *Advances in Nutrition* **9**, 1–8 (2018).
3. S. Tong et al., Understanding the value of the wellness visit: A descriptive study. *American Journal of Preventive Medicine: Elsevier* **6**, 591–595 (2021).
4. M. Klabunde, Traumatic Stress May Alter Boys' and Girls' Brains Differently. Livescience.com-health-not-hype, https://www.livescience.com/56846-boys-girls-brain-traumatic-stress.html, 2016).
5. P. Lockett, To curb the teacher shortage, we need to think bigger about the problem. Forbes Magazine Online. 2019.
6. N. Ziaian-Ghafari, D. H. Berg, Compassion fatigue: The experiences of teachers working with students with exceptionalities. *Exceptionality Education International* **29**, 32–53 (2019).
7. R. Pondiscio, Education's dirty little secret: Overworked and time-stretched teachers are relying on Google and Pintarest for lesson plans. US News. https://www.usnews.com/opinion/articles/2016-05-06/why-teachers-rely-on-google-and-pinterest-for-course-materials, 2016.
8. N. Doidge, *The Brain That Changes Itself* (Penguin, London UK, 2007).
9. C. S. Dweck, *Mindset: The New Psychology of Success* (Random House, New York, NY, 2006).
10. A. Rattan, C. Good, C. S. Dweck, "It's ok - not everyone can be good at math": Instructors with an entity theory comfort (and demotivate) students. *Journal of Experimental Social Psychology* **48**, 731–737 (2012).
11. R. Sykes, *Kindred: Neanderthal Life, Love, Death and Art* (Bloomsbury, London, 2020).
12. E. Dissanayake, *Homo Aestheticus: Where Art Comes From and Why* (Free Press, New York, 1992 and 2004).
13. C. Malchiodi, in *Handbook of Art Therapy*, C. Malchiodi, Ed. (The Guildford Press, New York, 2023), chap. 2, pp. 16–24.
14. J. A. Plucker, R. A. Beghetto, G. T. Dow, Why isn't creativity more important to educational psychologists? Potentials, pitfalls, and future directions in creativity research. *Educational Psychologist* **39**, 83–96 (2004).

15. R. Plomin, *Blueprint: How DNA Makes Us Who We Are* (Random House, London, UK, 2018).
16. M. Mikulincer, E. Sheff1, Adult attachment style and cognitive reactions to positive affect: A test of mental categorization and creative problem solving. *Motivation & Emotion* **24**, 149–174 (2000).
17. B. A. Hennessey, in *The Search for Optimal Motivation and Performance*, C. Sansone, J. M. Harackiewicz, Eds. (Elsevier Inc – Academic Press, Educational Psychology, 2000), pp. 489.
18. M. Csikszentmihalyi, *Flow: The Psychology of Optimal Experience* (Harper Collins, New York, NY, 2008).
19. S. Paabo *et al.*, A high-coverage Neandertal genome from Vindija Cave in Croatia. *Science* **358**, 655–658 (2017).
20. G. Kaimal, J. Mensinger, J. Drass, R. Dieterich-Hartwell, Art therapist-facilitated open studio versus coloring: Differences in outcomes of affect, stress, creative agency, and self-efficacy. *Canadian Art Therapy Association Journal* **30**, 56–68 (2017).
21. N. Hass-Cohen, J. Findlay, *Art Therapy and the Neuroscience of Relationships, Creativity and Resiliency: Skills and Practices* (W W Norton, New York, 2015).
22. W. T. Boyce, B. J. Ellis, Biological sensitivity to context: An evolutionary-developmental theory of the origins and functions of stress reactivity *Developmental Psychopathology* **17**, 271–301 (2005).
23. G. Von Petzinger, *The First Signs: My Quest to Unlock the Mysteries of the World's Oldest Symbols* (Atria, Simon & Schusster Inc., New York, 2017).
24. M. H. Immordino-Yang, K. W. Fischer, in *International Encyclopedia of Education*, V. G. Aukrust, Ed. (Elsevier, Oxford, 2010), pp. 310–316.
25. S. Magsamen, Your brain on art: The case for neuroaesthetics. *Cerebrum*, (2019): PMCID: PMC7075503.

Play Card

By Audrey Gallagher

Introduction

"Come quick, you are needed in Ms. Ludwig's[1] class!"

Radio calls can add a weighty slab of cortisol to even the funnest party. I had been there before. I knew what to do. Still, the overtones of panic, which were evident in the message, coursed through my lower stomach, giving me that dreaded icky feeling. I knew better, but there it was again. Oops, cortisol swimming around in my brain.

"This is what you do." I reminded myself, quickening my pace toward the corridor where Ludwig's classroom could be found on the left.

Breathe.

I gulped a deep inhale and held it for a long moment since my pace was close to sprinting. Turning the corner all appeared quiet. As I entered the classroom, however, I could see that same ugly momentum that I was feeling inside. Coats, bags, and books were strewn in disarray; three or four kids with resigned, frightened expressions were cowering together.

"Cortisol everywhere. Contagious!" I murmured to no one. "Just great!"

I came across Ms. Ludwig and some students who were sheltering with her. She reminded me of a mother hen with wings outstretched over her brood in the wake of a fox attack. Her nervous smile assured me that I wasn't the fox. I was the irate farmer following the trail of feathers. Except that, I was neither irate nor interested in hurting anything or anyone. I followed her eyes to overturned desks. The terrified boy was still inside the coop.

Stepping gingerly over books, coats, and other classroom paraphernalia scattered on the floor, I ignored the disheveled mess in Ms. Ludwig's class. There would be plenty of time for cleanup later. My priority was clear. I needed to locate the boy first, establish his disposition, check for any injuries, and then figure out the next course of action. Each episode of escalation, though bearing some similar footprints, was in fact quite unique and distinct. Each situation, thus, required a unique and distinct response on my part. This would be our introduction – our first interaction – everything I do in this moment matters. I look carefully throughout the mayhem in an effort to locate him – at the same time, seeking clues to help me connect with the child. Peripheral sharpness eliminated obvious "under-desk" places; I focused on more difficult-to-get-to hiding places. The room was as I expected. It looked like a tornado had ripped through – upturned desks, chairs strewn about, with children's bags askew on the floor. Several books had been thrown forcefully, and a large bulletin board's art was precariously dangling from the wall.

The schedule indicated that they were about to transition from writing to math. The children were supposed to have completed a writing task. When I see him, I pretend to be focused on the schedule and I stop moving. Keeping a fixed distance between us, I slowly lower myself so that we are at the same level. I have not forced eye contact yet.

Soundly barricaded under a table, Liam was obviously agitated, escalated, and distraught. Although it was our first meeting, I knew his name and had already perused his file. It was no secret that he was not doing well in the classroom setting and I was familiar with the struggles he was experiencing each day. The sounds that he was exuding resembled strange animal-like grunting and gurgle-growling. His face was flushed, his breathing heavy. I perceived tension in his tiny body; his clenched little hands were trembling. As I expected, he had been intently watching my every move as I slowly advanced toward the center – from the doorway toward his location.

In classrooms across North America, Liam's behavior and unpleasant outcomes are part of unfortunate scenarios that have become more prevalent in learning spaces as the stakes get higher. Crisis situations like these leave parents, teachers, administrators, mental health professionals, and the entire community wondering how best to respond.

There are immediate and long-term solutions that sometimes work. But something is missing? Sporadic solutions are not good enough. Any teacher will tell you – it's always the same kids. Why do the same children end up in the same dire destructive devastation every time they come to school? It's bad for the children themselves; it's bad for the other children in the classroom; it's bad for the teacher; it's bad for the parents; it's bad for the school; and it's bad for society in general. We know that evidence predicts that children who struggle in their early years of school fall behind and they stay behind. Rarely, if ever, do they manage to catch up (1). Their life trajectories are profoundly impacted by this failure to engage and thrive (2). Yet we know that all children are hardwired to learn (3). An American kid drops out of high school every 26 seconds. That's more than a million every year, a sign of big trouble for these largely clueless youngsters in an era in which a college education is crucial to maintaining a middle-class quality of life – and for the country as a whole in a world that is becoming more hotly competitive every day (4).

It was a series of firsts! The day I met Liam for the first time was the first day of school, and also my first day in a new school in a new district. Having browsed his IEP (Individual Education Plan), I was expecting to meet him that first week, but he preempted my plans … we were suddenly and calamitously thrown together under the desk in Ms. Ludwig's writing class. Liam always needed to be in control back then. That changed. It took time, patience, and especially knowledge about what might have been going on inside Liam's mind. The rest of this story relates to a magic journey that Liam and I danced together for the next two years.

As I sat with him on the floor that first time, I was searching for cracks in the wall, opportunities to get past the anger and frustration so that we could begin our journey together. He didn't know it yet but we had already started.

We began with enough distance between us so that Liam had personal space and freedom to move and think. Very soon the growling stopped. I was far enough away to give him space but also close enough that I could match my breathing with his. At first, it was quick, but I was able to slow it down a little. When it was ok, I made direct eye contact and showed him with stillness and a kind unmoving message that it was safe to do so. I continued a conscious engagement of his mirror neurons through a deliberate and slowed breathing technique, which would allow him to get more air into his lungs. I knew that more oxygen would get some focus into his breathing and eventually cause de-escalation where he could feel more calm and tranquil. I breathed loudly and deliberately slowly and waited for his breathing to mirror mine. Then I exhaled loudly. He unconsciously followed my lead, breathing in with me – holding – and then exhaling with me.

I whispered, "It's ok." Breathe!

"I'm here." Breathe!

"It's safe."

I tried to breathe more and speak slowly, quietly, calmly. Say less, be still, respect the space, and have deep breath. Repeat. Breathe. Sit still. Repeat. Breathe.

The growling stopped and I could tell he was willing to make eye contact. I waited. Then I opened a conversation with "wow" and "curiosity" – wondering. When the brain is in curious mode, it can't be in reactive screaming, throwing things mode.

"Wow … I can see you were pretty upset." Breathe. "I wonder what happened?"

He was breathing a little more easily by this time. I continued to mirror breathe with him. He opened up a little.

"My pencil…"

That was all he got out. His face told the pain of some story that I didn't yet know.

With a little prompting, he was able to articulate a sad tale. He told me his pencil "had broke" when he was trying to write his sentence.

"That sounds hard." I offered.

"…and when I tried to get a new one it was time to clean up…"

He was close to tears again. He was not done with his writing assignment. He knew he would have to stay in during recess.

I told him that did sound hard, and I wondered if he wanted some help cleaning up so we could get ready to see what his class was doing next. He began to free himself from his self-imposed hiding place, the prison that seemed safe while his world imploded.

"Where should we start." I was happy that he was engaging in the cleanup with me.

"Umm… books," he pointed at a familiar title that was facedown open.

I picked one up and put it back on Ms. Ludwig's bookshelf. Liam picked another and then two more. He was happy to see the order return to his space.

We talked about what he knew about which books went where and decided we both did not really know … so we would settle for putting them back neatly.

We progressed through the room quietly retrieving items that had been strewn across the floor. We helped each other, working easily and feeling a shared sense of purpose and mastery. Difficult tasks like turning chairs and aligning tables came easy. He was strong for his size. The physical labor was a welcome focus. Together we managed to staple the bulletin board back up and stopped to look around and see our work. It felt good to make things right with the room. This same sense of success and satisfaction was apparent on Liam's face, just as the sense of frustration and dread were so apparent on his features earlier. The grunting and growing gave way to smiles of delight.

I was fortunate that the class could give us time and space to co-regulate. When we were done, he was ready to join his classmates who had transitioned to the library.

I checked in with the teacher. She was frustrated and upset; it made sense – the room she had worked so hard to create had been destroyed on the first day. She didn't really understand why. The truth is neither did I at the time – I just knew it wasn't a choice for Liam … like which color do you like better … red or blue?

Looking at dysfunction and dysregulation with their attendant disruptive behaviors from a "classroom management" standpoint can be very disheartening. It's difficult to make progress; everyone loses, and it is increasingly frustrating to the point that teachers are questioning why they chose such a difficult profession (5). When we approach the situation from a cognitive and neuroscience direction, solutions are immediately accessible and offer long-term relief. Simply put, behavior like Liam's is an evolutionary "reactive" survival remnant. A reptilian residue of the survival brain, it is often referred to as the reactive, involuntary brain associated with freeze, fight, flight, and fawn (6). The following account describes the story of Liam's journey to his potential and how his classmates along with play became the intervention. I was a participant in this journey and it too taught me a lot. I was able to hone and adjust aspects of the play encounter so that the intervention easily transferred to new situations with different children.

That first year, I spent time with Liam meeting one-on-one and building a connection with the family, teacher, administration, IEP case manager, and the whole school community. I started to see growth in our one-on-one time, supported the teacher in creating a break space, and increased structure around transitions and unpredictability of changes in schedule, which were the times when I noticed he struggled the most. I was also able to partner with Liam's family who were struggling to support him at home.

Additionally, I spent time at recess watching his play and interactions with peers, sometimes coaching, sometimes playing, and sometimes observing. I noticed that he really enjoyed playing but, sadly, that only a few of his classmates would play with him – they would sometimes tolerate his need to be in charge and would help him with regulation when he needed it. I now know that he was experiencing amygdala hijack (7) on a regular basis. This had a cumulative negative impact in his world. It caused both adults and peers to be afraid and uncomfortable around him. I could see that he wanted friends, but he was not able to offer them a safe place in his companionship. I knew that in order to reach him I would need to work to repair the beliefs that his peers and adults had about him (8).

He made progress in our one-on-one meetings, developing coping skills and learning to acknowledge feelings, but I was concerned because it wasn't generalizing outside the "me plus he" meetings – transferring to activities in the classroom. I knew that he was keeping up with learning, but his challenges with regulation would have a significant impact on his future if we were not able to co-create a solution of support. The construct of near and far transfer were goals for me. Could Liam successfully bring what he was learning in small groups with me to a bigger setting like the playground with peers or the classroom with a teacher and fellow students (9)?

I had been considering a play-based intervention for some time. I spoke to the administrator of Liam's school and we agreed that in the fall I would create a small play therapy room to better address and support his needs. My plan was to change at least one place in his learning environment where he could guarantee psychological safety, fun, and autonomy. I knew that he would grow new neural structures for social engagement in the limbic region, which would connect pathways from his reactive hindbrain to his higher order rational and thinking brain. The question was … how long would this take? I went with excitement to review the play area. It was not a glamorous space; in fact, it was a classroom forgotten where old desks and abandoned classroom materials went to be forgotten. But it was a space and it was dedicated to play.

I cleared a space in a far corner near the sink with shelving and all the various toys that I had collected over the summer.[2] I was able to arrange with his teacher and managed to get a set time every week to meet with Liam in this play space. It turned out to be the end of the school day. This was good because Liam often arrived with many pent-up emotions that had spontaneously emerged from classroom and playground encounters, which resulted in amygdala hijack.

Play therapy in its purest form is very person-centered, accepting, and mostly without significant limits (10). One limit I needed to set because of the nature of the space was that the play occurred in the identified space. If play left the identified space, we would need to stop for that day and return another day. I learned to repeat phrases like "When your play is outside the play space we have to leave". In retrospect and in later programs, I changed my approach a little. I realized that it would work better when the child

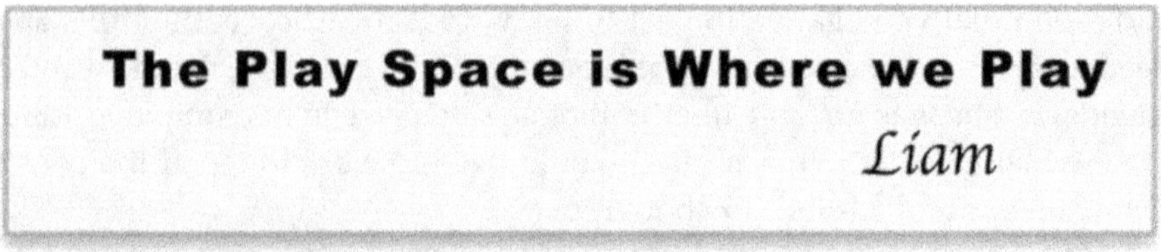

> **The Play Space is Where we Play**
> *Liam*

FIGURE 8.1 Liam's Play Area Sign

co-created the space with me. So we would make a colorful sign in large letters. He could see himself in charge of the play space. This was a deliberate first incursion into agency – stepping up to take ownership of our work together, knowing that sometime soon others would be joining us. Agency is a very powerful step toward intrinsic motivation with autonomy driving the bus (11). An example of signage co-created and signed by the student is shown in Figure 8.1.

I was concerned about this originally because this was a student who regularly stretched the limits in all his environments and although I felt I understood why, I also had a responsibility to ensure his safety during our time together. The primary reason I believe these limits worked was because I had worked with him at family meetings the previous year. He knew that I was consistent and caring and that I meant what I said and would follow through.

I had the privilege of seeing him one-on-one, which gave me the opportunity to have a great deal more time to play, affirm his strengths, and support the development of social skills. I believed in the transformative power of play. I liked how Stuart Brown described play. For him, it was … "an important mechanism for learning that allowed us to manipulate concepts and ideas in a context that removes concerns of time and risk of failure and provides opportunities for participants to experience flow" (12). It turned out that Liam loved to be in "flow" and our time together seemed to stand still when he was actively happy in play.

This time together allowed us to develop trust and connection. It would help me to better support him when his nervous system became overwhelmed, and he needed a regulation partner. Within the classroom, his amygdala hijack would often look like hiding under something and throwing things toward others. There were times when it was directed at specific people but overall it was a response to an unseen stimuli or request that was overwhelming.

I was convinced that we could make breakthrough progress by enhancing a play space with Liam. I immersed myself in reading theorists who espoused play. Their ideas intrigued me. I fully believed that my time with Liam in the play space allowed him to experience autonomy, mastery, and purpose in a way that gave him intense pleasure and personal satisfaction. As I documented his improvements week by week, I had real proof that his ability to play became critical not only to his being happy but also to sustaining social relationships (12). I too participated in the increased oxytocin, serotonin, and dopamine that were abundant in the play space. I knew that this change was sorely needed in the classroom where cortisol tended to be more prevalent. I couldn't help thinking about how contagious oxytocin or cortisol is!

In Kindergarten, we had made progress. However, it was clear to me that the skills we were learning one-on-one were having a hard time transferring to the classroom setting. I was fortunate to have a partner teacher who was consistent and firm, but also caring and willing to try something different to support Liam's growth. This growing relationship and his ability to co-regulate with adults meant that he had many successful days at school. Success begets success.

In Phase 1, Liam and I would play one-on-one for about 25 minutes once a week. It was not enough to instill cognitive rehearsal and consolidate myelination for skills and practices that occurred in class, so I looked around for more time. I adjusted my schedule to increase the intensity to two times a week. During this time, we were able to override his reflex response and myelinate a new response within the play. I introduced support routines in the non-declarative memory space (13). Non-declarative memory formation involved growing white matter neural structures in the medial temporal lobe, which connected hippocampal and amygdala regions with the executive function higher order processing functions of the prefrontal lobe. It might sound remote, but it is in fact very easy. Non-declarative brain functions involve classification exercises (e.g., sorting and making sense – like we did when Liam helped me clean up the mess he made on day one) and perceptual motor skills. These latter include teaching children movements related to time (e.g., moving fast vs. slow), direction (moving forward, back, or to the side), and spatial awareness (e.g., crossing their arm from the right side of the body to the left or tapping their heel to the ground). With practice and time, we were able to engage in activities that involved classical conditioning routines and associationism as Pavlov had figured out with his puppies (14).

I moved slowly and methodically and rarely engaged without first seeking his direction. This created a space in which he was "in charge" and the typical roles of adult and child were reversed. He was in charge and I was following.

During our play, there was a lot of barricading and throwing things toward me (primarily balls). I worked to narrate objectively what I saw him doing and ensure that I was seeking his feedback on how he wanted me to respond:

Example (whisper voice) "what should I be doing now?"

Through this process Liam was utilizing skeletal musculature (cerebellum) by throwing balls during play. We easily bypassed the amygdala by allowing the space to be child-led with permission to express self and unconditional acceptance. Through intentional priming, we were able to co-create a space, invite peers, provide autonomy and mastery, and gradually increase trust with fun.

What I knew more than anything was that Liam needed to be in charge and have a safe space to play. He had to be the person directing his world. Our sessions were chaotic, filled with noise and mess, with many items strewn about. Keeping with the traditional model of play therapy, I was very intentional about not expecting him to help with the cleanup (this went against all my normal school beliefs that had been activated by earlier classroom management training techniques). I made a commitment that I would plan my time so that I could clean up our space before my next activity.

This was honestly a challenge because our meetings were at the end of a very full day and generally before another meeting, but I knew from my readings that requiring Liam to clean up would change his play and could potentially become a battle that would impede progress in our time together. We continued in this way for six weeks. I would meet with him one to two times a week for 25 minutes. He would play and express himself. The play felt very much like Liam against the adult so I would need to remind myself before we entered our sessions that his choices were not about me specifically and that I was there to support his growth. This helped me to have the correct intention when we entered the play space.

Overall, he accepted the limits of the play space and when he no longer needed reminders, I knew we had successfully co-created with autonomy. I felt comfortable to begin phase II of the intervention.

Phase II involved inviting a peer. I had set up the time with the teacher at the start of the intervention to ensure that the timing would allow other students to be invited to play. I let Liam know that our goal was to invite everyone in the class so that he knew that we would be inviting different students each time we met. This was an important step.

It turns out that dyadic friendships are really vital for children to gain proficiency in social and articulative skills that matter (15). Researchers have established that friend, compared to non-friend dyads, would evidence more literate language in the form of talk about cognitive and linguistic processes. Findings suggest that different peer relationships differentially affect children's oral language in areas of conflict, social regulation, and metacognitive and literate language. Data support the proposition that different sorts of peer relationships and instructional settings affect children's interactions and early literacy development (16).

There were a couple of times that things could have become challenging because we did not have an agreed upon process. In the beginning, it was easy because anyone could be a choice. As time progressed, I relied on the teacher to help know which students were "available" to come with us.

In the beginning, I would model (co-create that leads to co-regulation) the expectation of the play being in the play space. Over time, Liam took over this explanation with each new peer who joined us. We started with one peer and together they would explore the space and negotiate the activity. Liam would often direct the play and I was always amazed at how his peers would allow him the space to lead. I spent many hours with the children barricaded and the balls being thrown at me.

As I watched the faces of the peers, I could see the look of confusion. Is this really ok? Can we really throw balls at this adult? And then, the look of pure joy as they realized that there would be no recriminations and that they could enthusiastically join the fun.

I watched as his peers began to look at Liam in a different way. They were more accepting and compassionate; they became his healers (17). Research has shown that active play selectively stimulates brain-derived neurotrophic factors, which stimulate nerve growth in the amygdala where emotions get processed, and in the dorsolateral prefrontal cortex where executive decisions are processed (12).

As Liam's skills grew with regulation (18), he wanted to invite more peers to our time together. The group grew to a maximum of four, which was a lot for our tiny space. The play became more organized and cooperative and advanced into what theorists refer to as "deep" play. Play transforms into deep play when it is mentally absorbing, offers challenge, offers new context to use prior skills, and has the same satisfaction as work, but rewards are more clear and offer connections to players past (19). The deep play with his peers where his peers modeled cleaning up and our time together ended with the students working together to clean up the space; they taught him a school expectation without the need for adult direction. It happened quickly then. In the classroom,

Liam began to successfully engage in learning activities with peers and navigate transitions and changes to the schedule. Calls for support stopped.

The feeling of safety and the satisfying sense of belonging that he found in our play area transferred over time and with practice to the classroom. This was huge. He was able to make adjustments to his expectations, his transition skills, and his collaboration techniques so that other children were able to encounter and engage with him seamlessly. I gradually reduced the number of times I was seeing him and by the end of the school year, we were able to remove my support entirely from his IEP.

He had learned skills of regulation, belonging, and safety from and with his peers. Furthermore, those skills consolidated with time and transferred to second grade. I had the privilege of joining his class on a final class trip the next year and was delighted to witness his full acceptance and assimilation into the class structure so that he clearly was able to enjoy the event with peers who were friends and playmates on a day that was exciting and full of unpredictability. From my part, what I learned from Liam, I was able to incorporate and adjust, as needed, with and for the next child who came along and needed a play date with an adult who could help them find their potential.

Play is fundamental to our growth and development. Play that affords safety, belonging, and unconditional acceptance is transformational. The principles of this intervention can be applied to any classroom setting. Research carried out by Dearybury and Jones (19) is influential:

> The evidence from scientific research on learning is that a playful learner and a playful teacher form an extraordinarily effective learning system.
>
> (Dearybury, p. xix)

Thinking about this through a neural lens, the principles of play therapy are rooted in relationship, agency, autonomy, and a sense of purpose. It also supports the child as the change agent in their own life through a supportive environment that contributes to growth, healing, and is rooted in connection. Their ability to engage in playful sociability allowed them to move from THEM vs. Us to see only WE (19). The play increased neurotransmitters for both Liam and the class – additionally, it increased the support for the teacher – who understood that we were partners in success and that success translated from Liam to the entire classroom increasing both social and academic goals for the class.

Sadly, too often play is seen as primarily childish – something that a child should grow away from (12). However, there is ample evidence from research in child development studies that, for children, play "is a way to test the possibilities of their environment without consequence" (20). Parents and teachers would do well to understand how a supportive environment would enhance growth, healing, and connection, that fosters a child's journey to maturation and in particular self-regulation.

What I have learned is that play is fundamental. It is how we learn. It is the language by which we speak. We cannot "teach" regulation; we cannot teach safety or a sense of belonging – one has to experience these primal feelings as a sense of being, through repeated practice and exposure in a psychologically safe place and with someone we can trust. Play is an essential element of this process. In most mammalian species, play is akin to preparations for adult life in all its complexities. Children thrive in such spaces. Play helps us problem-solve in real time. It is through that problem solving that we are able to grow neuronal structures, circuits, and synaptic connections as we architect powerful potential through our brains.

Notes

1. All names have been changed to protect participants.
2. Toys included miniature people, balls, a pop up tunnel, blankets, babies, helpers, puppet show frame with puppets, art supplies, and more.

References

1. University of California, California high school dropouts cost state $46.4 billion annually. *UC Santa Barbara*. 2007 (http://www.ia.ucsb.edu/pa/display.aspx?pkey=1643).
2. C. Rowe, How much do dropouts cost us? The real numbers behind 'pay now or pay later' in *The Seattle Times* http://blogs.seattletimes.com/educationlab/2014/01/03/how-much-do-dropouts-cost-us-the-real-numbers-behind-pay-now-or-pay-later/ (Seattle Times, Seattle WA, 2014).
3. J. Medina, *Brain Rules: 12 principles for surviving and thriving at work, home and school* (Pear Press, San Francisco, 2008).
4. D. Feldman, A. Smith, B. Waxman, *Why we drop out: Understanding and disrupting student pathways to leaving school* (Teachers College Press, Columbia University, New York, 2017).
5. E. Madfis, *How to stop school rampage killing: Lessons from averted mass shootings and bombings* (Palgrave MacMillan, Switzerland, 2020).
6. K. O'Mahony, *The brain-based classroom: Accessing every child's potential through educational neuroscience* (Routledge, Taylor & Francis Group, London, UK and New York, ed. First, 2021).

7. J. Willis, *Research-based strategies to ignite student learning: Insights from a neurologist and classroom teacher* (Association for Supervision and Curriculum Development, Alexandria, VA, 2006).
8. B. Perry, *The boy who was raised as a dog: What traumatized children can teach us about loss, love and healing* (Basic Books, New York, NY, 2006).
9. D. Sears, D. L. Schwartz, The Effects of innovation versus efficiency tasks on recall and transfer in individual; and collaborative learning contexts, paper presented at the ICLS, Indiana, July 2005.
10. J. Piaget, *Play, dreams and imitation in childhood* (original title: la formation du symbole chez l'enfant: Imitation, jeu et reve image et representation) (Norton, New York, 1962, 1951).
11. A. Gallagher, T. K. O'Mahony, in *Learning and the brain conference*, K. O'Mahony, Ed. (Neural Education, San Francisco, CA, 2023).
12. S. L. Brown, C. C. Vaughan, *Play: How it shapes the brain, opens the imagination and invigorates the soul* (Avery, New York, 2009).
13. L. Squire, S. Zola, Structure and function of declarative and nondeclarative memory systems. *Proceedings of the National Academy of Science* **93**, 13515–13522 (1996).
14. D. Todes, *Ivan Pavlov: A Russian life in science* (Oxford University Press, Oxford, UK, 2014).
15. I. Jones, Social relationships, peer collaboration and children's oral language. *Educational Psychology* **22**, 63–73 (2002).
16. J. W. Aslington, in *Individual differences in theory of mind: Implications for typical and atypical development*, B. Repacholi, V. Slaughter, Eds. (Psychology Press, New York, NY, 2003), pp. 13–38.
17. J. Panskepp, *Affective neuroscience: The foundations of human and animal emotions* (Oxford University Press, New York, NY, 1989).
18. S. Warren et al., Anxiety and stress alter decision-making dynamics and causal amygdala-dorsolateral prefrontal cortex circuits during emotion regulation in children. *Biological Psychiatry* **88**, 576–586 (2020).
19. J. Dearybury, J. Jones, *The playful classroom: The power of play for all ages* (Wiley, San Francisco, 2020).
20. Trezza V, Baarendse PJ, Vanderschuren LJ. The pleasures of play: pharmacological insights into social reward mechanisms. *Trends Pharmacol Sci*. 2010 Oct;**31**(10): 463–9. doi: 10.1016/j.tips.2010.06.008. Epub 2010 Aug 3. PMID: 20684996; PMCID: PMC2946511.

9

Belonging

By Paige Wescott

David's mom and dad were going through a huge mess. There were so many stressors, ultimatums, and accusations at home; divorce was threatened almost daily.

David was in the sixth grade. He was beginning to get used to phrases like "domestic violence", "alcoholic behavior", and "adverse childhood experiences". Though normally an attentive, interested, and capable learner, David was finding it more and more difficult to cope. The challenges, the guilt, and the fear he had been experiencing at home were clearly affecting him. All of it weighed heavy and was showing up at school.

In the middle of a loud, violent, domestic moment, where David's dad, who was drunk, once again, had ripped his mom's shirt and was hitting her; David was alarmed. Although he had thought a lot about his parents' arguments – the fighting and hurtful verbal and physical abuse – this time he wasn't thinking ... David reacted in a moment of fear, dread, and exasperation. Stepping up to his father – he found himself in between his mom and his dad – something he had only rehearsed in his mind, before. After quickly taking in a huge breath, he looked up to his father. Calmly he said, "Please, Dad. Stop! You're having an amygdala hijack! You're not thinking right. Breathe with me!"

David's dad did stop, and he stepped back, a few paces. "What the F_ _ _? What the hell is an 'amygdala hijack'?"

Calmly, again, David continued, "It's okay Dad, just breathe with me." He used his outstretched hands – palms up to gesture breathing in, twice, quickly, through the nose, and then showed his palms down for slowly, breathing out, ... with a sigh, and a long pause in between.

David's dad just stared at his son. He stepped further back as if someone had slapped him sober; he didn't move. David listened. In the screaming silence, it was as if he could hear the cogs of his dad's brain churning. Suddenly, his dad just turned and walked out of the house. He did not return until the next day.

Early that next morning, David was still asleep when his dad showed up at the house. Downstairs, David's dad asked his mom to explain what David had said. "What the hell did he mean, amygdala hijack?"

David's mom explained as best she could. She began by telling how David's teacher had taught him and his class everything (and that David had taught her) about the body's response to stress. David's teacher had shared some of her own current stressors and some of those she, herself, had experienced growing up. David's teacher had then practiced breathing exercises with David and his class and explained why the breathing worked and how the body responds. The class, too, had discussed domestic violence, alcoholism, and drug abuse, and even talked together about how best to respond to friends and family going through these challenges. David had even believed that he might be able to someday get through to his dad to stop beating his mom.

In the silence that followed, David's mom watched her husband, closely, and could almost see him working through the memories of the night before.

Then, abruptly, in an emotional sob, David's dad broke down in front of his wife in tears after processing all she had explained. A massive feeling of emptiness, regret, and shame seemed to overcome his physical frame. He dropped his knees to the floor and begged her for forgiveness. The two had a first, real discussion, together, about David, about raising children, and about stress ... It was the first discussion in a long time that had truly made sense. The potential outcome was hopeful for both of them. That morning they promised to get counseling, to help David's father stop drinking, and to work together to repair their marriage.

Apparently, David's heartfelt plea had hit home. David had not judged his dad; he had practiced with his teacher, learned how to lower his own stress levels, and was able to "school" his dad in a nonthreatening and nonjudgmental way. This all had hit his father so hard, and his Dad knew, clearly, this was his time to change!

Many months later, David's mom shared this account and details of their ongoing journey with the school team. She and David's dad did not get divorced. They are still seeing a counselor, rebuilding their marriage and family relationships from scratch. The school counselor brought up the longitudinal impact of ACEs on David to the team. This was definitely not on the radar.

Most educators today are very familiar with Felitti's 1998 groundbreaking study on ACEs (Adverse Childhood Experiences) (1). Student teachers are usually introduced to Felitti's work sometime in their second semester. Freshmen educators who are preparing for classroom connection and relationship-building are typically exposed to a lot of this new knowledge. The big takeaway boils down to the fact that the higher the ACE score, the more likely the individual will have a difficult journey through life – often with ongoing emotional disorders, prolonged mental health issues, and, in addition, physical health problems that can be life-threatening. For most beginning teachers, Felitti's work is intense and unimaginable – that a young child could suffer such abuse and neglect as outlined in categories that are highlighted in the research.

At the same time, many new teachers are not aware of the powerful backstory to the groundbreaking discovery that forever changed learning spaces for all of us. The following summary[1] illuminates the puzzling series of events, which lead to Felitti's breakthrough. A routine questionnaire and an unintentional mistake were responsible for changing education, juvenile justice, public health, and so much more. The word unintentional is important because, back in 1985, Felitti was not focused on exploring anything related to school, learning, or education (2).

> The ACE Study had its origins in an obesity clinic on a quiet street in San Diego. It was 1985, and Dr. Vincent Felitti was mystified. The physician, chief of Kaiser Permanente's revolutionary Department of Preventive Medicine in San Diego, CA, couldn't figure out why, each year for the past five years, more than half of the people in his obesity clinic dropped out. Although people who wanted to shed as little as 30 pounds could participate, the clinic was designed for people who were 100 to 600 pounds overweight.
>
> A cursory review of all the dropouts' records astonished him—they'd all been losing weight when they left the program. That made no sense whatsoever. Why would people who were 300 pounds overweight lose 100 pounds, and then drop out when they were on a roll?[2]
>
> "I had assumed that people who were 400, 500, 600 pounds would be getting heavier and heavier year after year. In 2,000 people, I

did not see it once," says Felitti. "When they gained weight, it was abrupt. If they lost weight, they regained all of it or more over a very short time."

But this knowledge brought him no closer to solving the mystery. So, he decided to do face-to-face interviews with a couple hundred of the dropouts. He used a standard set of questions for everyone. For weeks, nothing unusual came of the inquiries. No revelations. No clues.

The turning point came by accident. Felitti was running through yet another series of questions with yet another obesity program patient:

- How much did you weigh when you were born?
- How much did you weigh when you started first grade?
- How much did you weigh when you entered high school?
- How old were you when you became sexually active?
- How old were you when you married?

"I misspoke," he recalls. "Instead of asking, 'How old were you when you were first sexually active,' I asked, 'How much did you weigh when you were first sexually active?' The patient, a woman, answered, 'Forty pounds.'"

He didn't understand what he was hearing. He misspoke the question again. She gave the same answer, burst into tears and added, "It was when I was four years old, with my father."

He suddenly realized what he had asked.

Although it was my class of mostly new teachers to the profession, I had a colleague who was co-teaching with me that day. The plan was to get this cohort of enthusiastic educators prepared for classroom connections. We were building foundations for fostering safety and belonging, and there was great energy in the room. I was excited to share the teaching load with my longtime friend and mentor (let's call her Maria). We had decided on an overarching theme that centered on fostering a sense of belonging, connection, and relationship building. On this day, we divided the load to suit our strengths. Maria was tasked with introducing stress-related encounters and had chosen Felitti's work and ACE scores. I had planned to work through content integration with SEL and hands-on activities. All our classes were designed to be inclusive, engaging, and fun.

Maria went first. I was curious and expectant to also fill out the ACEs form (*CDC-Kaiser Permanente Adverse Childhood Experiences Questionnaire*) with my team, which she distributed to each participant. She had decided to focus most specifically on the impact that Felitti's findings might have on educators' daily routines, mindsets, expectations, and attitudes toward learners.

I had heard of the study, but I was unaware of the specific methods and uncanny circumstances in which the research had emerged. I sat down to fill out my own survey with the team. That's when it happened!

Looking back, I remember being fully shocked. As I read through the questions, I was overcome, as if each question had stunned my senses. Feelings welled up from deep down and surfaced quickly. I felt so embarrassed; scared. Ashamed. So many emotions. I couldn't look up from the survey. My head was swimming and I remember finding it difficult to focus. Cautiously, I looked around the room. Everything seemed blurry; everyone was moving in slow motion. I watched; I listened, but I couldn't hear. Sounds were unrecognizable; I remember hearing a wash of waves…

In retrospect, my brain was overloaded; it had shut down. Emotions associated with early, buried experiences, and traumatic memories had overwhelmed my processing system. This was new. I had never worked through my memories in THIS context; I had never looked at these specific past occurrences all at once and assessed their impact. It was a numbing experience.

My colleague Maria was in her element picking up energy from the enthusiastic high-spirited teachers. She shared later that the questionnaire was invoking a deep-seated response from individual teachers, as they calculated and recognized their ACE scores. She followed up by inviting individuals to share their results. There was a palpable level of collaboration and collective empathy in the room. Several teachers reported having at least one ACE; a few had three, and it seemed that everyone was able to share how much more understanding they now felt for students, families, and fellow staff members, who might have experienced challenges, trauma, and adversity during early developmental years. Apparently, the class was progressing with much discussion, excitement, and discovery.

Out of the dull drone, I heard my name. A strong sense of panic followed the knowledge that I was apparently "on deck" to share with the group.

What about you, Paige? Do you have any ACEs?

"What? Oh, sorry. Yeah, uh … hmmm … I have a LOT." I whispered through a nervous laugh.

My voice was in that soft, barely audible place that I recognized from far back in my past. I could feel the blood rushing to my neck and into my cheeks. It was the heat that I sensed when my face turned fully red. There was dryness in my mouth. I could feel my heart beating fast. It was pounding in my chest, and I couldn't seem to catch my breath! Everything felt so restricted. My mouth was open, but no sounds came out.

Suddenly, I was standing. "Oh; I have to go get my lunch," I blurted out to a silent room. Their faces looked surprised.

I quickly exited to the hallway and went straight to my car. The exercise and fresh air helped. My breathing had eased a little, and I felt like I was returning to safety. I opened the car door and got in quickly. I locked it immediately. That seemed like the right thing to do.

Alone in the car, I thought about what had just happened. I had never abandoned a class full of students before – I was supposed to be in charge. Had this ever happened to anyone else – all these ACEs? Am I an anomaly? I kept thinking back to the score. Did I add them up correctly?

I was off the ACEs charts. NINE out of TEN!

Each one was visible inside my brain – father incarcerated, alcoholic parents, verbal abuse, physical abuse, sexual abuse, emotional abuse, divorce, death of a parent, domestic violence … nine out of ten!

This score seemed so significant. How could I have not seen it before? It gripped me with fear. What does this mean? What kind of a monster does this make me? How can I face my colleagues and team? How can I face my students again?

I took my phone out and, as if through habit, started searching. I needed more information, and I needed it now. Where could I find out more information about ACEs? I found a myriad of correlational outcomes associated with Felitti's research that high ACE scores seemed to predict. I remembered my training. Correlation or causal … or both?

It was clear. My adverse childhood experiences were causative with a list of negative physical, emotional, and cognitive health outcomes – sickness, disease, and death. The science was staggering – negative health outcomes were strongly correlated with individuals who had higher ACE scores. These were not stated as causal, but somehow I knew they were being interpreted as such…

I had to stop there. Breathe.

My first inclination was to agree with the multitude of studies and organizations that were making blatant causal connections, even if it was apparent that they were willing to do so in the pursuit of some agenda. My head was swimming, again. Breathe! I closed my eyes, as if darkness would bring some clarity. But there was no darkness, just memories.

I was finally able to take SEVERAL CONSECUTIVE quick, deep, cleansing breaths through my nose; hold and release…

With each breath, I found a little more clarity. I began to slowly revisit my past and I remember choosing to see events within a new frame. I invited myself to step back to observe those messy, hurtful, terrible events of my childhood – that had persisted during my growing-up years between the ages of 6 and 13. "Formative years" was a phrase I had used when discussing developmental psychology with my students. I knew my "formative years" could destroy me. They could also inform me, I decided.

If I were to accept (like many experts who wrote articles and reported news stories about early traumatic experiences) that verbal, sexual, emotional, and physical abuse and neglect would always revisit the next generation … that knowledge would end up possibly defining my life, tempering my thoughts, and edging its way into my belief system, expectations, and self-efficacy.

The idea that the abused could become the abuser was a somewhat common societal belief and one that I had entertained often during my younger adult years. But even as I visited my unsavory and regrettable past, I knew that my story was not this story.

These ideas would always be in my mind and at times haunt me. But they did not define me. I had begun to reframe them, over many years. This was important so that I could positively inform my parenting, my relationships, my marriage, and my teaching. I thought I had broken the chain. These ACEs would end with me. Yet, the exercise of looking at them all at the same time was unexpected, initially overwhelming, and new for me – it had completely taken me by surprise. I couldn't let it hijack me in front of the new teachers.

I was still processing a response toward regulation. I had never worked through the ACEs scorecard before. These memories, experiences, and thoughts – taken all at once – were almost as powerful as the emotional surge that I had just experienced in front of the new district team. I recommitted to my decision. These would inform me and teach me, but more than anything, they would END with me.

I took several more deliberate, full breaths, from my diaphragm, cognizant that I was sending a signal to my 10th cranial vagus nerve. I needed to slow down my heart rate, lower adrenaline and cortisol levels, and fine-tune my nervous system before I returned. Knowing I am a strong contagion, I learned early on as a principal that it was my responsibility to bring the nervous system state I wanted to foster in my team and my students into the room with me. Gratefully, I could feel a sense of calm and clarity return. Rest and digest. Lunch! I had forgotten that it was lunchtime. I finished my final slice of apple.

I looked at my phone; I still had a few minutes. I knew I would have to go back inside and be transparent with everybody. Could I openly share my story? The story wasn't all negative. Miracles had occurred. How did I get here? Despite so many challenges, I was here. Where did the resilience originate? Every experience I chose to share had the potential to help others. Good or bad, right or wrong, these young teachers were now part of my story, and they did need to hear it.

Even though I was missing important team discussions, by the end of the week I had a glimmer of how this unintended segue had been incredibly useful. My story shed new light on how longitudinal impacts in our lives are invasive and complex. As I had done most of my life, I had to intentionally and vividly recall my memories of empowerment from my resilience makers – the amazing people who had sheltered and supported my journey throughout my life. Their voices, though also soft and caring, were consistent, non-judgmental, emphatic, and real.

Teachers!

Yes, they were kind, loving people – but most of all – they were teachers. It's why I am a teacher today. It's why I was so energized to go back into the room and be with my people. Two elementary teachers and two high school coaches! They journeyed along with me, supported me, withholding judgment, and always met me right where I was.

I was able to recognize their caring, loving, and consistent influence in my life. They held me together; building strong, committed, and lengthy relationships over 40 years, especially during my early school experiences. They were committed to supporting and believing in me, simply by their consistent presence and availability in my life. They remained steadfastly connected with me through years of deep struggle.

"They are still reaching out to me today," said my own voice, once timid, that was now replaced with a strong, inner vocalizing that reminds me of my growth during my journey with them.

They never asked. I never told them. But they knew they had connected. I am convinced that they have no idea how much impact they have had on my life. I still feel their love and possess so much gratitude for them. To this day, they have no real understanding of what was happening in my world during those heavy, struggling years.

They were and ARE my superheroes! They suspended judgment; they unfailingly believed in me and spoke belief into me. They recognized my capacity to withstand life's struggles. They helped provide and foster the belongingness, safety, and trust I longed for; they refused to become offended by my frequent dysregulation and "disrespectful" behaviors.

I have always loved Dr. Bruce Perry's work. I read The Boy Who Was Raised as a Dog over and over. His words spoke truth to me. "The more healthy relationships a child has, the more likely he will be to recover from trauma and thrive. Relationships are the agents of change and the most powerful therapy is human love" (3).

The teachers and coaches in my "four-member support group" were NOT therapists. They were, simply, therapeutic. And THAT is what has made all the difference…

The sixth graders had matured over the summer and had arrived fairly regulated into a new position of leadership. They seemed excited to take on their role, as the big fish in the pond for the year ahead. Our K-3 group, however, would have no part in assuming their new roles (or even consider the posture) of regulation. Counselors, paras, admin, and our support Dads were fully onboard, however, and at the ready. We had spent the first three weeks attempting to simply hold our classes together, but the stress responses were a rapid moving contagion (for both adults and students), and our youngest students were arriving dysregulated and remaining so for large parts of each day.

Even as teachers introduced basic understandings of the brain, like what happens when we experience an amygdala hijack, and shared with transparency their own struggles with regulation and compassion, younger students continued to show challenging behaviors. Even with planned fun activities and high expectations fostered by the Associated Student Body (ASB), many of our students continued to remain victims of stress. Staff and faculty were showing signs of weariness and burnout fatigue a month into this constant behavioral dysfunction. It was difficult for teachers to not become offended. To make matters worse, we began having parental crises as well, and this became the impetus for mandatory morning meetings – just for us.

> "We need to slow down in order to speed up." That was the motto for our first morning.
>
> "What do you mean?" one of the teachers complained. "Running out of time is my greatest stressor right now; I am so far behind already. I refuse to end up like last year … with upper grade teachers being disappointed by our grade level team!"
>
> "No disappointments here … we're all having a challenging start," offered one of our sixth grade teachers.
>
> "It's not anyone's fault." I wanted to keep the meetings upbeat. "This is a classic 'revert to default' situation. Our default neural pathways!"

I was met with a lot of raised eyebrows. Revert to default appeared to be a new concept for this group.

"Ok", I started again. "We all – well at least 60 percent of us – elementary school teachers and staff have been trained with 40–50 hours of educational neuroscience. Several of you have completed a two-day advanced course as well and have been working this summer within your grade level teams. This all happened less than a month before the start of school. I was with you … We were excited when we finished that PD. We had a new framework. We were inspired. We had momentum. We believed in each other, in ourselves, and in our students and families. I don't remember a year feeling better equipped as a team AND with this much energy and dopamine flowing in our systems."

"Right! But what has that got to do with reverting to default? What does that even mean?" You could always count on Marjorie to ask the right question at the right time.

"Exactly. 'Revert to default'. Glad you brought that up."

"It was you who brought it up." Marjorie was smiling.

"I did. Yes. Bear with me. Whew; let's breathe." I took two quick, deep breaths in through my nose, held it long, and released a long, audible sigh … JUST so that everyone in the room was forced to mirror my thinking and breathing (4). "At the end of summer, before school had even started back, we were using this new framework – it's based on a solid combination of learning science and neuroscience (5). I know because each of us was using a new and 'empowering' (as many of you called it) vocabulary."

I waited. I watched faces search their memories for "vocabulary entrees" that hadn't been used in a while.

"Remember … phrases that changed how we understand learning and teaching, like 'myelinating new structures and pathways', 'emptying out working memory', 'practicing Long Term Potentiation', 'using disequilibrium', 'chunking', and especially 'amygdala hijack'."

I deliberately walked the phrases slowly through their minds, used our co-created TPR motions, and I allowed each construct enough time to gain a footing again, in brains that were scrambling to catch up. It reminded me of a midwestern farm that had just survived a direct hit from a tornado.

> "Team! NO SHAME that our deadlines and time pressures have pulled us from our mark! No SHAME in the Brain! We got this. We can readjust our neural thinking caps right now. It's as easy as that. When we change our words, use our neural vocabularies – our mental models shift in relation to our understanding of what is going on in our own and in our students' learning brains (6). This matters, because we are in charge of the ONLY THING that we CAN change – our learning environments (7)."

I was met with a stony silence. Individual teachers were revisiting the place in their memories where our summer Professional Development knowledge that was so critical for our success resided and was still accessible. The application of that knowledge had been somewhat suspended. Light bulbs were going on, however, and our hopes, beliefs, and expectations were resurfacing.

> "We can choose to become STUDENTS of our STUDENTS! They will guide us when we co-create the space with them. These students have brains ... they are hardwired-learning machines (8). We can make time for disequilibrium and LTP because we know that the attention span of elementary school learners is no bigger than a goldfish's!" I could feel momentum beginning to build ...

> "Who needs Lacrosse balls?" The changed subject energized the group.

> "The key to the neural equipment storage is in my inbox," I reminded them. "Check-out whatever is needed to produce more fun, focus, and more movement! (9) As you plan your lessons, think about your commitment to intrinsic motivation – drop the sticker stars and any reliance on extrinsic rewards – let's focus on giving our students opportunities for choice! Fostering autonomy increases the connection to intrinsic motivation (10). Highlight every evidence of their mastery. Call it out to them and co-discover a purpose that flows directly from their appetite (11)."

I double-sniffed a deliberate long breath and held it; releasing it with a sigh ... so the others could join me in the next in-breath. Maintaining collective connection and collective care throughout this day and in the months to come was certainly going to be critical.

> "Above all, I would like to see us begin to 'greenhouse' our students with intentionality (12); that means pulling back from our frantic pace. Stick with the plan; go slow to ultimately go fast. Begin to re-work your solid foundations. Let's think carefully about that sense of belonging that we felt so passionately at the end of our recent PD (13)."

As morning meetings gained momentum, I could see the change. The "I" began to become "WE". It was as if a switch had been pulled and suddenly, the neuroscience of learning was regaining its foothold, front of mind. Together, we came up with a couple of co-created ideas, which shifted the energy that would sustain us through the rest of the school year. Here is a list of what we planned to accomplish, in our co-created learning spaces ... WE

- Identified sensitive "orchid" students (14)
- Focused on becoming even more "students of our students"
- Identified our students' appetites – knowing full well that aptitude would follow (15)
- Celebrated only positive effort in our students' daily activities – avoiding all inclinations to punish/shame or judge (16)
- Planned to give "all the joy to ALL the students" so that we were not "othering" children or introducing unwanted "social evaluative threat" (17)
- Were intentional about calling parents (green-housing our students at home) by sharing success stories with regard to their child (18)

We felt that when parents receive positive feedback about their children, homes change, parents change, and students' lives change for the better.

By year-end, six families spoke warmly about the fact that telephone calls that focused on their child's amazing performance were catalysts for change in behavior, attitude, and expectations. Two families also mentioned that the positive nature of calls had changed the relationship (which used to be aggressively corrective and fiercely negative) between father and daughter in one case, and father and son in the other. Ten of the families stated that the positive calls had improved trust about the school and contributed to increased pride and belief in their students.

I noted in these calls that as many as 15 parents cried during the engagement and they were extremely thankful to the school and teachers. Over half of the parents stated that they had NEVER received a "positive" call from the school – but had gotten many difficult and negative ones. As a result, students were celebrated at home. Consequently, change, growth, and an increase in self-efficacy soon became obvious in these children.

That intentional shift to recognize good, call out good, and celebrate all apparent growth within our students and families made a spectacular difference. We avoided stress responses that forced team members to prioritize "pushing" the pace or "catching up". In fact, we removed the word "push" from our lexicon. We knew that pushing some students didn't really make a difference – they were so resilient that it didn't seem to matter. But pushing sensitive, hyper-vigilant students and staff was proving to be counterproductive in so many ways (19).

Joshua's Story

It was Rebecca's fourth-year teaching. She had experienced "enough" frustrations in the pre-neural education system – the traditional behaviorist model – with rewards and punishments. She was ready to "get" the freedom of switching to a brain-based program (20). She was fully onboard and embraced neuroscience vocabulary, methods, and constructs. She immersed herself in reading articles and books that fostered the implementation of research and practices about how human brains work and how children learn. She was especially keen to hone her skills in how to build white-matter structures that helped her students increase learning with deep understanding. As a fitness enthusiast, her neuroscience heroine was Wendy Suzuki and she seemed to surface Dr. Suzuki's research in her work and conversations with staff and students on a daily basis (21).

Joshua was an active second grader in Rebecca's class who consistently appeared to experience fear in social contexts (22). We discussed in our weekly get-together how social evaluative threat appeared to be a major challenge to Joshua's self-image, his difficulty in accessing his true potential, and his seemingly incessant negative chatter and self-talk in the classroom, at recess, and before and after school.

To make matters worse, Joshua's parents were going through a divorce. The disruption of his safety and stability seemed to reach him at his core. His sister, Hannah, was an eighth grader whom he adored, and who attended a neighboring middle school. She was a perfect student (in his mind), and she inspired him, greatly. Joshua continually looked up to her; her daily desire for excellence, her many loyal and caring friends, and her consistent dedication to her studies, assignments, and projects. Nevertheless, the inspiration soon dissipated, as he, unfortunately, began to compare himself to her level of performance. He became increasingly fixated on his many imperfections that seemed to consistently fall short of her excellence in everything she pursued. Although Joshua's first grade year had been stellar, this year was different. Looking back, he remembered how his family and extended family celebrated his success. This became a constant reminder that this year was different. It had become clear that his "moment in the spotlight" had been short-lived. Mom left dad during the summer and things went downhill fast. Rebecca and the team fought hard to stay ahead of his adversity, but it ended up being a disaster in so many ways.

Rebecca inferred that he no longer had any sense of safety at home and Joshua's grades had been dropping dramatically. He was miserable. He had become the epitome of the phrase, "hurt people hurt people". We actively co-regulated with him daily, using a 2 X 10 approach (connect with him for at least 2 minutes per day for 10 days), and then continued to foster trust-building with the counseling team, throughout the fall and into the winter.

He loved to hike, walk, and jog. So did Rebecca. Eventually, Joshua began to open up about his sister. It was clear that he was able to express how much he loved her. At the same time, there was an underlying feeling of pressure and negative comparison. We detected a growing urgency about learned helplessness (23). He was not in control anymore. He felt that she constantly judged him – checking up on his grades and comparing his performance to her second grade year. He was convinced that she frequently criticized him for not being perfect like herself (24). We decided to put it all out on the table.

We set up a three-way Zoom call with Hannah, Joshua, and me. Hannah began the conversation and talked about their relationship. I stayed in the background stepping in only when there was a need to sustain the discussion. I allowed the two siblings to hear each other's perspectives. Joshua began to lead a lot of the conversation. Hannah and I seemed surprised! He spoke his mind.

It was becoming obvious that Joshua had been imagining the worst in almost all situations. Misunderstandings, preconceptions, misconceptions, and so much hurt became vividly apparent in the discussion about their relationship. As the distance between them, seemingly caused by offense (especially, perceived offense), waned, Hannah spoke up about her complete belief in her brother. She shared that she was aware of the power she wielded in Joshua's life and admitted that at times she may not have been as encouraging, loving, forgiving, or kind as she could. She admitted also that she had allowed her fear and hurt about her parents' separation and divorce to ruin her relationship with her brother. She teared up as she apologized. Joshua lit up! Hannah's transparency and honesty affected him greatly and he began to lower his defenses.

Joshua was so very pleased to learn that Hannah had a very different conception of his capabilities, his gifts, and his potential. Joshua's demeanor changed. His body posture and facial expression began to reflect a new hope and encouragement. By the time the 25-minute zoom meeting approached a close, both were coming away visibly changed, and in many ways, restored. Ending the conversation with the idea of potential meet-ups for the two at different times during the upcoming quarter was the icing on the cake. Hannah committed to staying close to her brother with care and encouragement and becoming less of a judge of his grades. Several visits were scheduled, where Hannah was allowed to connect with Joshua during lunch and recess and sometimes for part of a class period later in that year.

Although their parents never reunited, Hannah and Joshua continued to co-regulate with one another and cheer each other on. As the year progressed, brother and sister grew closer. Joshua's self-talk grew more positive, his self-efficacy began to thrive, and his grades greatly improved. As he engaged in healthy teacher relationships, he also began to interact in much more meaningful ways with his friends, classmates, interests, and pursuits. The school became these siblings' safe place, where they were able to connect, heal, thrive, and belong.

Notes

1. ACESTooHigh is a nonpartisan traditional online news site that reports on research about positive and adverse childhood experiences, including developments in epidemiology, neurobiology, and the biomedical and epigenetic consequences of toxic stress. They also cover how people, organizations, agencies, and communities are implementing practices and policies based on research. This includes developments in education, juvenile justice, criminal justice, public health, medicine, mental health, social services in cities, counties, and states.
2. The mystery turned into a 25-year quest involving researchers from the Centers for Disease Control and Prevention and more than 17,000 members of Kaiser

Permanente's San Diego care program. It would reveal that adverse experiences in childhood were very common and that these experiences were linked to every major chronic illness and social problem that the United States grapples with – and spends billions of dollars on.

References

1. V. J. Felitti *et al.*, Relationship of childhood abuse and household dysfunction to many of the leading causes of death in adults. The Adverse Childhood Experiences (ACE) Study. *American Journal of Preventive Medicine: Elsevier* **14**, 245–258 (1998).
2. J. E. Stevens, The Adverse Childhood Experiences Study — the largest, most important public health study you never heard of — began in an obesity clinic. ACES Too High. https://acestoohigh.com/ 2012.
3. B. Perry, *The boy who was raised as a dog: What traumatized children can teach us about loss, love and healing* (Basic Books, New York, NY, 2006).
4. R. Feuerstein, R. S. Feuerstein, L. H. Falik, *Beyond smarter: Mediated learning and the brain's capacity for change* (Teachers College Press, New York, 2010).
5. J. D. Bransford, A. L. Brown, R. Cocking, *How people learn: Brain, mind, experience and school* (National Academy Press, Washington, DC, 2000).
6. D. Hebb, *The organization of behavior* (Wiley & Sons, New York, 1949).
7. K. O'Mahony, *The brain-based classroom practical guide; Regulate relate reason* (Brain-Based Solutions, Seattle WA, 2023).
8. J. Medina, *Brain Rules: 12 principles for surviving and thriving at work, home and school* (Pear Press, San Francisco, 2008).
9. J. Ratey, *Spark: Why exercise and play are critical for healthy brains* (Little Brown, New York, NY), 2008.
10. D. Pink, *Drive* (Riverhead Books, New York, NY, 2009).
11. R. Plomin, *Blueprint: How DNA makes us who we are* (Random House, London, UK, 2018).
12. D. Dobbs, The science of success. The Atlantic. 2009.
13. L. Darling-Hammmond, Building a belonging classroom. Edutopia: Classroom Management. https://www.edutopia.org/video/building-belonging-classroom/ 2019.
14. W. T. Boyce, B. J. Ellis, Biological sensitivity to context: An evolutionary-developmental theory of the origins and functions of stress reactivity *Developmental Psychopathology* **17**, 271–301 (2005).
15. J. D. Bransford, L. Darling-Hammond, P. LePage, in *Preparing teachers for a changing world: What teachers should Learn and be able to do*, L. Darling-Hammond, J. Bransford, Eds. (Jossey-Bass, San Francisco, CA, 2005), pp. 1–39.
16. D. Sobel, B. F. Skinner, the Champion of Behaviorism, is Dead at 86 in New York Times, https://www.nytimes.com/1990/08/20/obituaries/b-f-skinner-the-champion-of-behaviorism-is-dead-at-86.html, 1990.

17. A. Woody, E. D. Hooker, P. M. Zoccola, S. S. Dickerson, Social-evaluative threat, cognitive load, and the cortisol and cardiovascular stress response. *Psychoneuroendocrinology* **97**, 149–155 (2018).
18. L. Darling-Hammmond, B. J. Barron, P. D. Pearson, A. H. Schoenfeld, E. K. Stage, *Powerful learning: What we know about teaching for understanding* (John Wiley & Sons Inc, 2008).
19. T. Boyce, Differential susceptibility of the developing brain to contextual adversity and stress. *Neuropsychopharmacology* **41**, 142–162 (2016).
20. K. O'Mahony, *The brain-based classroom: Accessing every child's potential through educational neuroscience* (Routledge, Taylor & Francis Group, London, UK and New York, ed. First, 2021).
21. W. Suzuki, *Healthy brain happy life: A personal program to activate our brain & do everything better* (Harper Collins, New York, NY, 2015).
22. W. T. Boyce, *The orchid and the dandelion: Why some children struggle and how all can thrive* (Knopf Doubleday Publishing Group, New York, 2018).
23. M. E. Seligman, Learned helplessness. *Annual Review of Medicine* **23**, 407–412 (1972).
24. C. S. Dweck, *Mindset: The new psychology of success* (Random House, New York, NY, 2006).

10

Soft-Start

By Taylor Cassidy

Introduction

It was my first year of teaching and I was doing exactly what it was that my college courses and mentor teachers had prepared me to do. At 8:15 when my students walked into the classroom, I had "Morning Work" ready for them. Reading skill practice, math review from the day before, and instructions to "read quietly" to themselves when finished. I circled the room helping "struggling" students and checking to be sure that their planners were signed from the night before. "Come in, do your work, sit quietly." It was the same instructional system I had grown up in, the same system I had trained in. This was "what we do." It was what they did across the hall, next door, and in every intermediate classroom I had been a part of. It quickly became known as "Bell Work" in comical Pavlovian fashion, but I didn't think there were any alternatives.

Paradigm Shift

In March 2020, I had the opportunity to attend a conference with my colleagues in Seattle, Washington. It was the annual conference put on by NCCE – The National Council for Computer Education. Just over halfway through my first year of teaching, it seemed like a wonderful opportunity to spend 5 days on professional leave and continue to learn and develop myself as a new-to-the-field educator. Not to mention, just over halfway through my first year of teaching, at 22 years, the prospect of a "mini-vacation" to the "big city" was attractive in and of itself.

I attended this conference with a multifarious mix of coworkers from my rural Montana school. Our IT director, Robotics coach, STEM Lab supervisor, technology committee member, and I took the just under 2-hour flight to Seattle. We each had different goals. Many of my coworkers were in search of software updates, robotics, and opportunities to bring coding and gaming into the classroom. I had other goals. Beyond wanting to be entertained and social, I was seeking out something to challenge my thinking – something that might improve my classroom management. What I got was much more. Sure it was entertaining, and it was designed to improve classroom management, but I wasn't expecting to be completely "wowed" by the information and brain-fried by the opportunities. Who would have thought that what I learned in that room would change my life and my students' lives deeply? The course that I had signed up for turned out to be a day-long institute on the "Neuroscience of Learning". I had always been interested in the brain and was drawn to the neuroscience of learning, but this was not what I had expected. It not only captured my attention but also ended up shifting my entire educational philosophy and methodology. And the best part is that I found an active community of amazing teachers who were already changing education in their schools wherever they worked. I call them my peeps.

I knew, just like everyone else, that stress was not good for us and especially not good for our kids, but when I attended a class on "Stress in the Classroom", I was blown away. I learned the basic fundamentals of how the brain works and realized that stress invaded every element of my classroom. But worse, I realized that I was the cause of much of that stress for my young learners. No wonder my students were struggling when I created difficult transitions, when I changed my body language, and/or when I handed them an assignment first thing in the morning. I saw the world through a different lens. I began to understand the incredible power of the brain to either make or break my class. I was excited to see my part in that as well.

I like to think of the brain as organized in three basic systems – back survival, middle emotional, and front abstract thinking. I learned that near the center of our heads we have two amygdalae – one in each hemisphere. These almond sized/shaped structures protect us by reacting to incoming sensory stimuli from the world around us (1). When those amygdalae sense that we are safe, with no imminent danger, they route information to the executive center so that we have access to the front part of our brain. That front part of the brain, I found out, is the prefrontal cortex (PFC). This is the "smart" part of our brain, the part that learns, thinks, and reasons. It's where we want our children to access every day in our learning spaces. Conversely, if our amygdalae sense danger or stress, even perceived stress or danger, it impedes our access to the PFC and we end up in Freeze, Fight, Flight, and Fawn (2). I kind of knew about Fight Flight – I had heard of them before … but I had no idea how important they were and I was glad to learn about freeze and fawn. I was able to "see" some of my children in freeze and fawn immediately I learned about those constructs. This was just the tip of the iceberg.

I haven't thought about perception – about how children perceive certain things and these things can add to their understanding of the world around them. For instance, it's important to note that the danger or stress detected by the amygdala can be real "imminent" or not real "perceived". Our amygdalae have the same reactions to stress, whether a vicious tiger is chasing us, someone is upset with us, or we have a math test slapped on our desk (3). What I, as an educator, also find important to remember is that I don't dictate what it is that is stressful to students. The amygdalae react specifically depending on an individual's personal and lived experiences (2). In other words, what is stressful for Johnny might be a cool walk in the park for Jamie. This doesn't make it easy for me as a teacher – I have to assume that the behavior that I observe in a child might have something to do with the perception of danger, fear, or anxiety. The good news is that I learned how to recognize stress and to apply one of many tools to alleviate the stressful situation. I can change the learning environment so that the child can be successful.

This learning opened my eyes to the reality that so many of my students walk into the classroom under a great deal of stress. The list of reasons "why" is as numerous and unique as the students in my classroom. Those reasons can also vary from day-to-day and minute-to-minute. The act of coming to school itself is very stressful for many children (4). When you add in the variety of things that can happen before a student even walks through the doors in my classroom, it becomes clear that many students are coming into the classroom in a state of stress, and therefore without access to the learning part of their brain. The bad news is – the brain is always learning something. However, instead of learning the things I wanted them to learn, they were learning that school is scary, teachers make it worse, and that they are not good enough (5).

With this newfound knowledge, it became clear to me that "morning work" was not effective in my classroom. A majority of my students were coming in a stress response and therefore unable to access their thinking, reasoning, and logical PFC. Having students walk into the room, and expecting them to access information from the day before, much less apply it, requires a great deal of reasoning, logic, and access to that executive learning center of their brain. Moreover, I realized that what happens first thing in the morning has huge repercussions for children right throughout the day. It also began to dawn on me that maybe it had repercussions also for the rest of the week, or the month or longer. In order to make room for executive functioning and learning, I would need to allow opportunities for healthy emotional regulation in my classroom – first thing. This was my first Neural Education Shift in Practice – the first step of many in an overall paradigm shift.

I needed to uncover and unpack Bruce Perry's understanding of the child's brain so that I could adjust my learning environment to meet the needs of every child. I had been introduced to Perry's work at the conference and it spoke loudly to me in my early morning preparation mood. It seemed simple enough – Regulate first, Relate second, and finally Reason. That was the schema that he introduced in his writing (6). I needed to figure out how to invite the children into a learning space that was psychologically safe so that they could first co-regulate with me and with peers, then build strong connections while they relate to each other and to me. Finally, I would expect then that the environment would invite all children to be able to articulate, solve problems, and have fun as they reason using their executive higher order thinking brains.

WIN/BINS

Practically speaking, how could I reduce stress in my classroom to prime the brain for learning? In the fall of 2020, in place of my usual "Bell Work", I created a system called "WIN/BINS" in which students had the opportunity to regulate and relate with one another before being asked to reason. These became my 3Rs for classroom management.

"WIN" Stands for Whatever I Need

During this time students had an easy opportunity to finish breakfast, sharpen pencils, fill their water bottles, use the restroom, and take care of any of their other needs. Intentionality with regard to time, space, and structures to meet most basic needs resulted in eliminating the frustration of interruptions that heretofore ensued 15 minutes into the first lesson. I didn't notice it at the time, but soon it became apparent that the autonomy associated with the children being able to take care of their own needs on their own time was my initial step into Intrinsic Motivation. Autonomy was key. Then as they found they had some Mastery in that process, they were able to find Purpose. I adhered to the definition of Intrinsic Motivation that I learned in Seattle – Autonomy, Mastery, and Purpose beat Rewards and Punishments any day in my class.

After taking care of "whatever they needed", the children had access to bins that were put together with careful planning and intention. As shown in Figure 10.1, these "bins" included board games that had been abandoned in a closet, old math manipulatives that were collecting dust, stem materials donated by community members, lacrosse balls (ball bouncing became part of my co-regulation effort), stuffies, toys, and lots more. My goal was to give students free access to materials that would help move them out of any "amygdala" stress response and prime them for work in their executive PFC.

In addition to managing stress, introducing soft-start bins into my classroom offered a variety of other benefits to my students in our

FIGURE 10.1 WIN/BINs

post-COVID space (7). Stress reduction was primary. As I watched students use STEM materials to engage in open-ended activities, I observed stress levels decrease in a matter of minutes. It was clear that these fun choices helped restore joy and calm to our learning space (8). Additionally, the soft-start gives students opportunities to build resilience and grit that would transfer to other situations (9). Building a tower of blocks requires a lot of concentration, focus, and careful accuracy. If the tower falls down, it can be frustrating and difficult. I was aware because of my newfound knowledge in cognitive neuroscience that the children were achieving mastery through persistence, experiencing fun while trying and failing in a safe space, and that they were myelinating new white matter structures in places like the superior longitudinal fasciculus that would improve their life trajectory going forward (10).

The conversations I heard students having were representative of the kind of growth mindset, critical thinking skills that so many scripted curriculums seek (and often fail) to instill in our students. As students encountered frustrations in building, creating, or figuring out a puzzle, I watched them learn to regulate, and relate with their peers, to ultimately reason more effectively. Specifically, I recall a group of students working on a hexagonal puzzle. The variety of odd shaped pieces only fit one way, and as an adult with a fully formed PFC, I have to admit it's quite a daunting puzzle to solve. I watched students, who typically shut down in the face of challenging situations (11), start to take deep breaths, utilize positive self-talk (12), and collaborate with their peers to find new strategies to attack the problem in front of them.

"Man this is tough…"

"What if we tried it this way…"

"I know there's a solution, I just have to keep trying…"

If practice does indeed make permanent, and we have to build structures in the brain around growth mindset and resilience, it makes sense that I watched students start to transfer these skills to reading and math. Struggling students' attitudes around difficulties in reading and math started to transform as they utilized those same skills and strategies they had unknowingly been myelinating during their morning "free time". The student who previously put his head down at the first sight of a difficult word problem now had the structures and myelinated pathways in their brain to persevere.

I also watched students learn and practice social skills that so many of them were lacking, especially in the post-COVID space. Students had ample opportunities to practice resolving conflict, take turns, and build positive relationships in low-stakes situations. These observations convinced me of the genius of schools where children are allowed to experiment and make mistakes in a place where there are no serious scary repercussions; a safe psychological environment that honors everybody's effort.

"Hey, can I play with you?"

"When you're finished, can I have a turn?"

Slowly the rules and guidelines I had set around the materials started to transform as they set their own norms. Students began resolving situations themselves, rather than relying on the teacher to settle disagreements. One situation that stands out is how the students managed the sharing of particularly popular materials. Instead of having to intervene and "referee" who could play with what, I heard students start to solve social ambiguities.

"What if I play with it today, and you can play with it tomorrow?"

"Can we split up the materials?"

"Let's build something together."

It's not lost on me that these skills are incredibly difficult for a third grader, but I watched these same conversations translate to the playground resulting in diminished write-ups and behavior issues at recess. It turns out that similar results have been documented in schools that are in that same neural concept methodology no matter where in the world, e.g., India, Africa, and New Zealand (4).

Case Study 1

Two students come to mind when I think about the benefits of the soft-start in my classroom. The first account describes a child who arrived to class from a trauma enfeebled home environment that, though very tough to witness, is not uncommon in many schools anywhere in the country.

John (*name changed) enrolled as a new student at our school the day before classes began. Like many of my students, John came to me with a history of "difficult" family and previous school situations. He had recently moved to our school and was looking for a fresh start. For the first month, John could be found with his face up against the outside wall – refusing to enter the building. The transition to school created a stress response. It was clear to me that he was experiencing a hijacked amygdala, so he was unable to access his PFC to even enter the building, much less learn. As I implemented the soft-start in my classroom, I noticed that, day by day, it took less coaxing and less support to get him into the building. By the middle of the year, John was skipping down the hall with glee. He was one of the first children in the door, ready to check in and start his morning soft-start routine. Coming into a classroom where he had an opportunity to play, build friendships, and relate with his peers reduced any stress response and helped him develop a more positive relationship with school. At conferences, his guardians were awestruck and overjoyed. They had tears in their eyes by hearing that their child, who had for so long struggled within the school system, was now thriving. It was a good reminder for me that all children want to thrive, that all children can thrive, and that all children will thrive when the learning environment is adjusted to meet their needs (5).

The second account described a child who arrived at class in a perennial state of hypervigilance. This little girl was anxiety ridden and fearful. Sometimes freeze described her, sometimes fight, sometimes flight, but always fawn.

Jill (*name changed) bounced between virtual and in-person instruction during the COVID-19 pandemic. Returning to full-time in-person instruction, she struggled with regular attendance. (We've seen this schoolwide and regionally as well). In addition to other therapeutic measures, we found that the opportunity to connect with her peers with the morning soft-start increased her attendance by more than 20%. Knowing exactly what awaited her in the classroom each morning helped ease her anxiety and reduce the stress around attending school. The predictability, consistency, and kindness that she experienced each morning helped defray any retroactive inhibitions that were causing her to not be in school. She knew that each morning when she walked into my classroom, she would have time to connect with her friends, chat with her teacher, and prepare for the day. Instead of walking into an ever-variable assignment or environment, she knew what the first 15 minutes of her day looked like.

Morning Check-in

Another practice I implemented in the soft-start routine was a digital morning check-in. I made it part of their morning routine as students ate breakfast and transitioned to their "BINS", they logged on to their Chromebooks and completed a quick Google form I created (see Figure 10.2). This form

FIGURE 10.2 Morning Check-in

served two major purposes. On the one hand, it was incredibly practical because I used it to take attendance and complete the lunch count for the day. The second part of the form gave students the opportunity to check-in with themselves; to give real data with regard to areas I had learned were essential to their success. Students reported on their perceived quality of sleep the night before (see Figure 10.3), their current emotional state (see Figure 10.4), and anything else they felt I should know (see Figure 10.5).

Students like Jill were able to let me know if they were having an especially difficult time. Other students used this space to let me know what was going on at home, about an upcoming trip, or things that they were struggling with. Their responses varied:

"We're getting a puppy"

"I would like to check in with the counselor"

"I had a fight with my mom this morning"

Knowing this information about my students allowed me to move from Perry's "regulate" to "relate". I was giving my students a safe space

FIGURE 10.3 Morning Check-in Mood

FIGURE 10.4 Morning Check-in Feeling

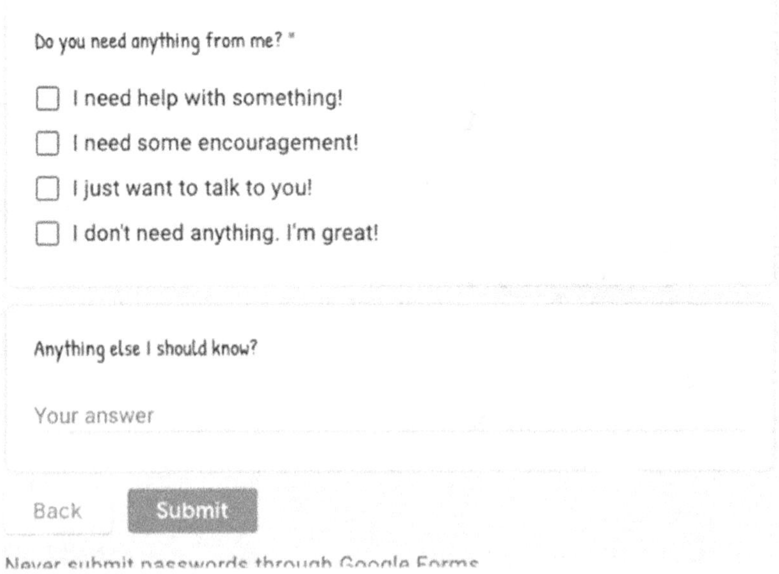

FIGURE 10.5 Morning Check-in Needs

to routinely share with me things of importance to them. I was able to touch base with students regarding this information and connect with them on a deeper level. From "What kind of puppy are you getting…" to "I'm sorry you're having a tough time – I'm here for you", I was able to bring our morning check-in into conversations throughout our day. The old adage "everyone is fighting a battle you know nothing about" is true. Each one of our students walks into our rooms with "things" we might know nothing about. The knowledge that a student slept poorly the night before or that they were feeling sad, mad, or stressed allowed me to adjust my teaching to better serve the whole-child in front of me.

In addition to allowing me to build relationships and be better aware of the brain-body states of my students, this practice gave my students the opportunity to be mindful and reflective. Having a moment in the morning to check-in with themselves is a skill not many of my students are familiar with. This integration of mindfulness and Social Emotional Learning has been incredibly helpful for students as they navigate life in a post-pandemic classroom (13). This practice also increased our ability to greenhouse students and provide them with the highest level of care. This check-in process provided an immense amount of data and information that could be shared among teachers and service providers to better support students in a holistic way.

Case Study 2

Jim (*name changed) was a student in my class whose performance, attitude, and demeanor were quite variable.

He had ok days and really tough days. It was seemingly impossible to know what version of him would walk in the door on any given day. Somedays we got sunshiny, ready to learn Jim, and other days we got a Jim who was upset, stressed, and chronically shut down. I mentioned to the school counselor that it felt like it was every other Monday that Jim was having a particularly difficult time. The school counselor and I sat down and reviewed Jim's data from his morning check-ins. We found a clear pattern! Indeed, every other Monday Jim was self-identifying as angry, stressed, and tired. This matched the unexpected behavior I was encountering in the classroom. Our school counselor recalled that Jim's family had just moved to a new parenting plan. In talking with the parents and Jim, we discovered that he was spending every other weekend with a different set of parents. We hypothesized that the change in behavior was due to a change in routine at home. With this information, we were better able to support Jim. We were able to anticipate these changes at home and put supports in place to alleviate the stress and reduce difficult classroom behaviors as a result. Knowledge was power in this situation as we were able to understand the potential CAUSE of behavior, possibly even before the student realized it himself. With that knowledge, we had the power to increase and refine support to better meet the needs of Jim at specific times.

Jane's (*name changed) story was disturbing and also inspiring.

Jane experienced a heartbreaking amount of trauma in her lifetime. Positively, by the time she found herself in my classroom, she had a large greenhouse of support. I fall back on Bruce Perry again to show how we built a greenhouse for Jane. We were able to identify four consistent caring adults who were there for Jane every day. And she knew this. She had multiple teachers, counselors, and caring adults in her corner ready to support her however they could. Still, she struggled. Her morning check-in became a safe space for her to routinely connect with her support systems and advocate for needed support. She utilized the "what else should I know" section to do so.

"I had terrible nightmares last night…"

"I'd like to check in with the counselor today…."

"I'm really sad today"

Giving Jane the space to communicate within the safety of her greenhouse allowed her to be a vital participant in her system of support.

It was clear that my soft-start and practice of "WIN/BINS" was improving student outcomes in my classroom. I was sure that this would be the "new normal" in my educational space. I planned to repeat the exact process the following year. However, to my consternation, it didn't work. This beautiful brain-aligned idea that was PERFECT the year before was not working for this new class in a new year.

My instinct was to revert to default (14, 15) – to return to my myelinated pathway and just go back to "morning work".

"It isn't working, so it doesn't work, I will just not do it."

Luckily, my background in Neural Education and my Neural Lens support and "greenhouse" group pushed me to think about the WHY behind it not working!

I took the time to observe the new class. It didn't take long for the penny to drop. It was an amygdala situation – I should have known. I was causing them to hijack. Many of the kids struggled with the social time. They didn't yet have the skills. They were missing white matter structures to be able to engage with the morning BIN time. That too had to be taught to them! It was a profound realization. The exact thing that was supposed to regulate my students was hijacking them. The big takeaway for me was even more profound. I could easily have punished them for not having the white matter structures to be able to engage in what should have been a simple matter – instead, I got busy growing those structures for them. I often heard muttering about growing the superior longitudinal fasciculus and the uncinate fasciculus in the faculty room. I didn't care because it soon got the children to a place where they could engage with the WIN/BINS.

Instead of "it doesn't work", I shifted my thinking to how can I adapt this activity to meet the needs of all students? I had to address the lagging skills of these students who were entrusted to my care. I felt it was a grand privilege. I got busy adjusting the soft-start. I made several small tweaks and a couple of new items were added. As a result, today it is much stronger.

For this class I had to expand my thinking. It involved offering more options, such as seasonal packets of puzzles and mazes. I found items that were explicitly designed to support social skills and play. Very soon, I was able to envision many other ways to soft-start the day. I involved the children and together we co-created a new soft-start routine. Bins had additional choices that sprang from finding out from students what they enjoyed doing with their friends and sometimes alone. The idea of following the child's "appetite" before looking for their "aptitude" was huge for me (16). I was developing a rich inventory of what worked to regulate them and I was beginning to realize that one size didn't fit all – Duh! Sometimes what is obvious is just simple!

Coming from my first Neural Education institute, I wanted strategies, the process, the "thing" to do in my classroom – but no one strategy meets the needs of all kids in our classrooms. It's the Neural Lens that matters – the intentionality to realize that the brain is malleable and that the brain is always learning. It is better that the child is learning that "I am capable", "I can succeed even if it's hard" allows us to change the way we view our careers and professional capacity. I learn from and with my students. It gives me the mindset necessary to tackle challenges and keep tackling them day in and day out.

The kids in my classroom are diverse. The kids I had in 2021 were different from the ones I had in 2022, and even those kids were different from September 1 to May 31. I too am different. I shudder sometimes, when I think about how my attitude, my first teacher training that delivered my sharp and unkind words, and my unpredictable body language could have contributed to inducing stress and amygdala hijack for those early-day classes. Not anymore! This is why co-creation is so essential to my work. My soft-start has evolved and looks different in the years that followed that first "ground breaking" year, but the "why" and the intention behind the construct have remained the same – how can I reduce stress for my students as they enter the classroom to begin their journey through school and life?

References

1. J. Willis, How to teach students about the brain. *Educational Leadership* **67**(4), 2–4 ascd.org/el/articles/ (2009).
2. B. Perry, *The Boy Who Was Raised as a Dog: What Traumatized Children Can Teach Us about Loss, Love and Healing* (Basic Books, New York, NY, 2006).
3. R. M. Sapolski, *Why Zebras Don't Get Ulcers* (Henry Holt and Company LLC, New York, NY, ed. Third, 2004).
4. K. O'Mahony, *The Brain-Based Classroom: Accessing Every Child's Potential through Educational Neuroscience* (Routledge, Taylor & Francis Group, London, UK and New York, ed. First, 2021).
5. K. O'Mahony, *The Brain-Based Classroom Practical Guide; Regulate Relate Reason* (Brain-Based Solutions, Seattle, WA, 2023).
6. O. Winfrey, B. Perry, *What Happened to You? Conversations on Trauma, Resilience, and Healing* (Macmillan Publishers, New York, NY, 2021).
7. Greenberg, J. Decety, I. Gordon, The social neuroscience of music: Understanding the social brain through human song. *American Psychologist*, http://dx.doi.org/10.1037/amp0000819, (2021).
8. D. Pink, *Drive* (Riverhead Books, New York, NY, 2009).
9. M. E. P. Seligman, *Flourish* (Simon & Schuster, New York, NY, 2012).
10. R. W. Fields, White matter in learning, cognition and psychiatric disorders. *Trends in Neurosciences* **31**, 361–370 (2008).
11. C. S. Dweck, *Mindset: The New Psychology of Success* (Random House, New York, NY, 2006).
12. L. Donati, in *Learning and the Brain* (Institute for Connecting Neuroscience with Teaching and Learning, Neural Education 2.1, 2020), p. 24.
13. Teachers in Action, in *Singularity Event in Schools*, T. K. O'Mahony, Ed. (Institute for Connecting Neuroscience with Teaching and Learning, Seattle, WA, 2020), pp. 1–3.
14. M. Richey, T. K. O'Mahony, M. Prince, F. Zender, B. MacPherson, Revert to default - Insights on transfer of expertise in a complex competitive workplace, paper presented at the American Society of Engineering Education, Seattle, WA, June 17, 2015.
15. D. Lortie, *Schoolteacher* (University of Chicago Press, Chicago, 1975).
16. R. Plomin, *Blueprint: How DNA Makes Us Who We Are* (Random House, London, UK, 2018).

11

10/10 Would Recommend

Using Choice to Transition from Co-Regulation to Self-Regulation

By Gunner Argo

Introduction

Amelia was fairly vocal about her general distaste for English. She was a junior and told me on several occasions that she never liked her English classes and never did well in them.

"That's ok. I get it." I told her.

She wasn't trying to antagonize me; she was simply being honest and I appreciated that. In fact, I enjoyed having her in my class because she had very definite opinions and was one of the few students who would actively engage in our discussions.

We started the school year with a unit on narrative writing. The reason I chose narrative writing as my first unit was because it gave me a chance to learn about my students. The basic structure of the unit was to give them a prompt and then just let them write a draft. We would then move on to another draft with another prompt. I gave them several different options to choose from and introduced different writing techniques as they moved from one draft to another. The prompts were structured around different themes such as "a person of impact" or "a defining moment". My hope was that if a student struggled to come up with an idea for one draft, they might find inspiration in another.

At the end of the unit, students would choose from several different drafts to formalize and submit as a formal assessment.

Amelia's first draft was about losing her horse. The area where I teach has a strong equestrian program and Amelia had spent years training and working with her horse only to lose it to illness. She was devastated and wrote extensively about it for her first draft. When it was time to write the second draft on a new topic, Amelia struggled to come up with something new to write about. After several days, I asked her how she was doing and she told me that she was struggling with coming up with something to write about. She was obviously frustrated.

"Can I just keep writing about my horse?"

"Yeah, why not?"

"Really?"

She was surprised that I had so easily relented. I explained to her that the point of the unit was to practice narrative writing skills, and the topic of the writing was ultimately up to her.

She didn't write the next two drafts; she continued to write about her horse. She didn't turn in her formal draft on time; it took her almost another month to finally turn it in. But she did turn it in. She didn't complain about writing an essay; she turned it in when she felt like she was done writing her story. More importantly, she was happy with what she turned in even though she didn't like writing in general.

What is executive function?

Executive function is an umbrella term that is often used to describe a wide variety of neurological processes including things such as planning, self-monitoring, impulse control, time management, organization, task initiation, and attention. In reality, these are some of the diverse and complex neurological processes and sub-processes needed to achieve a desired goal or outcome. Executive function is often pointed to as the ability to get on track and stay on track until something is completed.

The development of executive function skills is usually associated with the development of the prefrontal cortex (PFC) or frontal lobe of the brain. As the brain matures and develops throughout our lives, the PFC continues to develop after adolescence (1) and into adulthood. The processes associated with executive function, such as organization and focus, are much more limited during adolescence than they are later in development. An adult's brain is better equipped for self-management than a child's or teenager's brain.

While it is commonly accepted that the development of the PFC is integral to increases in executive function, it is important to remember that skills such as organization or task initiation are incredibly complex and are the result of activity in several areas in the brain (2). It is not a simple causal relationship of one area of the brain firing to complete one task. Simply waiting for an area of the brain to "come online" does not guarantee that these skills will suddenly become available for use. We don't just wake up one morning with the ability to organize our schedule and stop procrastinating.

All regions of the brain don't necessarily mature in synch with each other nor at the same time.

The brain develops very rapidly in the first 3–5 years of life, and all the structure and building blocks are present by age 9. The different centers of the brain develop and become functionally connected over time. The last part to mature is the prefrontal lobe. This happens during adolescence (3, 4).

The general principles of biological growth and maturation are common in typical development, but it does not happen on a specified schedule and is different for each individual. It is not just a matter of waiting for an area of the brain to fully develop, but it is also practice and learning that can contribute to increases in executive functions. We might gain better tools, but we also need to practice using them to increase proficiency (5).

The human brain is an adaptation machine. It is constantly changing with respect to both internal and external stimuli (6). Basically, adaptation occurs not just when we are subject to an action or event, but also when we reflect or think about that action or event. The myriad of skills that make up an executive function are no different. They can be taught, they can be practiced, and they can be improved, even while the PFC is still developing (7).

Executive function is the base for all learning and development. The basic principles of learning require these skills. The more a student can focus, the more they will learn. The better they are at managing their time, the more they will learn. The sooner they complete a task and can move on to the next one, the more they will learn. In no uncertain terms, increases in executive function improve academic performance (7, 8).

Changing Course

Amelia did not turn into a model student overnight. By the end of the year, she still turned in her work late and most of the work that she turned in was on par with most other students. She passed the class with a C. But she never once told me she didn't know what to write about or refused to do an assignment. She liked it when I was willing to co-create the learning space with her input (9). She did ask me several times, "is it ok if I do this instead?"

"Sure."

And then she would get to work. Sometimes she asked if she could do something differently than the way I had described. Or she asked if she could choose a different topic, or work on something else. I very rarely told her no, and if I did, I explained why and she generally accepted my rationale and continued. It was the first English class that she said she liked. She told me that my class was "10/10. Would recommend."

One of the last projects we did in the class was a multimedia informational article. Students could choose their own topic and their own format. The primary goal was to share information about a topic that consisted of one primary subject and five secondary components of the main topic. For most students, this meant a one or two pages document with a few pictures broken up into five sections consisting of a paragraph each. Once again, Amelia's project came in late. But what she turned in was beautiful.

Amelia created a website with multiple pages of material and information. She included pictures and videos, it was well organized, and the layout looked amazing, from the color choices to the fonts and placement of materials. It was one of the best projects that I have seen from a student for that particular assignment. What was her topic? Horses.

When given the option over her topic, the freedom to create something without restrictions, and yes, a little extra time, the student who admittedly hated English class turned in one of the best English products I have seen as a teacher. More importantly, she was proud of what she did.

There were two primary reasons why she enjoyed my class. The first was the realization that she had a choice over her work in the class (10). The second was that she felt safe because I generally accepted her choices and let her make her own decisions (11).

Development and Scaffolding

Before I got my own classroom, I spent some time as a substitute teacher. While I tried to take jobs at the high school level, I occasionally subbed for an elementary school. One of the most noticeable differences between working with young children and older adolescents was the speed at which things occurred and the routine nature that was often implemented in elementary classrooms. Lesson plans were often broken down into 5–15-minute intervals. Sometimes shorter, accounting for nearly every minute of the day from the first bell to the last.

There was a routine for getting students from the door to their desks. Where to put their materials and how to organize them. Where to sit for different activities, how to line up for recess, how to form a line and walk to the library. Each activity was a practice in co-regulation. The students did not have to plan where to go or what to do when they got there. They did not have to decide who they should sit next to or weigh out the risks and rewards of which task they should work on first. The cognitive weight of deciding, of planning and organizing, and of managing workloads was facilitated by the routines established by the teacher leaving more time and cognitive effort to focus on whatever it was they were doing in class.

At the high school level, I often got sub plans that were a few short sentences or vague at best.

"Have students read this chapter and discuss it in groups."

"Have students complete worksheet 5A and then read the next section."

"Students are taking a test, and then working quietly on homework once they are completed."

Inevitably, without more specific instructions, without structured routines, and left to their own devices, I would be bombarded with questions.

"Can I switch seats with this person?"

"Do I need to write it in full sentences, or are bullet points ok?"

"What do I do when I'm finished?"

Often my response would be, "figure it out."

Or, in slightly different terms, "regulate yourselves so I don't have to."

Developmentally, at a young age, providing students with extensive co-regulation structures is appropriate. As they develop neurologically and practice those skills, the scaffolded supports should be removed, allowing students to transition to self-regulation. The difficult part is knowing exactly when and how to take off the training wheels and let them pedal on their own. Like watching a child fall over the first time riding a bike, it's a little scary for everyone involved.

Transitioning from Co-Regulation to Self-Regulation

There is a noticeable gap between co-regulation to self-regulation and this becomes dangerously apparent as high school students transition to college or post-high school careers. We've often heard stories about students who were highly successful at the high school level but struggled at a college or university. Without a parent to wake them up in the morning, a vice-principal monitoring the halls to make sure students are in class, or a daily schedule dictated by bells, it becomes more difficult for students to simply go to class and do the work.

This became abundantly clear in 2020 when most schools across the country transitioned into online learning institutions due to shutdowns amidst the initial spread of COVID-19. Students struggled to keep up with schoolwork, but it wasn't because they didn't know how to do the work. It was because they didn't know how to manage a new method of access and delivery. Educators drastically overestimated their students' level of self-regulation and underestimated the impact of the co-regulation practices that facilitated productivity in the classroom. Specific class periods for each class, bells, and designated locations for each class are all co-regulation practices that decrease the cognitive demand on students.

During the pandemic, students now had to decide when to get up, when to work on each class, which room of the house to join their online meetings from, when to eat lunch, and when to do their "homework". Each of these decisions seems simple enough to an adult, but to an adolescent or young child, this takes a level of decision-making, problem-solving, self-control, and personal motivation that they simply were not prepared for. They no longer had someone to tell them exactly what to do, how to do it, where to do it, and when to do it.

In order for a student to learn the skills of self-regulation, they need to practice those skills. The brain adapts to changes in stimuli, environment, and actions. Whatever it does, it becomes better at. If it always looks to an authority for guidance, it will get better at looking to an authority for guidance. If it practices relying on the bell to tell it when to start or stop, it will get better at relying on the bell when to tell it to start or stop. If it waits for a teacher to tell it what it needs to learn, it will get better at waiting for a teacher to tell it what it needs to learn. This is the basic principle of neuroplasticity, that the brain changes chemically, structurally, and functionally (12) to adapt to outside stimuli to become better at whatever it repeatedly does.

As teachers, we need to learn to help students transition from co-regulation to self-regulation. It should be a pathway, not a crutch. It can be very easy to use co-regulation as a short-term fix to improve classroom management, but it is not always something that students can take with them. Like taking off the training wheels for the first time, it can be difficult and messy when we allow our students to take on more responsibility in self-management, but without providing them the space to practice these skills, they may miss necessary development and growth opportunities.

Providing Opportunities to Practice

It is not an easy process for the teacher or the students. On one side, teachers have to let go of some of the control in their classroom, and this often feels like chaos. And it absolutely is. I would imagine it is what the first few billion years after the Big Bang felt like. A lot of unorganized material just vibrating around with no clear structure and nothing really getting done. But slowly, and it does seem like millennia, the first inkling of organization appears.

So, start with something small. I try to promote this development of self-regulation by asking students to create their own timelines for assignments and projects.

"How long do you think this will take?" "How many class periods will it take you to create a quality product?" Some will finish it in five minutes and some won't even start for five days. This is why I employ frequent check-ins and reminders. But simply by asking them to tell you how long they think it will take, they are practicing more self-regulation than being told what day it is due. It is then cemented when you actually honor that choice.

When a brain begins choosing and deciding for itself, it gets better at choosing and deciding for itself. When a student practices making decisions, creating plans, and developing timelines, they get better at those executive function skills. But it isn't always easy.

Providing too much choice, or choices that don't feel safe, can place students in a state of amygdala hijack (13). For some students, just deciding on a topic for an argumentative essay seems overwhelming. You may need to provide a box first. For example, "choose one of these three choices."

A teacher may tell them that they have a choice, but not value the choices that they make if they do not fall in line with preconceived notions about what a student should do specifically. When given the opportunity between practicing their own autonomy or safely folding into known routines, most teenagers will choose safety first, and that means giving the teacher what they expect to receive in return for the expected grade.

For example, if I gave my students a choice about what topic to write about for an analysis essay, most would stick with the safest options possible because that is what will get them the grade they are looking for.

If a student wants to write an analysis of a book by creating a soundtrack for that book if it were made into a movie and then explain why those songs would be particularly fitting for specific scenes, it is my responsibility to find the analytical value in that choice. If I were to simply say "no" or grade them down because it did not fit my preconceived ideas about what an analysis is, then there is a lack of safety for them to make more choices in the future. They will not depend on their own ability to problem-solve and self-regulate, but will defer to a co-regulation model where they will choose the option which is the safest possible choice.

From my own experience, I had to ask myself what was the biggest danger of letting students come up with their own topics, develop their own timelines, or try something new. One of the things that I was most afraid of was that they would abuse it. They would take advantage of the freedom and that they would be off-task, they wouldn't actually do the work. And for the most part, that is exactly what happened. I just had to realize that a student abusing their freedom looks very similar to a student practicing making choices. My job became helping them understand that is actually what they were doing, practicing. They were practicing self-regulation, and it was something that they could get better at. But if I immediately pulled back that opportunity, they would fall back into relying on co-regulation.

It was a painful experience for all of us, but growing up usually is.

From Practice to Application

Amelia's transition from co-regulation to self-regulation was challenging and developed over the course of an entire year. At the end of each semester, I give a reflection survey to my students. Among some of the questions that I asked, here is what she had to say in response:

- **What is one memorable thing you will take away from your time in this class?**
  It is ok to mess up on things and it is not always 100% because there are usually second chances and if you try your hardest, that's what matters. I can't think of much academically but I took away a lot from you specifically.
- **If you could sum up the one thing you learned from Mr. Argo in a single sentence, it would be:**
  I have tried to listen to the little things you say because I can read into those things and usually get lots from them. I learned that you are a pretty carefree guy but I know for a fact you have a soft spot and if we don't piss you off or frustrate you, then you seem to enjoy us in class, but more specifically as a person for sure. I have always tried to show my true colors to you and can easily talk to you and I can tell you enjoy me as a student, not to toot my own horn. Respect I feel like is also a big thing for you.

Amelia did well because she realized that I was giving her a choice. She learned that it was ok to make the wrong choice because she felt safe trying and failing. The informational product that she created took her a long time to complete and didn't fit the due date that I had planned in my own mind. But it also took task initiation skills, extensive planning, attention to detail, focus, organization, and a myriad of other executive function skills. Skills that she improved through practice over time.

Those are the skills I want her to have available once she graduates.

References

1. E. Sowell, P. Thompson, K. Tessner, A. Toga, Mapping continued brain growth and gray matter density reduction in dorsal frontal cortex: Inverse relationships during postadolescent brain maturation. *Journal of Neuroscience* **21**, 8819–8829 (2001).
2. R. Poldrack, Can cognitive processes be inferred from neuroimaging data? *Trends in Cognitive Science* **10**, 59–63 (2006).
3. A. Gopnik, A. Meltzoff, P. Kuhl, *The Scientist in the Crib: Minds, Brains and How Children Learn* (William Morrow, New York, 1999).
4. J. Medina, *Brain Rules: 12 Principles for Surviving and Thriving at Work, Home and School* (Pear Press, San Francisco, 2008).
5. C. Wendelken, E. Ferrer, S. Ghetti, S. Bailey, L. Cutting, L, S. Bunge, Frontoparietal structural connectivity in childhood predicts development of functional connectivity and reasoning ability: a large-scale longitudinal investigation. *Journal of Neuroscience*, 37(35): 8549–8558. https://www.sciencedaily.com/releases/2017/08/170807082201.htm, 2017).
6. N. Doidge, *The Brain That Changes Itself* (Penguin, London UK, 2007).
7. S. Espinet, J. Anderson, P. Zelazo, Reflection training improves executive function in preschool-age children: Behavioral and neural effects. *Developmental Cognitive Neuroscience* **4**, 3–15 (2013).
8. P. Zelazo *et al.*, The development of executive function in early childhood. *Monograph Social Research Child Development* **68**, vii-137 (2003).
9. K. O'Mahony, *The Brain-Based Classroom Practical Guide; Regulate Relate Reason* (Brain-Based Solutions, Seattle WA, 2023).
10. D. Pink, *Drive* (Riverhead Books, New York, NY, 2009).
11. L. Darling-Hammond, Building a Belonging Classroom. Edutopia: Classroom Management. https://www.edutopia.org/video/building-belonging-classroom/, 2019.
12. H. Johansen-Berg, E. Duzel, Neuroplasticity: Effects of physical and cognitive activity on brain structure and function. *Neuroimage* **131**, 1–3 (2016).
13. J. Willis, Three brain-based teaching strategies to build executive function in students. Brain Based Learning. https://www.edutopia.org/blog/brain-based-teaching-strategies-judy-willis, 2011.

12

The Dope Dealer

By Jeannine Medvedich

Introduction

My name is Jeannine Medvedich. I've been in education for over 25 years. Throughout those years, I've worn a number of hats. I've served as a teacher, a Special Services Director overseeing all programs but specializing in behavior, an elementary and secondary Building Administrator, a Director of Instructional Leadership, and as the Executive Director at Chief Leschi Schools. Currently, I am the Chief Academic Officer at Chief Leschi Schools (CLS) (see Figure 12.1).

I worked at Leschi in 2015 prior to returning in 2019. I was introduced to Neural Education while at Leschi in 2015 by Dr. O'Mahony and Missy Widmann, EdD. When I was introduced to Neural Education, it struck something inside of me. The training validated many of my hunches and intuitions that I had over the years. All of a sudden, my eyes were open to the fact that many of my successes were rooted in Neural Education and I didn't even know it. I now realize that I have brought Neural Education to a number of schools. In each of those schools, I was able to see miraculous transformations occur.

In 2019–2020, a new superintendent was appointed to CLS. Prior to his arrival, he reached out and asked me to return. He wanted to continue the great work that we had previously started when we were both at Leschi

FIGURE 12.1 CLS Two Worlds

serving in different roles in 2016. When we returned in 2019, the first thing he asked me to do was to take over all professional development. I started with Neural Education. Since teaching Neural Education to the CLS teachers, we have achieved amazing results. Our successes are hallmarked by nationally recognized accolades and featured in numerous news articles, magazines, and research publications (1, 2).

Being at CLS and utilizing a neural lens offers valuable perspective, as Leschi serves predominantly Native American youth, preschool through twelfth grade. Indigenous youth are underserved and the statistical outcomes speak for themselves. Unfortunately, indigenous youth have some of the lowest graduation rates in the country. For example, Washington state's graduation rate for indigenous kids was recorded as 67.8% in the 2020–2021 school year (3). Tragically, it is pretty much a coin flip whether a kid who is Native American is going to graduate high school. Horrifically, districts are not held accountable for this population, or any other underserved population, if their enrollment is less than or equal to 15%. This is incredibly problematic.

While these statistics are disheartening, I feel excited about the success we have had at CLS. In the 2022–2023 school year, CLS received two national Bright Spot recognitions from the Bureau of Indian Education (BIE). One was for our astronomically high graduation rate and the other was for our literacy program. In addition, Imagine Learning named us a Beacon School during the pandemic for our exemplary usage of Imagine Learning's digital programs. After the pandemic, the U.S. Department of Education named us a Green Ribbon School for implementing cost-saving, health-promoting, and performance enhancing sustainability practices (4).

The year before I arrived at CLS, the high school graduation rate was 53%. Now, in 2024, the graduation rate is 100%. Achieving a 100% graduation rate happened over a four-year period. During our first school year in 2019–2020, despite the last three months of learning taking place online, we raised the graduation rate to 75%. After having a fully virtual school year, our 2020–2021 graduation rate was 92%. We maintained that during the 2021–2022 school year. Cohort data from 2022–2023 will show about a 95.6% graduation rate. This is because one of our kiddos started the year so credit deficient that he decided he wanted to reclassify as a Junior. He will graduate in 2024, making the 2023–2024 school year a 100% graduation rate.

We really pride ourselves in making sure we have the infrastructure to support each one of our students. We go out and relentlessly pursue each and every kid and help them cross the finish line. What is most remarkable is that these gains happened during the global pandemic. In 2023 BethAnn Berliner, a senior researcher/project director from WestEd, interviewed me. During the interview, she shared that while she was researching schools across the nation, we happened to be one of the few schools that achieved growth during the pandemic, while other schools endured massive regressions.

Our literacy Bright Spot was achieved by having an engaging program where students could see themselves and their culture within the curriculum and instruction. Because of our great success, the Bureau has been our champion by providing us with vital funding to continue this great work. Moreover, we get calls from all over the nation asking how we support literacy in our schools. Literacy is so important because it is the gateway to everything else. It is necessary to have at least a sixth grade reading level to engage with the literature and reading materials of everyday life, as well as to maintain a successful professional career. So when I arrived, I ensured that we focused on literacy.

In the middle of the pandemic, Imagine Learning named us a Beacon School for our innovative use of their digital programs. In doing so, we

FIGURE 12.2 Tighten the Gap for Learners

displayed innovative and outside the box thinking to promote kid's acceleration in school during turbulent and unprecedented times. I specifically like to shift away from the term remediation and instead use acceleration. I do this because if you remediate a kid by taking them back to square one, they are never going to catch up. Acceleration happens when the steps to close the achievement gap are tightened (see Figure 12.2).

It is necessary to tighten those stepping stones to make sure kids can cross the finish line. One of the creative ways we utilized Imagine Learning's digital learning tools was by having teachers use the data that were generated behind the scenes of the program. This helped teachers see what skills their students were missing. Then, teachers paired the missing skills with an appropriate program to meet each student's individual needs within direct instruction. We also worked with families to show the value of how the program could accelerate each and every kid's learning trajectory.

On August 9, 2023, the U.S. Department of Education named us a Green Ribbon School. We received the award in Washington D.C. at a televised event. It was really exciting. We achieved this as part of our science curriculum as well as our career and technical education pathways. Our curriculum is engaging and phenomena based, meaning that it allows kids to experience science through actual phenomena. It lends career and technical education opportunities that help students become career and college ready within the sciences.

My interpretation of Neural Education is that it teaches educators to make sure students can see themselves in their education so they find a place to fit and belong. Our pathways do exactly that. Each pathway is linked to a tribal entity, meaning that we train kids to do jobs within their communities. In doing so, kids can envision themselves going into various professions. This creates more meaning in their education and makes kids more likely to engage in their learning. It is neurobiologically impossible to learn without some intrinsic investment, meaning they need to care about what they are doing. Our five career pathways encourage students to intrinsically invest in their education, their lives, and their futures.

One of our pathways is environmental science. Our environmental pathway is built on Next Generation Science Standard (NGSS) storylines. One teacher used her neural lens to make this phenomena-based experience possible. She did this by turning an on-site wetlands area, which was virtually unusable, into an outdoor classroom. Throughout this process, everyone at Leschi took risks. We wrote grants and ended up creating an on-site salmon hatchery, which resulted in something that students are extremely excited about. Students are now able to take the fish they grow from our hatchery and release them into Lake Leschi where they can reach the Puget Sound and continue their journey. This was all about taking what we had in front of us and looking at it in a new light. It was about dreaming and asking ourselves, "what would get the kids excited?" The best part is that this is possible at every school when educators use a neural lens. It is about working with what you have and exploring the potential of what is in front of you.

These awards are the culmination of years of work at CLS. I feel enthusiastic because if we can achieve this success at CLS district, with a population of students that have the lowest graduation rates in the country, I believe we can change the face of education in the United States. Additionally, the attention we've received is a big learning for me. I realize that putting on a neural lens no matter what role a person has within an organization is what allows kids to be successful. Whether you're a district administrator, a para-educator, work in facilities, transportation, or in the cafeteria, the kids are impacted by you. Everyone needs to know their value and everyone needs to be putting on their neural lenses every single day. We too often do the "ists" – racist, sexist, classist, ableist – and that is something that holds everyone back. When someone doesn't see the value in another, or thinks they are more important than another within an organization, we have done a huge disservice to our kids and ultimately can't serve them how we are supposed to. I truly believe CLS's awards and successes were achieved because so many of our Leschi teachers, administrators, and staff use a neural lens. It is important to remember that the focus does not need to be on content, rather it should be on the child. We don't start with children; we start with the teachers and support staff to serve the school and the systems. It is only when you start with the teachers and staff that we can show up in service of the "why", and "the why" is our children (5).

When we use a neural lens, it allows us to see through our student's eyes so we can find ways to ignite their excitement about learning. To do this, we make sure children can see themselves in their education by making it relevant to their individual lives. We also make sure children are neurobiologically supported in their learning process and environment. This is achieved by creating situations that allow children to generate supportive neurotransmitters, neuropeptides, and hormones in their brains, including serotonin, dopamine, and oxytocin. Without supportive brain chemistry, students are unable to access their prefrontal cortex or executive functioning, making learning virtually impossible (6).

I believe creating a space that enables learning-supportive brain chemistry is one of the most critical jobs I have as an educator. So much so that I bought a t-shirt with a brain on it that says "Dopamine Dealer" (see Figure 12.3).

FIGURE 12.3 Dopamine Dealer T-Shirt

I realized that I needed to learn how to "deal dope" in the form of connection, sense of belonging, and accomplishment to help our children generate the brain chemistry they need to have success in school. Far too often in meetings, I hear education staff say that kids need to see a doctor for prescription medications to help with their behavior. Teachers talk about how kids need medications like Ritalin to increase dopamine, which helps them focus. It makes me feel sick! Have you ever seen the pamphlets that come with these prescription medications? The pamphlets show molecular structures that are supposed to enhance brain chemistry, but, as educators, we have the ability to help the kids naturally generate learning-supportive brain chemistry (see Figure 12.4). As educators, we know medication clearly can't be our first line of defense – we can't prescribe them! While medical providers work with their patients and know what they need, we as educators need to work with our students to know what they need to succeed academically. We can't take our students to the doctor and we can't ensure our students have the insurance coverage they need to do so. But what we can do is work our neural magic. We have the ability to get what we want from students not from medication, *per se*, but by continuously exposing them to situations where they generate serotonin, dopamine, and oxytocin naturally so they eventually begin to figure out how to do it themselves.

As an educator, the trick is learning how to deal dope. By using my neural frame of mind, I figured out how to be the dope dealer!

You're probably wondering, what does dealing dope to increase serotonin, dopamine, and oxytocin look like in a school? Well, one of my tactics is having kids make their teachers coffee. One of the children I did this with was Lena.[1] Lena was in second grade. She was in massive trauma.

The picture in Figure 12.5 shows her little feet poking out, while she hides under the table. Lena was in an incredibly abusive situation at home which affected her brain chemistry on all kinds of levels. Her little brain was in complete shut down. She was in persistent amygdala hijack and was totally unable to access her prefrontal cortex. So, I decided I would be her dope

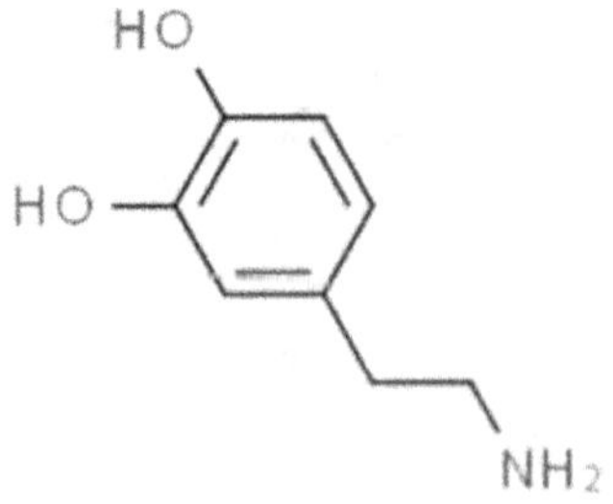

FIGURE 12.4 Dopamine Molecular Structure

FIGURE 12.5 Lena under Table

dealer. In doing so, I helped her release learning supportive neurochemistry and I did it through coffee.

I went to her teacher who was willing to work with me because she needed help. I asked her what I ask all my teachers once I had my neural lens in place.

I asked, "Do you want long-term change or a pound of flesh?"

No teacher is going to say they want a pound of flesh because I believe teachers are good people. But it is really hard because you have this little person, this tiny human, with really sharp teeth who might have just bit you, and opting for long-term behavior change is not reflective of the tiny ounce of disdain we as educators likely feel. I know I do. When enacting long-term behavior change, teachers have asked me, "Is this a reward?" I say, no! This is not a reward. I am releasing dopamine, serotonin, and oxytocin. I am literally drugging your child with the same chemicals that are the by-products of Ritalin. In doing so, the child can focus. It gives the kid access to their prefrontal cortex, opens up their executive functioning, and gives them everything they need to leverage learning because they are here to learn and they can't do that without the proper brain chemistry. So, I am going to dope them up!

When I approached Lena, I mirrored her by lying on the floor. I matched her positioning. When you mirror a child, it creates a sense of belonging and safety. It helps you sync with the child (7). When you sync with a child, your brain chemistry begins to match one another. I create oxytocin; she creates oxytocin. I release dopamine; she releases dopamine. Finally, when she was looking at me and I was looking at her, I put my hand out to her.

Together, we walked to my office and I told her we were going to make coffee for her teacher. I told her how much her teacher was going to love it and that her teacher cared about her, and wouldn't it be nice to take care of her teacher? Of course, she wants to take care of her teacher, as her teacher takes care of her. Caring for each other is an easy way to create oxytocin in the brain. The cool thing about oxytocin is that you can't refuse it. Kids can refuse serotonin and dopamine. For example, if you tell a kid you're going to tickle them and they fold their hands over themselves and turn away, they've refused the serotonin and dopamine. But they can't deny oxytocin. It is an implicit contagion.

I taught Lena how to make coffee and I talked to her. She was in complete control and was using motor control skills to make the coffee. She followed the rules and directions and put the coffee together just as her teacher liked it. Not how she wanted to put it together, but according to her teacher's wants. As she did this, she shared her feelings with me, her wants, and her dreams, and I continued to mirror her. When we got back to her classroom with the coffee, her teacher's face lit up! Sneaky me! I just created a situation where the teacher released oxytocin in her brain. Because oxytocin is contagious, Lena's brain released oxytocin too. This synchronized release of oxytocin helped Lena and her teacher establish a mutual sense of trust and safety, everything you need to be successful in a classroom.

A kid with big behaviors can be exhausting to us educators. So much so that there are times that we, with shame, breathe a sigh of relief because our day may be a little easier without them there. However, when a child who elicits this reaction brings their teacher a cup of coffee day after day, the teacher gets repeated hits of oxytocin. Day after day they come to my room and we make their teacher a cup of coffee. I knew repeatedly making coffee for teachers worked when I did this with a child named Amari (see Figure 12.6).

One day, Amari's teacher, Mrs. Hetlzer, called me up and said, "Amari isn't here, and I don't have any coffee! What am I going to do?" I said to her, "I don't know what you're going to do! Coffee comes with Amari!"

Amari was a kid I considered a "high roller" (see Figure 12.7). A high roller is a kiddo who makes it almost impossible for the teacher to teach and the kids to learn. This kid would run, run, run. We couldn't catch him. He made me lose many pounds and feel very frightened for his safety.

FIGURE 12.6 Amari Coffee Maker

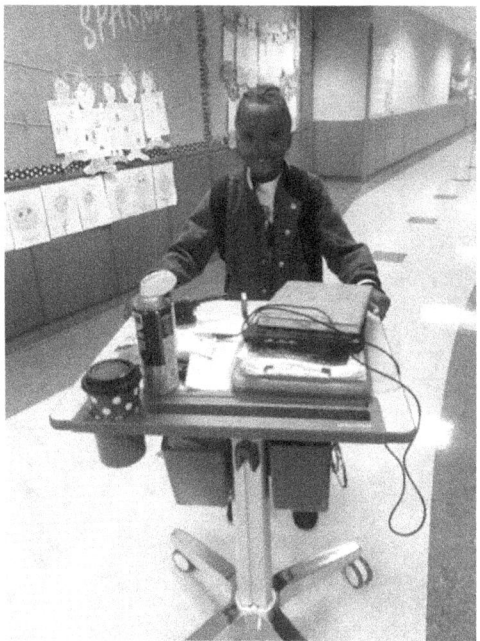

FIGURE 12.7 Amari Coffee Cart

So I made coffee with him, but because he was a high roller, I figured out that he needed to be dosed multiple times a day. His serotonin, dopamine, and oxytocin would wear off in the afternoon. So, I brought him to my office every afternoon to spin the brain-breaks wheel (see Figure 12.8). The brain-breaks wheel is a wheel he would spin and it would go tick, tick, tick, tick, tick until it randomly landed on a brain-breaks activity.

The tick, tick, tick is actually an anticipatory dopamine release, who knew? Well, apparently the famous American neuroendocrinology researcher and author Robert Sapolsky (8)! Then, we would do the activity for 30 seconds to one minute. This wheel is like crack for the kids. It sufficiently doses them and sustains learning-supportive brain chemistry throughout the day. Imagine that! Before I started to dose him, his teacher felt relieved when he was absent. Now, he was a kid that the teacher missed!

When I made coffee with Riley,[2] a tiny fifth grader who was living in a condemned RV, had been arrested, and was to be considered violent, I realized the power of the walk back to the teacher's classroom. As we walked, I mirrored her patterning while I listened to her talk and unload. As I mirrored

FIGURE 12.8 Amari Spins the Brain-Breaks Wheel

her, we synced. In doing so, I was able to help her get hits of oxytocin, dopamine, and serotonin. One day, when we got to the door of her teacher's classroom, I asked her if she wanted me to go in with her. She said, "No, I'm good! I got this by myself now."

She walked in, handed her teacher her coffee, and went on with her day. I knew at that moment that coffee, connection, mirroring, talking, and walking had stabilized Riley's brain chemistry enough for her to have the confidence to walk into her classroom alone and go about her day. This took repetition, cognitive rehearsal that myelinated new brain structures for lasting connection, and it made all the difference in the world.

I've made coffee with many of my students. In fact, when I worked as a high school special education teacher for kids with "behaviors" as well as academic deficits, I was able to start a coffee bar with them. Our success with the coffee bar made the cover of the South Sound Newspaper. The children felt vindicated with a big color photo.

The feature was called *Coffee, Confidence on the Menu*. The coffee bar was called Cafe O'ly.[3] Operating and managing this coffee bar made huge changes in my students' lives. Kids would come in struggling with basic math and literacy, but by having this experience, they found relevance in math and literacy through marketing and managing an actual coffee bar. This relevance leveraged the academic desire they needed to invest in their own learning.

Prior to working at the coffee bar, these students came in defeated. They did not see themselves as successful in the school community, and by the time I got them, they were pretty beaten down. However, they wanted an opportunity to be successful. I relentlessly encouraged them and "brainwashed"[4] them into believing in themselves. They made mistakes and were hard on themselves, but I was matter of fact. I would say, "you're going to make lots of mistakes, keep on making them, you're made for this." By simply standing near, I was able to support them without ever stepping in. They began to see themselves as leaders and for the first time I saw a beautiful arrogance about them that many kids with special needs rarely get to have in their lives. The popular kids would come to buy their frappuccinos and ask, "how do I get into this class?" My kids, with all their beautiful sass, would say, "You don't have the qualifications."

In the *Coffee, Confidence on the Menu* newspaper article, a student said…

"I kept on getting things wrong, so I thought I wasn't cut out for this. But learning a new job is a confidence builder for me."

(Cafe O'ly Barista, 2019)

Yes, they come in jumpy. Yes, they make lots of mistakes. Let them. Stand by them, reassure them, and let them know how magnificent they are. In my hardest times in life, I've lived by this quote and it is a quote I've shared with all my students…

"Whether you think you can, or you think you can't, you are right".

This is a direct function of the Reticular Activating System (RAS). The RAS is the part of the brain that holds beliefs about the self (9). These beliefs can be positive or negative. We have to be careful about how we approach conversations with kids and families when students are qualifying for IEPs. This is because a lot of times I find my confidence goes down. This happens because we are myelinating unhelpful RAS pathways resulting in children developing negative beliefs about themself. When it comes to special needs, what we need to remember is that a neurotypical kid needs a concept to be taught to them five times, while a neurodiverse kiddo needs to have the concept taught to them 15 times. We have to create access for kids to learn at the rate at which they are designed to learn. Truly, all kids can learn at high levels. That is on us. You, as an educator, have the power to build resilience in students through fostering and reinforcing positive beliefs about themselves in their RAS. When you do this, you architect and myelinate brain pathways that build confidence and help children succeed. Encouraging positive RAS brain pathways is like stringing up festive lights in a kid's brain. Flip on that light switch and let the kiddos shine.

Making coffee with kids continues to prove successful; however, sometimes, making coffee isn't possible. Many brand new students, such as kindergarteners, do not know how to focus. They need to learn how to excrete dopamine and use it to be successful in a classroom. For those who need it, I have invited them to join me outside of their classroom to teach them how to excrete dopamine. People don't realize how simple it is to deal dope! We dope children every day with childhood games. It teaches them focus and helps them learn to tune into adult expectations. For example, I have been known to dose kids with the games *Red Light Green Light* and *Simon Says*. A little one will focus intently on every single word you say when you frame it as a game. The trick is transferring this critical tool to the classroom. It could be as simple as taking a walk and asking them to anticipate your walking pattern with the tiles in your hallways. As we walk, I sync with them. Through syncing, I dose them! This has proven to be a simple way for me to help kids learn to follow directions. They magically stop when I tell them to stop. They tune into me and learn to listen and anticipate teacher needs.

This serves them to be successful, intellectually compliant, and engaged in classroom instruction.

Even with success, I think it is easy to have imposter syndrome. As educators we constantly question ourselves and if we are doing the right thing. I like to examine my successes as thoroughly as I examine my failures. I ask myself, "was it a fluke, was there some other factor that created that success?" I do tend to downplay the impact of the interventions that I put in place. I've done this throughout my educational journey. Then, I had a pivotal moment when the data was able to show me beyond a shadow of a doubt that putting on my neural lens, in fact, works. I was shocked and surprised by the data that I saw. There was no doubt in my mind that the one factor that contributed to the success was my implementation of wearing my neural lenses.

With little Lena and all my Elementary School kiddos, I knew they were finding success, but it wasn't until I concluded the year and looked at the data that I really fully understood the impact. You see, that Elementary school experience was one of the few times in my educational career when I started a year in progress. I arrived in February (halfway through a difficult year) to try to turn around an unusual situation. I stepped in the door and immediately rolled up my sleeves, put on my neural lenses, and got down to work as Assistant Principal. I was in charge of all discipline and behavior. I look at discipline also from the point of view of the brain – through my neural lens, I know that the word discipline derives not from punishment but from disciple. I know that education is not about filling up with content but about leading out a child's innate ability.

Laying on the floor, dancing on the playground, playing games in my office, and carting coffee to teachers truly paid off rich dividends. I inherited a very high rate of disciplinary stresses. Children were not responding well to the approach that the school was taking with these stressors. Very quickly, I saw dividends. Soon after I arrived in February, that ultra-high disciplinary data abruptly stopped rising and soon began a downward trend. It quickly settled to an all-time low and continued that happy trend through the end of the school year.

As shown in Figure 12.9, the moment February rolled around, discipline dramatically dropped from an all-time high to an all-time low. In looking at four years of data, it was clear to me that kids responded (and responded well) to dope.

Not only did kids respond to dope, but also teachers seemed to be responding well to "brainwashing". I "brainwashed" the teachers with a bulletin board that I posted outside the bathroom door. There was only one bathroom with one stall, and it was right next to my office. This meant that

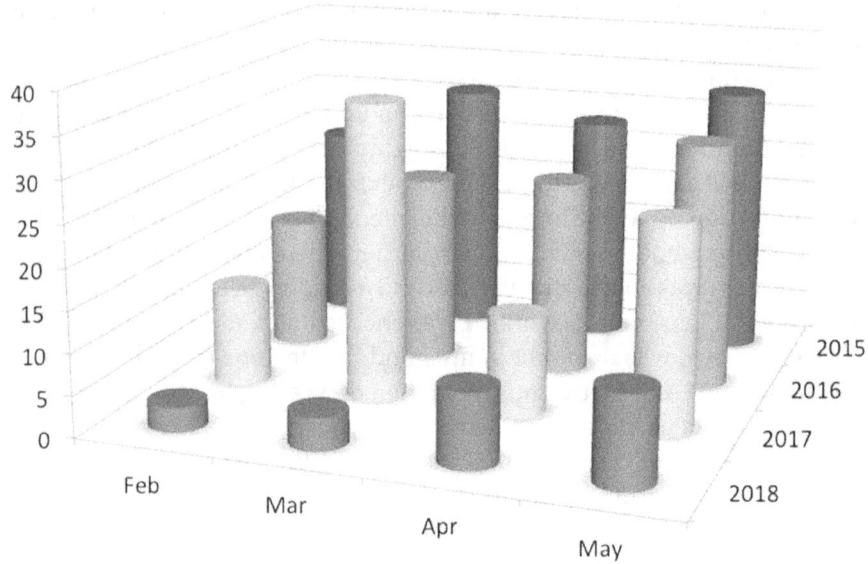

FIGURE 12.9 Elementary A Discipline Graph 2015–2018

while teachers waited in line for the bathroom, they could either talk to me or read the Neural Education quotes and research that I posted on the bulletin board. Miah ha ha! Yes, this was my little evil plan to get teachers to start thinking with a neural lens (see Figure 12.10).

Teachers would pace and dance while they waited for the bathroom. I knew they were engaging with the bulletin board when I heard them chanting, "be the thermostat, not the thermometer" and "I am the thermostat, not the thermometer!" Essentially during those moments, trials and tribulations, I found they were buying into my neural designs. If it seemed that my tactics were a bit unconventional, the research just outside my door seemed to lend me some credibility. After all, standing in line for the bathroom gave them ample time to read it!

Now that I knew Neural Education really worked and the data supported this work, I was ready to expand. The very next year I was able to go to Elementary B, one of the largest schools in the district. At that time, Elementary B had over 951 kids and one Assistant Principal, me! This meant I needed to tie my running shoes tight, roll up my sleeves, and slip on my neural lens. I started by purchasing myself a desk on wheels. Since my office was in the front of the building, I only saw the front door. I really wanted to be able to keep an eye on kids from my office. So, I decided to relocate to the P.E. teacher's office, with her blessing of course. I opened up the window,

FIGURE 12.10 Elementary A Bulletin Board by Bathroom Door

put a speaker in it, and played some music. The playground supervisors frequented my window. They brought me students who were struggling to manage their behavior in this big, open, crowded space. We would talk and plan for success, and the kids would return to play in a successful way. It was like having a McDonald's drive-through; they told me what they needed and I would make it happen. Would you like that super-sized? Then I would collect my pay, which was **NO REFERRALS** for me! Imagine a school with no discipline referrals!

This proved super successful, so I decided to dose the whole school with serotonin, dopamine, and oxytocin every Friday, like *every* Friday. We would go outside and have a giant dance party. Kids would put in their requests, choose the music, and orchestrate the moves. This gave the kids autonomy, mastery, and purpose. The kids felt part of the production. Sometimes I'd look over and there would be a kid climbing the wall. I'd make eye contact, just put my finger up and give the child a motion to get down … and the kid would get down. The recess duties' jaws dropped when this happened, but it was quite simple. Neurotransmitters that we shared, created, and fostered trust and meaningful relationships. I was "dosing" kids and syncing with them. Our office staff and nurse looked forward to Fridays. They would radio me saying, "Make sure you're on time to Friday dance party!" Why? Well, because Friday went from CRAZY office time to "nobody in the office" time. As a result of me syncing the kids, the office staff and nurse had time to finish their busy work in the sweet sound of silence. Not to mention, band-aid purchases went way down.

Because everything was going so well, I decided to take it one step further. When kids struggled with really big behaviors, I put my neural lens on to help them regulate, co-regulate, and sync. The only issue was that they were syncing with me. While that was a good thing, what I really needed was for them to sync with their teachers. Everything we do really is about leveraging academics. If a kid isn't in the class, the child isn't learning with the class.

After spending an entire summer with the staff delving into Neural Education, our teachers were invested. One particular second grade teacher received a kiddo in her class that came with extraordinary trauma. She agreed to step outside of the box, slide on her neural lens, and trust me as we journeyed through new territory together. Because of this kiddo's trauma, he would run at the slightest trigger. Not only did this make it difficult for him to excel at instruction, but it also was a safety issue. So, I asked the teacher to be the first person to sync with this child. I asked her to lie on the floor and mirror his little body, which was crumpled up under the table.

I asked her to slowly put her hand out and connect. Of course, it came naturally to her and to him. They both knew what to do. They were in sync.

Here is the catch. One-on-one like this takes up time and attention. To help her sync with him (instead of me), I stepped in and took her class. I had fun teaching her students, if not nearly as good as she did of course. This gave her the space to go outside with this kiddo to walk, talk, and dribble a ball. It was working. This little one was thriving. Every so often, I peeked into the classroom and snapped a picture to prove that he was working well with his peers. I proudly shared her successes with the staff and we all rallied by her side to help this kiddo continue to thrive. The recess duties took time outside of their responsibilities to sync with him, tossing hula hoops, dribbling balls, walking, and talking. He stopped running *from* the playground, and instead he ran *to* the recess duties.

The day I knew we had succeeded for this child was the day Child Protective Services (CPS) summoned him to the office. This visit triggered a time of great duress for this little one where in the past he would be in a full-fledged fight-flight reaction. The trigger was real and he immediately went into an amygdala hijack. He ran. This time he ran from the office – not to escape the school, but to his classroom and into the arms of his teacher. We had accomplished reverse eloping. He looked up at her and said, "I can do what I need to do as long as I can see you." He then walked into the workroom at the back of his classroom. He stood at the window and watched his teacher as he completed the CPS conference call. He kept his little hand on the window in the back of the classroom for the entire duration of the call. For the first time, a teacher was fully involved in the day-to-day trauma that we usually only see in the office.

It dawned on me that teachers thought kids were running to me because I was somehow rewarding them for their poor behavior. This magical team and I were able to flip that. Everybody saw it wasn't about punishment and rewards; it was about finding a way to manage and cope with the very difficult situations these tiny little ones were enduring. It was also about learning how to productively manage a child's big feelings. This is crucial.

When we solve the child, we solve the class, and when we solve the teacher, we solve the school. Think about it ... when we solve the school, we solve society.

It took some time to make big changes such as having a kid reverse elope, but changes don't have to be big to make an impact. Put on your neural lenses each day and look for something small that you can "neuralize". You might just be surprised at its level of efficacy. One day, I made a big discovery based on some unsolicited feedback. One of the things I do at Leschi every morning is take out my speakers and play happy music for the kids as they arrive at school. The staff and I dance and sing along while we greet and fist-bump the kids. The kids might show up grumpy and traumatized, probably from having to wake up! But this greeting helps them start to generate serotonin, dopamine, and oxytocin.

Last year, a principal told me that discipline was high on Mondays. She suggested I play calming music on Monday mornings instead of the happy, upbeat music I normally play. Interestingly, I wasn't playing music at all on Mondays because, instead of greeting the buses, I needed to be in professional development! I explained this to her and she curtly replied that I needed to find a way to start playing music on Monday mornings so discipline would go down. This was surprising and unsolicited data!

She was right. Sure enough, when I found a way to greet the kids with music on Monday mornings, the discipline data went down. It turned out that when the children had the opportunity to help me choose "good" music, it worked even better. By priming the students with oxytocin, serotonin, and dopamine through their music, Monday changed from being a stressful day to being a fun day – for everybody. All this to say, putting on your neural lens can be as easy as having a laugh at yourself or playing that song that makes your heart sing. If it works for you, your kids will be mirroring your energy. Easy peasy!

I want to finish on a serious note. Parents and educators, we can't afford to fail our kids. Our failure costs them and it costs us. There is ample research evidence (10) that if a kid doesn't graduate from high school, their life span decreases by 10 years. If we fail children in school, we negatively impact their health, wellness, and longevity (11). When teachers fail kids, we become participants in the school to prison pipeline (12). There is this naive idea that kids should just show up to school and do their part. After all, we as "successful" educators do that every single day.

Schools are not built for the kids that need us the most. We as educators have to be the change. We have to be willing to slip on those neural lenses even on those days we feel exhausted. I've always been told to work smarter, not harder, to which I will say, I am working as smart as I can. I would challenge everybody to put in the hard work upfront and give it some time.

- People will roll their eyes.
- People will accuse you of rewarding kids when they should be punished.
- People will accuse you of being a bigger problem than the child's behavior itself.

You will persist because you see an inkling of hope. We all have to stick with it. We have to teach others why you do the things you do. Trust me, it's exhausting ... but one day others will get it. When they do, things will change.

All of a sudden, working smarter by using Neural Education shows up in the data.

- You have fewer discipline referrals.
- You're spending less clerical time entering discipline data into the system.
- You see that kids are finally getting what they need and absolutely deserve.

Yes, you have to put in the time upfront. No, you're not rewarding them. No one would say it is ok to miss a dose of medication. So dose them with your dope! And while it is exhausting to lie on the floor, to cart the coffee, to spin the brain-breaks wheel, and pull out those goofy dance moves and groove (while everyone is watching), it pays rich dividends. And while you're busy doping up the kids, you're going to feel pretty dope yourself.

Notes

1. Lena is not her real name; it is changed to protect her anonymity.
2. Riley is not her real name; it is changed to protect her anonymity.
3. Pronounced "Au Lait", O'ly stood for Olympia High School. Cafe O'ly was word play in the phonological loop!
4. Here "brainwashed" literally means washing their brains. In doing this, the children got a fresh perspective on their own abilities.

References

1. T. Morgan, Chief Leschi Schools: Preparing students to walk successfully in "two worlds". Learn to Return, L2R Spotlight. https://t.ly/sqqRZ, 2021.
2. H. Wickersham, Lessons from a Pro: Jeannine Medvedich. South Sound Business. https://www.southsoundbiz.com/opinion/lessons-from-a-pro-jeannine-medvedich-puyallup/article_2f38060a-cffb-11ed-828a-f7a63be38d62.html, 2023.
3. Education, *Public performance review: Disparities in high school graduation rates & student success* (http://www.results.wa.gov), 2023.
4. *Green Ribbon Schools Announced: Chief Leschi Schools* (2023 https://www.ed.gov/news/press-releases/us-department-education-green-ribbon-schools-announced).

5. S. Sinek, in *Ideas worth spreading: How great leaders inspire action*, TEDx, Ed. (https://www.ted.com/talks/simon_sinek_how_great_leaders_inspire_action, 2009).
6. K. O'Mahony. The science behind sense of belonging and love: Child ANS reactivity and ASD, (Neural Ed Institute, iCNtl, 2019).
7. R. Feuerstein, R. S. Feuerstein, L. H. Falik, *Beyond Smarter: Mediated learning and the brain's capacity for change*. (Teachers College Press, New York, 2010).
8. R. M. Sapolski, *Why Zebras Don't Get Ulcers* (Henry Holt and Company LLC, New York, NY, ed. Third, 2004).
9. L. Donati, in *Learning and the Brain* (Institute for Connecting Neuroscience with Teaching and Learning, Neural Education 2.1, 2020), p. 24.
10. M. Matttos, Timebomb: The Cost of Dropping Out. Solution Tree, https://www.mikemattos.info/videos, 2017.
11. W. Haney, G. Madaus, L. Abrams, J. Miao, I. Gruia, "The education pipeline in the United States 1970-2000" (The National Board on Educational Testing and Public Policy, Boston, 2004).
12. B. Pettit, B. Western, Inequality in lifetime risks of imprisonment, (Yale.edu, 2002) http://www.yale.edu/ccr/western.pdf.

13

If I Only Had a Brain

Mirroring Neurons, Authentic Relationships (Regulate, Relate, Reason)

By Michelle Curry

I Can't Think!

"I wish I was smart … there is nothing in here." Toby was pointing to his head. His pained expression was sufficient to explain his frustration to his friend Mitch.

He proceeded to pound his fist on his head. "See empty. School's stupid, I want to go home and watch YouTube. I'm tired." Toby sputtered, throwing his hands up.

Mitch responded … "Yeah, me too." His head was downturned and he, too, was looking dejected.

Not a year has gone by that I haven't heard something similar from other students. Toby was already down and out and had given up and was taking Mitch down with him. The peers were mirroring each other's feelings and empathizing. I used to think of this as complaining, but I was now viewing things through a neural lens. This was communication.

What Had Just Happened?

For Toby, something in the "Objective" … how it was said, or what was said … caused him to have an Amygdala Hijack. We had just chorally read a **Learning Objective**.

We will practice and learn our short 'a' spelling words in a sentence.

I then told the class. "We are going to be having our spelling test on Friday, and we are going to learn different ways to practice the words in class."

No wonder he experienced an Amygdala Hijack. At least three items in that introduction were enough to shut his brain down. First, Learning Objectives are designed for teachers – most children have no idea what an objective is. Second, the mention of a "test" was enough to trigger negative memories of other tests where anxious fears of "not being good enough" and/or "looking stupid in front of friends" caused the amygdala to freak out and become hyperactivated. Finally, Friday is too far away. If it is not about me, right here, right now I can't engage.

An Amygdala Hijack is observed in a student when they freeze, fawn, flee, or fight (1). Toby was communicating; essentially looking for affirmation from other students around him that he wasn't alone in his thoughts. He couldn't think at the moment as he had come into class with his working memory already full.

I was ready for this mini-crisis because I had thought through my lesson plan with a neural lens for the first time … and I had a plan for what to do next.

I knew from the Brain-Based Classroom Workbook (Mirror with Peer, p. 27) that what was really happening could be that Toby's working memory was full of things that happened before he arrived at my classroom. I wanted to clear those negative spiraling thoughts from his and the other students' working memory. One way to do this was by using mirror neuron techniques (2). "Mirror neurons are sensory motor cells that react when a particular action is performed by someone nearby, or when it is observed by the child who is looking for relatedness. In other words, we mirror other's actions" (3). In this case, Mitch was mirroring his friend Toby, who was mirroring something he may have heard or seen as well.

So What Was the Lesson?

I wanted the children to Mirror me so I could move past the negative Amygdala Hijack. This is one of the techniques I learned from the Brain-Based Classroom Workbook. When Toby had his outburst, it provided the perfect opportunity for me to introduce information about how our working memory can be emptied when it gets filled up. I took a quick look at the "a" spelling words (can cat hat man nap tap). "How perfect," I thought, "I can use 'man' and 'hat' in the context of the scarecrow from The Wizard of Oz."

I called out **"Person"**.

The students had been taught to stand with their hands on their hips like a person to represent our first noun type.

I called out **"Place"**.

We put our hands above our heads to represent a second noun type: a roof.

I called out **"Thing"**.

The children and I pretended to hold a ball and bounce it, our last example of a noun.

Then I had the students put their hands out straight to their side and hang their heads to the side and I asked them "I can't move and if I was wearing a straw hat, what would I be?"

"Scarecrow" was the resounding excitement that came out of their mouths.

I queued up a short clip from The Wizard of Oz where the Scarecrow sang, **"If I only had a brain"**.

I told the kids how I had met him in real life (they always think this is cool). I explained that he told me how he really had his brain all along but he just needed to learn how to use it. Then we revisited the learning objective and read it aloud together:

> How will we practice and learn our short 'a' spelling words in a sentence?

I asked if we could use any of our spelling words to talk about The Wizard of Oz. There was a flurry of ideas. Toby suggested if you put a hat on a man and put him on a stick in a field, you have a **Scarecrow**. The can became the tin can from the **Tin Man**. The cat was the **Lion**. The scarecrow took a **Nap**. When you tap the Tin Man, you get a funny sound. Toby and his classmates' working memory had been freed by the Oz Mirroring activity and I overheard him say "this is fun."

We continued to practice mirroring techniques during the year and worked to develop positive growth mindsets. The day eventually came when I heard Toby say, "I love school, it's fun to learn things." Ah, deep breath.

What I Knew about Social Regulation and How It Causes Working Memory to Be Full

Toby and his classmates were profoundly affected by changes to their education due to COVID. Social distancing meant restricted play. Play is basic ... a foundation of learning and exploring so children can understand their world.

Toby's Kindergarten class experienced "distance learning" at the beginning of the year and then "masked up" for the rest of the year. Everyone had to abide by the 6-foot-apart rule – which meant enforced distance between desks and when walking in the hall. His cohort is that class of COVID social side-effects, with associated large gaps in learning (4).

They have had a whole different set of do's and don'ts than previous classes: do not touch one another, no playing tag, etc. One group can play here this day and the other group can play there another day. Clean after each playtime for the next group, repeat.

Now the masks are off ... the fingers are up the noses and the hands are all over each other. In the aftermath of COVID, floodgates opened and all bets were off. Not only that, but also this band of children did not learn how to play well together because of enforced distance and restraints. They struggle socially, especially with how to be nice to each other. And there are a lot of negative emotions. Any peer-to-peer mirroring opportunities had been restricted and/or masked.

Thus, with no masks and more freedom, I could see some students were worried because they couldn't read, and some who previously hid behind their masks were now mumbling what they didn't know. In addition, they were learning to cope with new norms surrounding social regulation, as students' and teachers' facial expressions were now more complete (4).

What Do You Do First? Regulate Yourself and Then Regulate Together

I thought about regulation and what I had learned from reading Dr. Perry's book (5). My previous practice had been to start the day by saying ... **Showtime!** I used to think that I had to perform like an actress in my classroom to get and keep my students' attention. That has changed. Now, I see it as regulating myself. Then I could go on to regulate with my students so they could learn what regulating meant. Instead of presenting myself to the class, I decided to implement a co-regulation and mirroring posture with this year's class. The idea of showtime changed and was replaced with a metacognitive question. I posed it to myself:

> Are you regulated so your students can reflect your regulation?

Toby had given me the moment I had been waiting for now that I was using a neural lens. I had mixed feelings. In the past and based on my early training, it was a moment I dreaded, filled with worries about how to handle children's negative emotions? "I wish I was smart, there is nothing in here," "School is stupid, I want to go home and watch youtube, I'm tired," "yeah, me too." In the past I would have brushed it off by countering, "You're smart," point out what the child was good at, and move on. *But that wasn't addressing the real problem.*

Co-regulate with Your Students so They Can See It Is Ok to Struggle, to Make mistakes ... I Had a Struggle with Learning to Read

I wanted my students to know that I understood their struggle to read. A typical response I receive is summarized in this voice:

> But you're a teacher, you know everything and never make mistakes.

Ah, the misunderstanding persists. As a child, I had this same vision of my teachers. And here it was again ... still present in my students. To make matters worse, I was responsible for conflating the notion of teachers with perfection. Most of my actions tend to complement the notion that teachers know everything and never make mistakes ... and bolster their misconception and ultimately propagate further the incorrect belief. No matter what kind of day I'm having, I project to the students that I know what I am doing and I am good at doing it. In retrospect, there are days when nothing could be farther from the truth. In turn, my projection to my students is mirrored and projected back to me. We mirror each other.

I told my students a few truths. I don't know everything. I love to learn new things. I especially needed them to know that as a child, I had struggled to read with my dyslexia. I shared with them that I often make mistakes with my backward b's and d's. I asked them to help me when they noticed I had written the wrong letter and that I would help them in return.

Finally, I drew on an **Anchor Chart** – a **BED** with the b being the headboard and the d being the footboard. We drew an arrow line over the e to represent the correct orientation for the belly parts of the b and d. The students and I referred to this throughout the year.

How Do I Take What I Know to Be the Best Teacher I Can?

Introspectively, I thought about all my school experiences and came up with my "toolbox of education". I started school in first grade, not kindergarten. I remember the day that my Teacher Joe sat down on the carpet with me and talked to me and told me that my tests demonstrated I had this new thing called dyslexia.

I attended a large Elementary in a small town in rural Washington. The big red bricked building is burnt into my memory. It was a Montessori school operated by the teaching college at the local University, located in what is now the Honors College building. Being part of the teaching college, we had many guest teachers come in and work with us. I had been told that sometimes the teachers would watch us in person and sometimes from behind mirrors and that there were tape recorders recording the teachers and the students. I was curious as to how this worked and found myself watching the teachers and students. I even made little notes to myself about what I saw, just like the teachers I had been watching. I would sit on this large window box seat to do my work, writing, reading the old blue books, and gazing out the window. I was trying to understand my brain and my dyslexia, and I was learning by mirroring my teachers.

Prior to becoming a teacher, I had spent 6 years as a para educator pre-k to fifth grade. One year as an art teacher (k-3) and another year as a 1:1 special ed para. During that time working in SPED, I had amazing authentic relationships with two students. I worked with a kindergarten boy who was essentially feral, leading us to communicate by whistling and hand motions. Then my yellow brick road led to a classroom where I worked with my son's old classmate's younger sister, a child with Down syndrome who loved to say, "let's run!" Running was her favorite thing to do at recess. Looking back on that experience now, I can see how regulation would occur during running and whistling. The most simple of tasks for many was a true celebration of mastery for these struggling learners. During this time, I had a lot of experience with social and emotional needs among early learners. I was on a pathway to becoming a certified teacher, so I returned to college. I was learning every new thing that I could.

As my thinking shifted, I realized that my pre-planning for entry into my classroom was dated. Recall how I used to begin my day teaching feeling like it was "showtime". I decided to make showtime into co-time. This involved stepping back, taking a deep breath, and aligning my thinking with my new knowledge about the brain.

Instead of pre-planning all the extra activities needed to occupy first graders, I set out to involve them – to find out what they liked. I asked them. I knew that these children have short attention spans and I wanted to build a structure that aligned with capturing and holding that attention. I also knew that I could grow their capacity for attention, but I had to be intentional about that. I'd planned a minute-by-minute schedule to create the structure needed to maintain a first grade classroom. I'd schedule wiggle breaks, appropriate first grade humor, brain breaks, videos, bins, and assorted activity centers. Intentionality and planning provided the students with structures that allowed them to free up their working memory and to be able to access new information.

When metacognition is part of the planning, I found that some students became more metacognizant. It is always gratifying when children begin shifting to that abstract place – able to think about their own thinking. A few were still egocentric and I had to find a way to break through to them. I liked what Principal Hunter (6) had said during a Neural Ed Implementation Workshop[1] with regard to this topic. "You can't have an authentic relationship with someone who you don't like." The words had deep meaning for me when he spoke them, and they were now part of my implementation of Neural Ed in my classroom.

I also remembered a thought expressed by Dr. Kieran O'Mahony, which he shared during a professional development session. "If students do not see themselves reflected in the classroom the teacher has already lost them" (2).

It seems silly. But I was able to use words in order to make the shift from my old classroom approaches to a neural classroom approach. Words reflected new knowledge, and that new knowledge helped me visualize new mental models that included my students. The new mental models were very different from the old models which I was able to walk away from.

I wanted to mirror my students and encourage peer-to-peer mirroring to regulate their social interactions. Mirroring in my classroom can only happen if the student is able to feel an authentic relationship with the teacher. The students must feel that the teacher really cares about their thoughts. Whether the students' thoughts are negative or positive, it is simply my job to listen to what they are trying to communicate and find ways to respond. It was only when I said the words, "This is not **MY** classroom. It is **Our** classroom", that there was room for the children to engage with their physical space. By co-creating the classroom with the students, it became clear that they could see themselves as a part of a room that they had helped create and embraced a collaborative responsibility every day to maintain.

I realized that, ultimately, I was planning things I liked and what I thought students would like, but I wasn't completely sure. The episode that caused some children (especially Toby) to become hijacked was based on my plan of enacting a choral activity to practice spelling words. I made a quick shift to a kinesthetic learning experience.

We ended the lesson with a fun talk about co-creating our classroom and making it our classroom family. I asked everyone to get out of their seats and, as I applied a neural lens to my teaching, shared in co-creating with the children. Although it may sound like a "disaster in the making" to share the keys with a 6- or 7-year-old, it's not. I asked them if they had ideas for those breaks, and boy … did they ever!

Why was I spending my time trying to figure out what this class would be like versus last year's class? All I had to do was take the time to ask … and listen. After our lesson where Toby blurted out his empty brain statement, we made a list of every child's ideas on the whiteboard. I snapped a picture to put the children in the planning phase. We discussed fun brain breaks and brought up the whole notion of safety – appropriate and safe breaks are best – but still can be fun when no one gets hurt or feels excluded (7).

Where Had I Seen or Experienced Mirroring?

Ray Bolger was the actor who portrayed the Scarecrow in the 1939 movie The Wizard of Oz. He had a slapstick dance, he could sing, and he fumbled about in the movie. He was filming a movie in the town I lived in as a child, and I discovered he was sitting behind me in church! My dad asked him if I could get an autograph and we were shuffled to a little room so as to not cause a crowd rush.

He looked down at me and said "Do you want to know why I wanted to be the scarecrow?"

I answered, "yes."

"Well, I wanted to be the first one to greet Dorothy and be her first friend and to enjoy the whole journey down the yellow brick road together." It was so easy to listen to his happy voice.

He told me the director said he had never seen someone so effortlessly look like a scarecrow come to life. Then he winked at me and said "I fumbled like I thought a scarecrow should. That is what I did to get the part," and he added that he really wanted to be the Scarecrow but was originally cast for the Tin Man.

He told me it was actually very hard for him to come up with the motions because the mask he wore and his makeup made it too hot. He told me he usually played the "little guy" in support roles. This was funny to me as a child, as he was pretty tall. I can remember thinking my dad (who was 6'8" and was standing next to him) wasn't much taller.

He laughed when I said "You're not little, you're a big guy!"

He told me his mother had read all of the Wizard of Oz books. I was surprised and exclaimed, "There is more than one?" He said, yes there was, and that I should have my mother read them to me.

Where Did I Learn That Authentic Relationships Are Valuable?

Ray Bolger was once quoted saying, "I was brought up on the books of The Wizard of Oz and my mother told me that these were great philosophies. It was a very simple philosophy, that everybody had a heart, that everybody had a brain, that everybody had courage. These are the gifts that are given to you when you come on this earth, and if you use them properly, you reach the pot of gold at the end of the rainbow. And that pot of gold was a home. And home isn't just a house or an abode, it's people … people who love you and that you love. That's a home" (8).

That quote has always felt similar to what I remember, but my recollection of that day was him telling me about his mom.

"My mother was a beautiful person inside and out and she was all the more a better person because she believed in the moral of the stories of Oz." He raised his right hand and pointer finger up when he asked, "Do you know what that is, a moral?"

"Yes," I said, "a story has a purpose and the moral to the story is the lesson you learn."

He asked, "do you remember me singing 'If I only had a brain'."

"Yes," I answered.

"Well, if you think about it … I've always had my brain all along during the movie but didn't realize till the end." He paused.

I thought about it and then nodded.

Dancing Down the Yellow Brick Road

"So this is the thing I want to tell you." Ray continued, "life is the journey through Oz and you walk it with others. You can learn something new from everyone you meet along the way, just like you learned something new from me today, that there is a whole series of stories about Oz. Now our paths crossed as we traveled on our own individual yellow brick roads," he continued, as he pointed to the brown speckled linoleum floor we were standing on.

"Just like I walked along the yellow brick road with Dorothy. We are connected because we just walked alongside each other on this yellow brick road in life. Also, because I was connected to Dorothy, so are you."

I asked him to show me how he danced and he laughed. "Now follow along with me."

He looked at the tiny room and said we will have to dance facing one another, you will mirror me. Then we danced.

We danced in that tiny room like a silly scarecrow together. When he stopped, he tapped his heels smartly together and pointed to mine.

I tapped in return and … I was on my merry way, a happy little girl who just tapped her red slippers and pretended to be Dorothy with the real Scarecrow.

That scarecrow gave me a framework to hold for life … I was traveling on my own yellow brick road, and it has remained a theme in my life and in my teaching.

My 8-year-old self walked to the car with scarecrow autograph in hand. I had a lot of questions for my mom who I also thought was beautiful inside and out, just like Ray thought his mom. She laughed when I asked "Why wasn't he dressed up like the Scarecrow? Isn't that who he is?"

I wanted her to immediately get all the books and read them with me.

What I learned were lifelong lessons the scarecrow had shared.

- Always show an interest in those that you meet, as you journey alongside them
- Talk with them and you will find you have so much you can learn from one another

My scarecrow asked me an important question that day.

Today, I ask my students the same question, "What do you think we can learn about each other as we travel the yellow brick road together?"

Then he did something more to reinforce my learning with kinesthetic actions. We were more than pretending to tap dance, and journey down the road together.

Walking Down the Yellow Brick Road Today

When I first encountered the Institute for Connecting Neuroscience with Teaching and Learning and Dr. O'Mahony, I saw him as the Wizard behind the curtain. I have long looked at my life through the lens of Oz. His book "The Brain-Based Classroom" and its companion workbook are the brain, the heart, and the courage behind my classroom and my new neural lens. Why is he the Wizard? Because neuroscience provides meaningful tools to understand what is happening in the student's brain. This helps me be a better educator.

I felt like the curtain was pulled back when I could "see" the neural substrates for behavior; I could feel the neural connections associated with attention and focus. Suddenly, learning made sense as a science and not just as an instinct that most teachers share. The human brain became malleable to me.

I felt, for the first time, that I was looking into the eyes of my students through a neural lens, and although I felt I always had a good connection, now I understood how to connect more deeply with them so that together we can learn. This neural gateway helps me find out how I can best help my students learn. I am better at what they are trying to teach me about themselves as we dance together along our roads mirroring one another.

How to Create Peer to Peer Mirroring Opportunities

Students and teachers, once Regulated, are able to Relate ... and from relatedness can access their Reason. These emotion-charged 3Rs refer to a primal journey that takes place inside each learning brain where first the reactive hindbrain is engaged enough to allow a learner access feelings and process relationship emotions in the midbrain limbic region. Finally, a two-way inter-activation between the midbrain and the higher order frontal regions allows the learner to make higher order executive decisions and access functions in the reasoning brain in the frontal lobes. This Regulate, Relate, Reason brain journey (9) from the back lower region to the front upper region is both physical and conscious. The more conscious we are about this structural connection to learning, the more easy it is for the children to be successful and thrive in school.

If not enough breaks are scheduled, children will make their own. How often have I looked out to see an orange crayon rolling across the floor with a bunny, lizard, cat, or whatever the student is imagining they are at that moment as they scramble after the "carrot" on all fours while wrinkling their nose and pouncing after it? After watching that exact scenario play out in my classroom one day with Porter, I had an aha moment. Porter is trying to teach me something. I need the students to have peer-to-peer mirroring opportunities.

I checked with Porter who had taken a break to see if we could let everyone join in and do a similar fun imagination game. Perhaps we could write about it in our journals afterward?

He agreed.

I thanked him for the idea mindful of his shy disposition.

But when it came time for Porter to share the activity, he was confident and bubbly. His peers and I could feel his excitement and enthusiasm. All the children were already excited to try the activity before they journaled. In preparation for the journal activity, I read an elephant story.

It was called "Forget Me Not". In it, the elephant thinks a blue bucket is the flower called a "Forget Me Not". I invited the students to pick their own colored crayon to represent a food or thing and decide on an animal that could be real or made up. Porter leads the class by explaining his imaginative game. He helped children understand what we were going to do and he demonstrated his version of it. The students each got to share what they had created after we journaled the activity. It was a great success. It was a clear example of a **Me Here Now** event where each child was able to generate ideas and contribute to the whole. We all learned so much about one another by seeing their choice of color and their favorite animal as well as the physical activity they chose to embark on. Everyone got to say why they liked the activity before we wrapped up.

Where Did I Finally Understand the Effects of Authentic Relationships and Mirroring Neurons?

Results of using my neural lens happened immediately and lasted a long time. My students helped me to see the effects of authentic relationships and mirroring when I looked through that neural lens. Sometimes, the classroom work spills over into the home in a good way for the children. More often than not it is usually the other spillover that occurs with negative repercussions that follow the children back to school the next day, week, or months.

I got an email from a happy parent. She wrote that while reading to her son, Thad, at bedtime, he looked up at her and said, "I think I will just stay in 1st grade, I like my teacher!"

This made me think of what an authentic relationship looks like from the perspective of the student and how it can have a positive impact. It follows too that when home is good, school can be good for a child. I made a note to connect with parents and guardians as well, and to build relationships around the children with the family where possible.

While bringing my students into the school one morning, I was pretending to pull them along, as if on a rope. We had crossed over the yellow bump we called the yellow brick road when Rose stopped the line with a concerned look on her face. She asked me, "why are you pulling my soul out of me?" She looked genuinely worried. We stopped the line and I told her I wasn't trying to do that and I pretended to push it back into her. I felt like I understood her emotions.

I took a step back and looked at it with my neural lens. Rose and I were connected through mirror neurons, and to her, it touched her very soul.

"Do you really feel connected to me, that I am linked to you?" I asked her slowly and quietly.

She shook her head resoundingly, "yes."

I said apologetically, "I didn't want to take your soul from you, but I think you're feeling that I care and that I want to walk with you side-by-side on the yellow brick road and work with you while you learn."

She smiled. We were side by side in a safe emotional connection. She had a choice and she had a voice. I liked that. I listened and I changed. It wasn't finished, however. Rose's emotional discussion had opened windows of opportunity for other children too.

I always do a "temperature check" with the children in the morning where my students look at the door and point to a feeling on the "feelings pineapple" emoji poster. This simple exercise shows me how they felt each morning. I had the matching plastic pineapple emoji "potato head" in the calm down castle nook to offer students a place to go and a way to deal with emotions.

Emotions are rich. Most of the time students would point to a happy emoji. Sometimes a student would point to a shy feeling. Other times an upsetting morning led to an angry emoji, or how they felt about breakfast or a sibling pestering them might cause them to point to a silly or crazy emoji.

That morning, I got a lot of silly looks and questions for the emojis after Rose and I had talked in the hallway. When everyone was safely in the classroom, we had a good discussion about connections and mirror neurons. We revisited our lessons about the brain, the yellow brick road, and about mirroring positive learning even when we are struggling.

As for Rose, she devoured her knowledge that year.

Oh, how amazing I thought, she was a real bloomer!

Note

1. The non-profit organization Neural Education with headquarters in Seattle, WA, introduced new information regarding implementation of neuroscience constructs with learning sciences methodologies through a series of online implementation workshops that began during COVID and continued thereafter.

References

1. K. O'Mahony, *The Brain-Based Classroom: Accessing Every Child's Potential through Educational Neuroscience* (Routledge, Taylor & Francis Group, London, UK and New York, ed. First, 2021).
2. K. O'Mahony, *The Brain-Based Classroom Practical Guide; Regulate Relate Reason* (Brain-Based Solutions, Seattle, WA, 2023).
3. R. Feuerstein, R. S. Feuerstein, L. H. Falik, *Beyond Smarter: Mediated Learning and the Brain's Capacity for Change* (Teachers College Press, New York, 2010).
4. M. H. Immordino-Yang, K. W. Fischer, in *International Encyclopedia of Education*, V. G. Aukrust, Ed. (Elsevier, Oxford, 2010), pp. 310–316.
5. O. Winfrey, B. Perry, *What Happened to You? Conversations on Trauma, Resilience, and Healing* (Macmillan Publishers, New York, NY, 2021).
6. J. Hunter, K. O'Mahony, Ed. (Brain-Based Solutions, Neural Education Implementation Workshop, 2022).
7. M. Widmann *et al.*, in *Healthy Schools Team*, SAGE, Ed. (Health Department Healthy Schools Grant, Tacoma, WA, 2016), vol. 1.
8. R. Bolger, Goodreads, Ed. (https://www.goodreads.com/quotes/9568890-they-were-great-philosophies-simple-philosophies-that-everybody-had-a, 1960).
9. B. Perry, *The Boy Who Was Raised as a Dog: What Traumatized Children Can Teach Us about Loss, Love and Healing* (Basic Books, New York, NY, 2006).

Index

Note: Page references in *italics* denote figures and with "n" endnotes.

2 X 10 approach 146

ability level 11, 33, 40, 47
Ability Society of Alberta (Ability 4 Good) 93
ableist 178
abuse: abused become the abuser 139; abusive home life 180; physical 133, 138–139; sexual 138
academic performance 1, 167
academics 8, 22, 39, 46–47, 50–54, 190
academic success 48
acceleration over remediation 177
access 153–154, 170; prefrontal cortex 180–181
ACESTooHigh (online news site) 147n1
achievement gap 11, 177
acquired brain injuries 72
adaptation 95, 167
ADHD 113
adolescence 22, 166–167
adult supervision 78
adverse childhood experiences (ACEs) 13, 22, 133, 135, 138, 147n1
advertising 105
aesthetical art 105; *see also* art
affirmations 28
after-school programs 95
agents of change 141
aging 71
alcoholic behavior 133
all Tiers to all students *see* Multi-Tiered Systems of Support (MTSS)
Amari 182, *183*

American Stroke Association 72
amygdala 9, 17, 24, 127–129, 151–152, 154, 161
amygdala hijack 6, 13, 17, 28, 61, 104, 124–126, 133–134, 141–142, 164, 171, 180, 191, 196–197
Anasazi ruins 115
Anchor chart 200
anchors of routines 100
aneurism 72; *see also* acquired brain injuries
anger 102, 122
animated conversations 23
anticipatory dopamine activity 184
anxiety 18, 66, 113, 152, 157
apathetic 87
Apgar score 87
aphasia 71
apneic 87
appetite over aptitude 115, 144, 163
architect brain pathways 186
Aristotelian Lyceum 7
Aristotle 3
Arm weakness 72; *see also* Spot a Stroke F.A.S.T.
art: aesthetical 105; cave 117; fine 104, 114; hominid cave 117; interdisciplinary 12, 102, 110; interpretative 105; making 104–105; novel 105; personal 106; pleasing 105; response 101–105, 107–110; and science 12; therapy 12, 102–103, 106, 110–113, *111–112*, 115; therapists 102–103, 111; useful 102, 105; utilitarian 113

arterial dissection 69; *see also* pediatric stroke
articulative skills 129
artistic skills 111
assessment 22, 166
assimilation 130
assisted living facilities 113
Associated Student Body (ASB) 141
associationism 127
atrophy 71
authentic relationships 203, 206–208; and mirroring neurons 206–208
autism 82
autonomic nervous system (ANS) 6
autonomy 8, 24, 28, 41–47, 83, 102, 125–128, 154, 190; *see also* intrinsic motivation
avoid scolding 96
awareness 20, 59, 72–73, 102; social 103; spatial 115, 127; *see also* conscious brain

baby dino embryo 42; *see also* dinosaur
bad behavior 4
balance 72, 88, 90–91, 95, 97
ball-bouncing activity 23
Band-aid 36; *see also* Mattos' medical model
Band-aid support 36
barricading 128
basic needs 103, 154
Beacon School award 176
beads 38, 40–41
behavior 181–182, 185, 190–191; alcoholic 133; bad 4; classroom 160; disrespectful 140; disruptive 8, 124; -focused punishment model 14; good 4; human 4–5, 116; novel (creative) 116; primitive 77; undesirable 5
behavioral health clinicians 111
Behaviorist Manifesto (Watson) 6
behavior modification 77
belief in oneself 22, 25, 186

beliefs: negative 21, 24, 186; permanent 24; positive 24, 186; and RAS 20–22, 24–25, 59–60; science behind 20; shared 105
"Bell Work" 150, 153
belonging 133–147
Berliner, BethAnn 176
bias(es) 21, 58, 60, 62; confirmation 60; implicit 10, 11; negativity 60; unique 20
bilateral hand use 49
bilateral integration skills 49
bi-manual training 93
biological growth 167
Bird Feeding Math Game 44
Bolger, Ray 202–203
bones 105
bored children do not learn 38
botox 93
Boyce, Thomas 83
brain 167; adolescent 115; based program 145; in curious mode 123; derived neurotropic factors 129; evolution of 105; feel-good brain chemicals 116; frontal lobe of 166; front part of 152; importance of 7; involuntary 124; learning-supportive brain chemistry 179–180, 184; neural lens 7–8; non-declarative 127; as organized in three basic systems 151; prefrontal cortex 13; rewiring of 12; survival 124
brain-breaks wheel 184, *184*
brain chemistry 179–182, 184–185
brain-derived neurotropic factors 129
brain injuries 72–74, 88, 113; acquired 72; traumatic 72, 113
Brain Injury Alliance 72
brain injury invisible 74
brain plasticity 71, 79; *see also* neuroplasticity
"brainwashed" 193n4
Bright Spot Award 176
Brown, Stuart 126

Bureau of Indian Education (BIE) 176
buried treasure 38
burnout 77, 103, 141

Café O'ly 185
camera on/off 101
Camp Korey 72
career and technical education pathway 177
career ready 177–178
caring 126–127, 140, 145, 160, 182
cartoons 29, 61
case studies 156–157, 160–164
Cat's Eye Marble 42; *see also* Dino Alphabet Pattern Game
causal: connections 138; relationship 167
CDC-Kaiser Permanente Adverse Childhood Experiences Questionnaire 137
celebrate students at home 144
Centers for Disease Control and Prevention 147n2
Centers Time 37, 45; *see also* kindergarten teaching team
cerebellum 8, 9, 48, 69, 128; *see also* pediatric stroke
cerebral palsy (CP) 12, 86–87, 93, 95, 98
cesarean birth 85
changing course 167–168
Chief Academic Officer 174
Chief Leschi Schools 174
child-individualized strategies 50
Child Protective Services (CPS) 191
children, thriving 131
child's dreams 49
Chromebooks 157
chunking 142
classical conditioning routines 127
classification exercises 127
classist 178
classroom management 124, 128, 151, 153, 170; cognitive brain-based approach to 7; techniques 4

cleanup 121, 123, 128
clinical art therapy 111
clinical therapy 102
clinical work 102
"Cocktail Party Phenomenon" 26
co-create: learning spaces 7–8, 14, 60, 63, 144, 168; signage 126; visuals 29
Coffee, Confidence on the Menu 185
cognitive demand 170; *see also* self-regulation
cognitive fatigue 72
cognitive overload 77
cognitive rehearsal 14, 127, 185
cognitive tasks 48
collaborative process 50
collaborative team effort 50
collateral blood flow 69, 74; *see also* pediatric stroke
college ready 177–178
coloring 106
comfort seeking 17
comfort tactic 16
community: -based mobile teams 103; -based programs 116; -based workshops 111; medical 95; professional learning 50; school 124, 185; in school initiatives 103; social 105; visual 109; well-being 103
compassion 23, 51, 73, 103, 141
compassion fatigue 103
compliance 17, 187
comprehension strategies 22
Conductive Education (CE) 12, 88–91, 93, 95–97; principles of 96; teaching strategies 96; therapy 12
Conductive Learning Center (CLC) 91
conductor 96
confidence 10, 185–186
confirmation biases 60; *see also* bias
confirm your belief 24
confusing instructions 77
confusion 33, 72, 100, 129

connections 9–11; causal 138; community 110; neural 205; neurons 95; synaptic 91, 131
conscious brain 20
consciousness 7
consequences 83, 147n1
consistent affirmations 27
consistent caring adults 160; see also Perry, Bruce
consolidate learning 127, 130
Constraint Induced Movement Therapy (CIMT) 93
contagion 18, 78, 80, 139, 141, 182
contagious behavior 77
context: ideas in 126; of punishment 83; social 8, 17, 145
coping skills 125
co-regulate 124, 127, 146–147, 153, 190, 199–200
co-regulation 82, 165–173, 199–200; transitioning, to self-regulation 169–170
correlation 48, 138
cortisol 22, 115–116, 120, 127, 139
COVID-19 pandemic 3, 100, 104, 157, 170, 208n1
COVID-19 quarantine 100
cranial vagus nerve 139
craniosacral 88
crawl 88–90
creative expression 35, 114
creative problem-solving 114
creative process 12, 39, 104, 105
creative scaffolding 105–107
creativity 105, 111, 113, 115, 117; creative roots 113–114
critical thinking skills 155
criticism 146
crutch 97, 170
curiosity 10, 17, 29, 62, 123
cyanotic 87
cycling 93

dance lessons 93
daydreaming 117
Dearybury, J. 130
death 102, 138
deep play 129
de-escalate 82
default mode network 116–117
defeating 33; see also self-talk
defense mechanisms 17, 105, 147, 180
deficits (academic) 185
deny dopamine 182; see also dopamine
depression 87, 113
desk on wheels 188
de-stigmatize art making 104–105
development 168–169
developmental milestones 22
developmental preschool 82
dexterity 40, 41, 111, 115; see also Mr. Tennis Ball Guy
Diagnostic Statistical Manual (DSM) 113
dignity 75–83; defined 79
dilation 67
Dino Alphabet Pattern Game 43
dinosaur 42
direct instruction 177
direction 43, 45, 127, 182, 186
disabilities 72, 93, 95
disciple 187
discipline 115, 187, 190, 192–193; artistic 105; of art therapy 102; mental health 113; school 5
discipline graph *188*
disease 71, 138
disquiet 33, 100
Dissanayake, Ellen 116
district administrator 178
district requirements 35
divorce 133, 135, 138, 145–146
domestic violence 133–134, 138
donuts 41; see also beads
dopamine 22, 29, 116, 127, 142, 179–182, 184–186, 190, 192

dope dealer 174–193
Dorothy 203–204
dorsolateral prefrontal cortex 129
Down syndrome 82, 200
drawing 21, 41, 101–102, 106, 114
dreams 65
drop out 135
Dweck, Carol 34
dyadic friendships 129
dyslexia 200
dysregulated 8, 65, 80, 141

Early Intervention and Home Care programs (Alberta Health Service) 91–93
embodied cognition 117
embroidering 106
emojis 105, 207
emotional disorders 135
emotional drama 78
emotions 32, 82, 137, 205, 207; amygdala 129; feelings and process relationship 205; negative 17, 198–199, 205, 207; positive 117; and sense of control 83; teaching and learning 95
empathy 117, 137
energy treatments 88
engagement 4, 7, 11–12, 38–39, 43, 46, 49, 103, 105, 109, 122, 125, 145
engagement scale 38
engaging trigger index finger 42; *see also* small motor skills
enlightenment 64–74
enthusiasm 23, 46, 80, 117, 206
environmental science 178
epigenetics 8
episodic memory 17
ER 67, *67*, 68, 74
escalation 78, 80–81, 121–122
evidence-based intervention 51
executive function 13–14, 72, 127, 153, 171, 173, 179, 181; defined 166; development of 166; and PFC 167

expectations 8, 78–79, 129–130, 137, 141, 143–144, 186
express latent emotions 102
external behavioral health providers 103
eye-hand coordination 35
Eye Spy 41; *see also* fun

Face drooping 72; *see also* Spot a Stroke F.A.S.T.
face masks 100, 102
failure model 35
falls 72; *see also* traumatic brain injury
fear center 17; *see also* amygdala
fear of failure 18
feedback 21, 24, 41, 107, 109, 128, 144, 191
feeling part of 27; *see also* social evaluative threat
feelings 134, 137, 146, *162*, 207; of despondency 77; gut 8; of isolation due to COVID-19 100; of safety 130; as a sense of being 131; teachers 35
feeling threatened by 27; *see also* social evaluative threat
feeling vulnerable 104
Felitti's study 13, 135–138
feral 200
fidgeting 16
fight flight reaction 103, 124, 152, 191
fine art 104, 114
fine motor skills 35, 39, 46–49, 51, 53; and academic coactivation 48
first line of defense 180
Fish, Barbara 102
fixedness 17, 23, 104
flight 13, 17, 103, 124, 152, 157, 191
flock of birds math game 45
flow 28, 69, 74, 126, 142, 143; *see also* teacher voice
fluke 50, 187
focus 26–28, 71, 137, 155; identifying topic/intention to 107; on knowledge 10; on neuronal connections 10; positive 62

focus on child 10, 25, 144
focus on content 28, 59, 107, 179
follow directions 186
Ford, Henry 62
forgiveness 134
formative years 139
foster care 22
fostering trust 136
framing difficult subject matter 102
Free2BMe 93
frustration 32, 78, 79, 122, 124, 145, 155
full potential 88, 93, 98, 113
fun: work disguised as 41
fun in a box 32–54; big ideas 38; collaborative team effort 50; fun characters 40–41; literature search 38–39; motivation 41–47; OT dilemma 36–37; overview 32–33; replication 50–51; results 48–49; school as three-ring circus 33–34; TTWWADI 34–35; *see also* fun

gallery walk 109
"Game Box" pilot program 47–51
Game Box time 46, 47
gamification 21, 41, 46–51, 89, 154, 186–187, 206
gaming 151
gastric nasal tube 87
Gen Ed 18
genes 114–115
Glenrose Rehabilitation Hospital (Edmonton) 91
go big or go home 43
good behavior 4
Google form 157
graduation rates 175; high 176; low 178
graffiti 114
graphic organizer 22
grasp objects *see* fine motor skills
gratitude 140
Gray Nuns Hospital in Edmonton, Alberta 85

greenhouse students 159
Green Ribbon School 176–177
greet with music 192
grip strength 41; *see also* Mr. Tennis Ball Guy
grit 155
Gross Movement Function Classification System (GMFCS) 93
growth mindset 27, 34, 155, 198; *see also* mindset
guilt 133

habituation 27
handprints on cave walls 105
handwriting skills 36, 51
hardwired learners 85–99
hardwired to create 116
Hass-Cohen, N. 115
headaches 1, 64–65, 72
healers 129
helplessness 77
hemorrhagic stroke 85
high roller 182, 184; *see also* behavior
hindbrain 125, 205
hippocampus 17
hippotherapy 93
hominid cave art 117
Homo sapiens 105, 115, 117
honesty 80, 147
hope 11–12, 22, 97, 102, 117, 143, 166, 193
hormones 179
hula hoops 191
humans: hardwired to create 116
"hurt people hurt people" 146
hyper-vigilant students 145

"I am no good at math" 25
icky feeling in the belly 22; *see also* cortisol
imagination 41–42, 117, 206
Imagine Learning digital program 176–177
imminent danger 152

impending doom 77
implicit contagion 182; *see also* oxytocin
imposter syndrome 187
impulse control 166
incarceration 138
inclusive: classes 136; of manipulative materials 38; opportunity 63
incoming sensory input 20, 60, 151
independence 28
Indigenous youth 175
Individual Education Plan (IEP) 18, 74, 82, 117, 122, 124, 130, 186
Individualized Health Plan (IHP) 74
information is freeing 23
innate ability 187
inner critic 107
Institute for Connecting Neuroscience with Teaching and Learning 205
intellectual disability 86
intense sensory experiences 88
intentional intervention group 21
intentional pause 61; *see also* teacher voice
intentional priming 128
interdisciplinary art 12, 102, 110
internal bleeding 86
International Alliance for Pediatric Stroke 72
interpretative art 105; *see also* art
interventions 1–2, 14, 18, 21, 35–36, 38–39, 44, 47–49, 51, 54, 71, 93, 95, 113, 124–125, 128, 130; collaborative 51; evidence-based 51; within failure model 35; fine motor 39; Gen Ed for 18; impact of 187; learners 18; mental and social 113; motor skill 36; play-based 125; principles of 130; research-based 38; systematic 35; task-specific approach to 48; of teacher 1–2; Tier 1 48; Tier 2 47; Tier 3 47
intrinsic investment 178
intrinsic motivation 37, 126, 143, 154
introvert 21
invention 113

isolation 4, 14, 54, 100–101
iterative cycle 24

jeering 80
joke 113
Jones, J. 130
joy 7, 10, 29, 45, 113, 114–115, 117, 129, 144, 155
Juvenile justice 135, 147n1

Kaiser Permanente's San Diego care program 135, 147n2
key to motor development 37
kindergarten teaching team 37
kinesthetic learning experiences 202
knitting 105, 106

labeling 18
lagging skills 162
laminated list of sight words 38
language delays 82
language encoding 71
latent emotions 102
laughter 26, 29
lay on the floor 66, 182, 187
learned helplessness 77, 146
learners 137, 200–201, 205; capacity to predict, plan, and assimilate information 10; in early Greek society 7; hardwired 85–99; interventions 18; multilingual 29; playful 130; tighten gap for 177
learning: as fun 39; objectives 196–197; professional 50; with deep understanding 145
learning-supportive brain chemistry 179–180, 184
left-hand dominant 69
letter: Naming Fluency 47; patterns 42; Recognition Automaticity 41
licensed Marriage & Family Therapist (LMFT) 103
lifespan decrease 192

life support 36; *see also* Mattos' medical model
literacy 185; Bright Spot 176; development of children 129; program 176
literate language 129
lived experiences 12, 152
lobes of the brain 8–9, 22, 205
lockdown 101
logic 13, 153
longevity 192
long term change 181
Lortie, D. 2, 4, 6
Lucky Charms 41; *see also* beads

magnetic resonance imaging (MRI) 68, 86, *86*
Magsamen, S. 116
Makah Tribe 115
making connections 9, 21
making mistakes 7; *see also* learning
Malchiodi, Cathy 105–106, 118n1
malleability 14
manage feelings 191
manipulatives for math 35
marriage counseling 134–135
Marriage & Family Therapist 103
massage 88
mastery 10, 24, 41–47, 60, 82, 123, 127–128, 154–155, 190
math 24–26, 29, 35, 39, 44–45, 47, 49, 62, 104, 121, 150, 152, 154–155, 185
Mattos' medical model 36
maximal potential 11, 33–34, 37, 51
meaningful relationships 190
meaning making 105
medication 77, 88, 93, 180, 193
medics 66–67
Me Here Now 60, 206
meltdowns 88
memory: deficits 72; episodic 17; non-declarative 127; semantic 17, 19; working 196–198, 201
mental health discipline 113

mental shift 24
metacognition 201
midbrain limbic area 205
middle school 22, 145
Miller's Law 79
mindset 17, 23, 27, 34, 104, 137, 155, 163, 198; changes in 14; cognitive 9; growth 27, 34, 155, 198; of improvement 74; teacher 11
mirroring 202–203; peer to peer 205–206
mirroring neurons 206–208; and authentic relationships 206–208
mirror neurons 17, 122, 196, 207
misconceptions 146
missing school days 22
mistakes 27, 156, 185–186, 199–200
misunderstandings 72, 146
modern mind 115–117
molecular structure *180*
"moment in the spotlight" 146
mommy dino 43; *see also* Letter Recognition Automaticity
Montessori: practical life activities 39; school 200
mood swings 72
morning check-in 157–159, *158*
motivation 9, 41–47; intrinsic 37, 126, 154; personal 170; and RAS 27; science of 22
motor control 182
motor learning 37, 45
motor skills plus academic skills 37
motor vehicle accidents 72; *see also* traumatic brain injuries
Mr. Tennis Ball Guy *40*, 40–41
multilingual learners 29
multimedia informational article 168
multitasking 22
Multi-Tiered Systems of Support (MTSS) 36
muscle tone spastic 72, 88, 95
mutual sense of trust 182
myelin 14, 17, 28–29, 71, 80, 127, 155, 161, 185–186

myelinated structure 17
myelinate neural pathways 29, 71

narrative writing 165–166
National Council for Computer Education 150
national currency 105
National Education Association 3
national flags 105
Native American youth 175
navigate transitions 130
Neanderthal burial site 105
negative beliefs 21, 24, 186
negative chatter 145
negative comments 23; *see also* self-talk
negative emotions 17, 198–199
negative self-talk 21, 25
negativity biases 60; *see also* biases
Neonatal Intensive Care Unit 85
neural concept methodology 156
Neural Ed bulletin board 62–63, 188
Neural Education 13, 62, 153, 161, 163, 174–175, 178, 188–190, 193, 201, 208n1
neural fatigue 20
neural historical considerations 115–117
neural lens 7–8, 13–14, 161, 163, 187–188, 190–192, 199, 205–207; educators use of 178–179; importance of 7; play therapy 130; use in teaching 202; utilizing 175
neural plasticity 12
neural substrates 17, 205
neuro-aesthetic researchers 116
neurobiology 178–179
neurological change 36, 46
neurons: mirroring 206–208
neuropeptides 179
neuroplasticity 22–23, 71, 74, 95, 97, 170; defined 95; knowledge and application of 97; positive effects of 95; principle of 170; *see also* brain plasticity
Neurosequential development (see Bruce Perry)

neurotransmitters 22, 49, 60, 116, 130, 179, 190; dopamine 22, 29, 116, 127, 142, 179–182, 184–186, 190, 192; feel-good 29; and fun 49; intrinsic 10; oxytocin 116
Next Generation Science Standard (NGSS) 178
night terrors 65; *see also* dreams
non-declarative memory 127
non-dominant hand 47
non-judgmental 104, 107, 134, 140
nonthreatening 134
NO REFERRALS 190
norms 3, 77, 156, 198
not good enough 18, 62, 121, 152
novel art 105
novelty 17, 29, 43, 60

obesity 135–136
obsess 18
occipital 9, 69, 87; *see also* pediatric stroke
occupational therapist (OT) 38, 47, 49–51; school-based 36
occupational therapy 11, 46, 49, 50, 71
off-task 172
olfactory bulb 20
Olympic rings 39, *52*
one-room schoolhouse 34
online classes 101
oral-motor/sensory 87
organizations 38, 72, 74, 91, 138, 147n1, 166–167, 171, 173, 178
OT-designed motor supports 37
outdoor learning 29, 178
Outdoors for All 72
outsider 117
overlap *vs.* side-by-side 39, 51; *see also* Olympic rings
override negative self-talk 25
oxygen levels 66; *see also* medics
oxytocin 10, 22, 29, 49, 116, 127, 179–182, 184–185, 190, 192
Ozette, WA 115

paleoanthropology 12, 115
palm to fingertips 41; *see also* small motor skills
pandemic regression 176
panic 120, 137
paradigm shift 150–153
para-educator 11, 76, 82
parents of severely disabled child 86
parent-teacher conferences 23
Pavlov, Ivan 127
pediatrician 65, 93
Pediatric Intensive Care Unit (PICU) 68–69; *see also* pediatric stroke
pediatric seizure 67
pediatric stroke 68, 72
Pediatric Stroke Specialist 68; *see also* pediatric stroke
Pediatric Stroke Warriors 72
peer to peer mirroring 205–206
perceived danger 152
perceptual motor skills 127
permanent positive impact on brain 93
Perry, Bruce 83, 141, 153, 159–160, 198
perseverance 96
personal art history 106
Peto, Andras 95
petroglyphs 115–116
phenomena based curriculum 177–178
phonemes 71
photography 29
physical abuse 133, 138–139
physical development interventions 35; *see also* interventions
physical therapy 71
piano lessons 93
pilot study 45, 48
"Pinterest Perfect" 27
pipe cleaner worms 44, *see also* Bird Feeding Math Game
pitch 28; *see also* teacher voice
planning 13, 45, 154, 166, 169, 173, 201–202
plant-based dyes 105

Plato 7
play 7–8, 12, 120–131, 156–157, 190, 198, 206; based intervention 125; described 126; imaginative 114; with modeling clay 90; as primarily childish 130; purposeful 32–54; sense of 80; space 125–127, *126*, 128–129; therapy 125, 128, 130
playmates 130
pleasing art 105
pods 76
point of view 27, 107, 187
pons 10, 69; *see also* pediatric stroke
positive: affirmations 28; attitude 96; beliefs 24, 186; feedback for parents 144; self-talk 62, 68, 155
posterior temporal lobe 87
post traumatic stress disorder 72, 87
posture 90, 141, 147, 199
potential 11–12, 22, 33–34; academic 49; imaginative 42; maximal 11, 33–34, 37, 51; notable 42
pot of gold 203
pound of flesh 181
practice makes permanent 155
preconceptions 2, 146
prefrontal cortex (PFC) 10, 13, 17, 48, 129, 152, 166–167, 179–181
prescription medication 180
prescriptive 36; *see also* occupational therapist (OT)
primal: expression 105; feelings 131; outcomes 10; survival characteristics 116
priming 128, 192
prisons 113
privileges 77, 79, 98, 126, 130, 162
proactive interventions 35, 88; *see also* interventions
processing speed 72
procrastination 167
professional development 26, 102, 143, 175, 192, 201

Professional Learning Community 50, 69
projectile vomit 87
protective wellness strategy 102
psychological safety 125
psychomotor improvement 88
Puget Sound 64, 113, 178
pulled out 18, 36
pulse 66, 166; *see also* medics
punishment 1, 4–6, 14, 83, 145, 187
pupils 65; *see also* pediatrician
purpose 10, 24 41–47, 123, 127, 130, 154, 159, 190
pushing children 145

quality of life 51, 88, 93, 122
quarantine 100, 102; *see also* COVID-19 pandemic
quiet rooms for calm down 77

racist 178
rainbow 203
Ramachandran, V. S. 5–6
RAS *see* reticular activating system (RAS)
reading phoneme segmentation 51
realia 29
reasoning 7, 153, 205; spatial 116
Red Light Green Light game 186
reflexes 65; *see also* pediatrician
reframe 28, 73, 139
regret 134
Regulate, Relate, Reason brain journey 195–208
regulation 198–199
rehabilitation 69–71; *see also* pediatric stroke
reiki 88
relationships: authentic 203, 206–208
relearning to live 70, 71
relevance 117, 185; *see also* motivation
remediation *vs.* acceleration 177
reminders 128, 146, 157, 171
remove scaffold supports 169; *see also* scaffolds/scaffolding

repetition 38–39, 43, 49, 71, 95, 185
repetitive uninteresting tasks 37
replication 50–51
research-based intervention 38
reset 82, 83
resilience 12, 113, 140, 155, 186
resiliency 73
resistance 40; *see also* Mr. Tennis Ball Guy
response art 101–105, 107–108; art therapy 110–113; creation 107; defined 102; educator 108–110; Zoom-based 108
Response to Intervention (RtI) 36, 54n1
rest and digest 139
reticular activating system (RAS) 10–11, 17–25, 57–63, 104, 186; attached to brain stem *19*; classroom strategies with 25–26; confirms beliefs *25*; as filter 25; instigators, teachers as 26–28; and novelty 29; parents use of 26; and realia 29
retroactive inhibitions 157
reverse eloping 191
'revert to default' situation 141–142, 161
rewards 1, 4, 6, 33, 129, 143, 145, 169, 191
rewire the brain 70
rhythm 28, 116; *see also* teacher voice
rigor as fun 52
risk-taking 22
Ritalin 180, 181
ritual 116
rollercoaster 78
rote motor repetition 39
routines 4, 66, 78, 100, 116, 127, 137, 169, 171
rubrics 26
ruminate 18

safe space 21, 128, 155, 159–160
safety 9, 17, 60, 161, 171–172, 182, 202; feeling of 130; fostering 136; psychological 125; sense of 146; teaching 131
salmon hatchery 178

Sapolsky, Robert 4–6
scaffolds/scaffolding 26, 47; creative 105–106; and development 168–169
scarecrow 14, 197, 202–204
school-based occupational therapist 36
school expectation 129
school nurse's office 64
school to prison pipeline 14, 192
seahorse 17
Seattle Children's Hospital 68, 69, 72
Section 504 Plan 74
self-actualization 113
self-awareness 22
self-contained classroom 81
self-directed goals 113
self-fulfilling cycle 24
self-fulfilling prophecy 60, *60; see also* RAS
self-monitoring 166
self regulate 62
self-regulation 14, 82, 165–173; transitioning from co-regulation to 169–170
self-talk 18, 24, 145, 147; conversations about 23; negative 21, 25; positive 62, 68, 155
semantic memory 17, 19
sense of belonging 17, 28, 116, 130–131, 136, 144, 180, 182
sense of control 83
sense of pride 176
sense of responsibility for action 96
sense of smell 20
sensory filters 88
sensory overload 88
sensory paradise 113
serotonin 10, 29, 49, 116, 127, 179–182, 184–185, 190, 192
severely disabled 86
sexist 178
sexual abuse 138
shame 134, 144, 182
shared gallery walk 109
short attention spans 201

Shriners Hospital for Children 93
shut down 137, 155, 160, 180
shy 206–207
sickness 102, 138
Simon Says game 186
simplicity 7, 77, 79
a single box 39
sit cross-legged 88, 90
skeletal musculature 128
skiing 93
Skinner, B. F. 4–6, 77, 82, 83n1
sleep 20, 65–66, 87, 95
social awareness 103
social distancing 100, 101, 198
social emotional learning (SEL) 35, 159
social evaluative threat 144–145
social interaction 37, 50, 201
social regulation 198
soft-start 150–164; case studies 156–157, 160–164; morning check-in 157–159, *158*; paradigm shift 150–153; "WIN/BINS" 153; "WIN" stands for whatever i need 153–156
soul of educators 33
South Sound Newspaper 185
spatial awareness 115, 127
spatial reasoning 116
Special Ed 18, 36–37, 46, 49–50, 75, 85–86
special needs 47, 185–186
specifically designed activities 47
Speech difficulty 72; *see also* Spot a Stroke F.A.S.T.
speech pathologist 71
speech therapy 71
spin brain breaks wheel 184, *184*, 193
spiral down 17
splints 89, 93
sports injuries 72; *see also* traumatic brain injury
Spot a Stroke F.A.S.T. 72
Stallone, Sylvester 97
standard classroom tasks 47
STEM Lab 151

step-by-step visuals 45
Stollery Children's Hospital (Edmonton) 91
stress 18, 22, 104, 109, 134, 141, 145, 151–157, 160, 164
stressors 103, 117, 133–134, 187
stroke 72; *see also* acquired brain injuries
stroke survivor 72
struggling learners 18
student pods 76
student voice 29
subconscious brain 20
summer camps 91, 95
superior longitudinal fasciculus 155, 162
support personnel 36
survival 60, 116, 124, 151; brain 13; information 26; robust defense for 17; and smell 20
sustainability practices 176
Suzuki, Wendy 145
swimming 17, 93, 120, 137–138
switch-tasking 22
synchronized release of oxytocin 182
sync with the child 182; *see also* mirror neurons
systematic interventions 35; *see also* interventions

tailoring fine motor activities 47
take risks 22
talent 14, 21, 114
tantrums 65, 78–79, 82
task initiation 166–167, 173
task-specific approach 48; *see also* interventions
teacher(s): intervention 1–2; neural lens 7–8; as RAS instigators 26–28; voice 28–29
teach to the test 35
teenager brain 167
terminal 32, 36; *see also* Mattos' medical model
test anxiety 18; *see also* anxiety

That's The Way We've Always Done It (TTWWADI) 34–35, 53
THEM *vs.* US 130
therapeutic process 111
theraputty 38
thermostat or thermometer 188
thoughtful exploration 39
Threat response 105, 116
three-marble series 42; *see also* Letter Recognition Automaticity
three-ring circus 33–34, *34*
throwing balls 128
Tier 1 36; *see also* Multi-Tiered Systems of Support (MTSS)
Tier 2 36; *see also* Multi-Tiered Systems of Support (MTSS)
Tier 3 36; *see also* Multi-Tiered Systems of Support (MTSS)
TikTok 29
time 66, 68, 71, 72, 75–76, 79, 80; *see also* pediatric stroke
time management 166
time out 82–83, 107
Time to call 911 72; *see also* Spot a Stroke F.A.S.T.
Tin Man 197, 203
token-economy 4, 77, 83n1
tone 28, 45, 61, 72, 87, 88, 95; *see also* teacher voice
tongs 41, 44; *see also* small motor skills
tradition 116
transfer 68, 80, 130, 155, 186; activities 125; goals 125; information 117; intervention 124; learning 127
transference 49
transitioning from co-regulation to self-regulation 169–170
translation 41; *see also* small motor skills
transparency 141, 147
trauma 13, 16, 18, 22, 69, 80, 102–103, 137, 141, 156, 160, 180, 190–191
trauma-informed healthcare 103
traumatic brain injuries 72, 113

trigger 42, 80, 116, 190–191, 196
trust 2, 21–22, 24, 71, 116, 126, 128, 131, 144, 182, 190
TTWWADI 34–35
tumor 72; *see also* acquired brain injuries
tune into adult expectations 186
tweezers 41, 44, 47; *see also* small motor skills

uncertainty 1, 100
uncinate fasciculus 162
unconditional acceptance 128, 130
underserved population 175–176
University of Alberta Hospital, Edmonton, Alberta, Canada 87
useful art 102, 105; *see also* art
utilitarian art 113; *see also* art

vaccinations 102
vagus nerve 139
vertebral artery 69; *see also* pediatric stroke
violent child 184
visceral involuntary gag 20
visual aids 29, 61
visualize 18, 26, 201
visually pleasing classroom 27
visual symbolism 100
vulnerability 104

Waldorf School 114
walk upright 88
Watson, John 4–6
WE 130, 144
well-being 21; community 103; emotional 111
wellness 102–103, 109, 192
wellness visits 103
WestEd 176
wetland outdoor classroom 178
Whole Words Read 47
"WIN/BINS" 153–156
witness not evaluate 107
The Wizard of Oz (book) 197, 203
The Wizard of Oz (movie) 202
work disguised as fun 41; *see also* fun
working memory 198
working with families 51, 69, 71–74, 103–105, 144–146
World War II 95
worry 18, 102

yellow brick road 14, 200, 203, 204–205, 207–208

Zoom-driven school experience 101
Zoom school 101

The Third Space and Chinese Language Pedagogy

Negotiating Intentions and Expectations in Another Culture

Edited by Xin Zhang and Xiaobin Jian

LONDON AND NEW YORK

First published 2021
by Routledge
2 Park Square, Milton Park, Abingdon, Oxon OX14 4RN

and by Routledge
52 Vanderbilt Avenue, New York, NY 10017

Routledge is an imprint of the Taylor & Francis Group, an informa business

© 2021 selection and editorial matter, Xin Zhang and Xiaobin Jian; individual chapters, the contributors

The right of Xin Zhang and Xiaobin Jian to be identified as the authors of the editorial material, and of the authors for their individual chapters, has been asserted in accordance with sections 77 and 78 of the Copyright, Designs and Patents Act 1988.

All rights reserved. No part of this book may be reprinted or reproduced or utilised in any form or by any electronic, mechanical, or other means, now known or hereafter invented, including photocopying and recording, or in any information storage or retrieval system, without permission in writing from the publishers.

Trademark notice: Product or corporate names may be trademarks or registered trademarks, and are used only for identification and explanation without intent to infringe.

British Library Cataloguing-in-Publication Data
A catalogue record for this book is available from the British Library

Library of Congress Cataloging-in-Publication Data
Names: Zhang, Xin, editor. | Jian, Xiaobin, editor.
Title: The third space and Chinese language pedagogy : negotiating intentions and expectations in another culture / edited by Xin Zhang and Xiaobin Jian.
Description: London ; New York : Routledge, 2020.
Identifiers: LCCN 2020031876 (print) | LCCN 2020031877 (ebook) | ISBN 9780367364267 (hardback) | ISBN 9780367364281 (paperback) | ISBN 9780429345890 (ebook)
Subjects: LCSH: Chinese language—Study and teaching—Foreign speakers. | Language and culture.
Classification: LCC PL1065 .T44 2020 (print) | LCC PL1065 (ebook) | DDC 495.180071—dc23
LC record available at https://lccn.loc.gov/2020031876
LC ebook record available at https://lccn.loc.gov/2020031877

ISBN: 978-0-367-36426-7 (hbk)
ISBN: 978-0-367-36428-1 (pbk)
ISBN: 978-0-429-34589-0 (ebk)

Typeset in Times New Roman
by Apex CoVantage, LLC